The Divin

Exploring the Philosophy of Religion

Series editor: Michael L. Peterson, Chair of the Department of Philosophy, Asbury College

This is a series of individual volumes on classic and contemporary themes in the philosophy of religion. Each volume introduces, examines, and discusses the main problems and arguments related to each topic. Each book also considers some important positions of major philosophers, offers thoughtful critiques, articulates new positions, and indicates fruitful directions for further investigation.

The Divine Attributes

Joshua Hoffman and
Gary S. Rosenkrantz

Blackwell
Publishers

Editorial Offices:
108 Cowley Road, Oxford OX4 1JF, UK
  Tel: +44 (0)1865 791100
350 Main Street, Malden, MA 02148-5018, USA
  Tel: +1 781 388 8250

First published 2002 by Blackwell Publishers Ltd, a Blackwell Publishing company

Library of Congress Cataloging-in-Publication Data has been applied for.

ISBN 0-631-21153-5 (hardback); ISBN 0-631-21154-3 (paperback)

A catalogue record for this title is available from the British Library.

Set in 10.5 on 12.5pt Bembo
by SNP Best-set Typesetter Ltd., Hong Kong
Printed and bound in Great Britain
by TJ International Ltd., Padstow, Cornwall

For further information on
Blackwell Publishers, visit out website:
www.blackwellpublishers.co.uk

Contents

Series Editor's Preface

Philosophy of religion is experiencing a kind of renaissance. From the last quarter of the twentieth century onward, we have witnessed remarkably vigorous activity among philosophers interested in religion. We are likewise seeing college and university students seeking courses in philosophy of religion at an unprecedented rate. To reach this point, philosophy of religion had to weather the harsh and hostile intellectual climate that persisted through most of the nineteenth and twentieth centuries. Absolute idealism depersonalized deity, naturalism supplanted a religious worldview, and positivism deprived theological claims of cognitive status. Yet, partly because of incisive critiques of these viewpoints and partly because of new, first-rate studies of religious concepts and beliefs, this field of inquiry has once again come to the fore.

The Exploring the Philosophy of Religion series, then, comes into a very exciting arena. The books it contains treat some of the most important topics in the field. Since the renewal of interest in religion has occurred largely among Anglo-American philosophers committed to the best in the analytic tradition, these works will tend to reflect that approach. To be sure, some helpful general introductions and anthologies are available for those wanting a survey, and there are many good, cutting-edge monographs dealing with technical issues in this burgeoning area. However, the books in this series are designed to occupy that relatively vacant middle ground in the literature between elementary texts and pioneer works. They discuss their stated topics in a way that acquaints the reader with all the relevant ideas and options while pointing out which ones seem most reasonable. Each volume, therefore, constitutes a focused, intensive introduction to the issue and serves as a model of how one might actually go about developing an informed position.

Philosophy of religion is dynamic and growing. The issues it addresses are of primary significance for understanding the divine, ourselves, and our place in the universe. With this sense of magnitude, the present series has been conceived to offer something to all who want to think deeply about the issues: serious undergraduates, graduate students, divinity and theology students, professional philosophers, and even to thoughtful, educated lay persons.

Michael L. Peterson

Acknowledgments

The authors would like to thank the following:

Kelly Trogdon, for his editorial work and help in compiling bibliographical information, as well as for his useful suggestions about ways in which we could improve this book.

The University of North Carolina at Greensboro, for subsidizing Kelly Trogdon's work for us under the auspices of its Undergraduate Research Assistant Program.

Cheryl Cross, for proofreading the manuscript and making a number of helpful observations.

Michael Peterson, the editor of the Exploring Philosophy of Religion series; his valuable suggestions are very much appreciated.

Finally, we would also like to express our gratitude to a number of philosophers who, over the years, have encouraged or assisted us in our work in the philosophy of religion: William Alston, Robert Audi, John Fischer, William Hasker, Norman Kretzmann, William Mann, George Mavrodes, Thomas Morris, Philip Quinn, James Ross, William Rowe, and Eleonore Stump.

Authors' Note

The Divine Attributes can be used as a text in undergraduate and graduate courses in the philosophy of religion. We have included a glossary that explains the meanings of philosophical terms that may be unfamiliar to students who are taking their first course in the philosophy of religion or to the general reader. Terms included in the glossary appear in **bold face** the first time they occur within the text or within the notes.

It is Infinity, which, joined to our Ideas of Existence, Power, Knowledge, &c. makes that complex Idea, whereby we represent to our selves the best we can, the Supreme Being.

John Locke, *An Essay Concerning Human Understanding*
II. xxiii. ¶ 35 (1690)

Introduction to Rational Theology

In this book we will analyze the idea of God (understood as a maximally great being). This exercise belongs to a philosophical discipline known as rational theology. In developing our analysis, we will go through the following stages: (i) describing the nature of rational theology, (ii) differentiating the idea of a maximally great being from other historical ideas of the divine (and identifying the core great-making qualities of a maximally great being), (iii) defending the coherence of maximal greatness and the mutual coherence of the divine attributes it includes, and (iv) elucidating those divine attributes. At the end of this book, we will provide an overview of the prospects for justified belief in the existence of a maximally great being from the perspective of rational theology.

Theology is the study of God, the gods, or the divine: it seeks to answer questions about the nature and existence of God, the gods, or the divine. *Rational theology* is a theology that accepts the canons of rationality. These canons consist of the laws of logic (both those of **deductive** and non-deductive inference), together with other principles regulating the use of sources of evidence such as introspection (or inner awareness), perception (or outer awareness), and memory. Thus, rational theology cannot accept an account of the divine which logically **entails** a contradiction, or which flies in the face of probability. For instance, according to the logical **Law of Non-Contradiction**, nothing can both be and not be at the same time. This law implies that it is absolutely **impossible** both for God always to exist and for God never to exist. Similarly, it is absolutely impossible that there exists a spherical cube. Therefore, if there is an account of the divine that logically entails that it is within the power of God to bring it about that he both always exists and never exists, or to bring it about that there exists a spherical cube, then that account of the divine is unacceptable to rational theology. Furthermore, the canons of rationality imply that we cannot rationally attribute to God a source of evidence or knowledge that is incoherent or appears to be inconsistent or impossible.

From the perspective of rational theology, if the concept of God is logically incoherent, then he cannot exist. Consequently, a rational defense of the existence of God requires a coherent conception of God. A conception of God is coherent if and only if the divine attributes are intelligible taken both individually and in combination. Finally, the existence of God should be not only formally consistent, but consistent with the **necessary** truths of **metaphysics**, **epistemology**, and **ethics**, at least to the extent that these can be ascertained.

As the reader will have noticed, we use masculine pronouns to refer to God. We do this for stylistic reasons; this should not be taken to suggest that God has gender. Indeed, assuming that God is nonphysical, and that a nonphysical being could not be biologically gendered, it is impossible that God is biologically gendered.

The relevant canons of rationality, cited earlier, require us to seek truth and to seek to avoid falsehood. They are the canons of *epistemic* rationality or justification. **Epistemic justification** is the sort of justification that is necessary for knowledge. More specifically, a belief can count as knowledge only if that belief is both true and epistemically justified. Rational principles of other kinds require one to seek other valuable goals, such as maximizing one's own happiness, or maximizing happiness for oneself and others. It follows that one should distinguish epistemic rationality, which is fundamentally and essentially truth-seeking and falsehood-avoiding, from nonepistemic rationality, which is not. It is **possible** that we will be happy if and only if we believe in God, and we could have such a prudential or practical reason for believing in God even if we are not *epistemically* justified in believing in him. But rational theology, in our sense of the term, has no place for a belief which is not epistemically justified, for instance, unreasoning faith, a "**will to believe**," or a belief whose only justification is prudential or pragmatic.[1]

Rational theology is committed to the following two general principles of epistemic rationality. First, if a **proposition**, p, does not have **intrinsic credibility** for a person, S, then p is acceptable for S only if S has adequate evidence for p.[2] In other words, one ought to accept a proposition only if one is epistemically justified in believing that proposition. Second, the *degree of confidence* a person, S, has in the truth of a proposition, p, should be in proportion to the evidence S has for p, or in proportion to p's intrinsic credibility for S. That is to say, the degree of confidence one has in a proposition ought to be in proportion to one's epistemic justification for believing that proposition.

A theology is rational *to the degree* that it conforms to the canons of rationality. *Ideally*, a rational theology *completely* conforms to those canons. On the other hand, the failure of a theology, T, to conform completely to these canons is consistent with T's being *highly* rational.

This book is a study in rational theology. Thus, we assume that any defensible theology must meet the demands of reason. More specifically, our main purpose is to give a rational account of the *nature of God*, that is, of the God of the three major Western religions of Judaism, Christianity, and Islam.[3] The conception of God that these religious traditions have come to accept is the conception that Anselm (1053–1105) expresses: the being than which none greater is possible, that is, a perfect being.[4] This notion of maximal greatness or perfection will serve as a regulating definition on the basis of which we will attempt to derive and analyze the fundamental divine attributes, such as divine power, knowledge, and goodness. From this notion we will also try to decide whether God is to be understood as being eternal, as within or outside of time, as **existing necessarily** or **contingently**, and as a physical or a spiritual being. We believe that the systematic construction of a coherent conception of God based upon the foregoing rational principles is instructive, and of theological and philosophical interest.

The notion of *rational religion* parallels that of rational theology. Rational religion is a belief in God, the gods, or the divine based upon reason. Accordingly, rational religion accepts the possibility of revising its beliefs in response to rational criticism. (Rational religion may base the belief that God exists upon *experience*, even upon an apparent experience of *God*, but only on the assumption that the belief that God exists is revisable in response to rational criticism.) In contrast, *revealed religion* is a belief in God, the gods, or the divine based upon the absolutely authoritative revelatory experiences of one or more historical individuals. Such revelations may be codified in what is accepted as an infallible sacred text, for example, the Bible. Unlike rational religion, revealed religion rejects the possibility of revising its beliefs in response to rational criticism. For example, an advocate of rational religion who believes that God exists would be willing to abandon that belief in response to rational criticism, whereas an advocate of revealed religion who shares this belief would *not* be willing to do so. This is consistent with the fact that some advocates of revealed religion are willing to revise their beliefs about the correct *interpretation* of their sacred texts in response to rational criticism. On the other hand, some advocates of revealed religion are strict fundamentalists who maintain that there is a unique *literal* reading of their sacred texts that is not open to further interpretation.

Relative to a particular conception of God, the gods, or the divine, *theism* asserts the existence of God, the gods, or the divine; *atheism* denies their existence; and *agnosticism* neither asserts nor denies their existence. Relative to the Anselmian conception of God, theism asserts that such a supreme being exists. Traditional forms of Judaism, Christianity, and Islam have a shared commitment to theism in the sense just specified.

However, the philosophical task of *defining* or **analyzing** the nature of God is, we believe, prior to the task of deciding whether or not God exists. After all, before one can tell whether or not something exists, one has to know *what it is* one is inquiring about in this way. As we indicated earlier, our main purpose in this book is to carry out this definitional or analytical task. Although this book is not primarily about the *existence* of God, we nevertheless will have a few things to say in our concluding remarks about how rational theology addresses the question of the existence of God. In what follows, we give a brief summary of each chapter of the book.

Chapter 1: *The Idea of God*. In section 1.1, we distinguish different understandings of the divine, such as polytheism versus monotheism, a personal versus an impersonal god, pantheism versus a divine being separate from the universe, and so forth. In section 2.2, we focus on the regulating idea of the divine as the greatest or most perfect possible being. This idea has been at the core of traditional Western theism at least since the Middle Ages. We discuss how this regulating idea entails various salient divine attributes that together comprise the nature of God, attributes such as omnipotence, omniscience, omnibenevolence, incorporeality, and necessary existence. Nevertheless, we reject the idea that maximal greatness entails certain attributes that have been ascribed to God, such as omnipresence and timelessness. In later chapters, it is argued that attributes of this kind cannot meet the test of coherence.

Chapter 2: *Substantiality*. In section 2.1, we discuss the notion of categories of being, including substance, and show why God is properly understood as a substantial being. In particular, we show why God must be understood as a *person*, rather than as an impersonal being. In section 2.2, we show how substance is to be understood in terms of a kind of independence (which God as a substantial being would enjoy). Lastly, in section

2.3, Spinoza's nontraditional theory of God as an independent substance is assessed.

Chapter 3: *Incorporeality*. In section 3.1, we define the notion of a soul or spiritual substance. We also show how the nature of God, in particular divine spirituality, precludes God's being literally omnipresent, but allows for some metaphorical sense in which God would be omnipresent. Section 3.2 defends the intelligibility of souls against various philosophical attacks. Section 3.3 defends the intelligibility of **body–soul interaction** against philosophical objections. It is also argued that God's being omnipotent entails that God is a soul, rather than a body. In section 3.4, we argue that God's being a soul entails that he is **simple**, that is, without parts. In addition, we distinguish this sort of simplicity from other, more radical and arguably incoherent forms of simplicity.

Chapter 4: *Necessary Existence*. Section 4.1 discusses the **necessity** or **contingency** of propositions, of properties, and of the existence of beings. In section 4.2, we explain the concepts of a **necessary being** and a **contingent being**. We also defend the coherence of the idea of a substantial necessary being against Humean objections. Section 4.3 provides an account of divine necessary existence, divine **necessary properties**, and divine **contingent properties**. In addition, we defend the standard, possible-worlds analysis of **modalities** such as necessity and contingency. In section 4.4, we distinguish the notions of a necessary being and a self-existent being and argue that the latter notion is problematic.

Chapter 5: *Eternality*. Section 5.1 discusses the debate over the nature of divine eternality and the motivation for the claim that God is timeless. In section 5.2, we argue that this motivation is misguided and that divine eternality is fully intelligible only if it is temporal eternality. Section 5.3 explains the distinction between immutability, or strict unchangeability, and incorruptibility, or the impossibility of diminishment or decay. We maintain that God should be understood to be incorruptible but not immutable.

Chapter 6: *Omniscience*. In section 6.1, we show why omniscience is not to be understood as knowing every truth, but rather as knowing as much as any being could know. We also discuss what sort of knowledge an omniscient being would have, and what the limits of knowledge are for an omniscient being. Included in the latter is a discussion of the possibility of knowledge of future contingent and first-person propositions. Based on the discussions in section 6.1, we offer a definition of omniscience in section 6.2. Finally, in section 6.3, we survey the prominent arguments that figure in the debate over the compatibility of divine foreknowledge and human **freedom**. We maintain that divine omniscience would *not* include foreknowledge of human choices and actions that are free in the **libertarian** sense.

Chapter 7: *Perfect Goodness, Perfect Virtue, and Moral Admirability*. Section 7.1 discusses the relation that God would bear to morality, and argues against the **divine command theory** of ethics. In section 7.2, we examine the relation between divine goodness and a **consequentialist theory** of right and wrong. The problem of evil, we maintain, usually assumes that some form of consequentialism is true. We will argue that certain puzzles arise about the nature of divine goodness given such a theory of ethics. In section 7.3, we examine divine moral perfection on a **deontological theory** of right and wrong, and its implications for the problem of evil. Finally, in section 7.4, we answer an alleged **paradox** according to which maximal greatness and moral admirability are incompatible.

Chapter 8: *Omnipotence*. In section 8.1, we show that the case of omnipotence is analogous to that of omniscience, in that the former is to be understood as *maximal* power, and not as the power to bring about *every* **state of affairs** (or even every *contingent* state of affairs). We also argue that there cannot be two coexisting omnipotent beings, and hence that God would be uniquely omnipotent. Section 8.2 discusses in detail what sort of power an omnipotent being would have, and what limitations there would be upon the power of such a being. Included in this section is a discussion of whether an omnipotent being can bring about impossible states of affairs, necessary states of affairs, past states of affairs, and free human actions. Based on the preceding sections, in section 8.3, we construct a formal analysis of omnipotence. Finally, in section 8.4, we argue that our analysis allows divine omnipotence and omnibenevolence to be reconciled. We also argue that our analysis of omnipotence implies that God would be a free agent in a robust sense.

In the postscript, *Concluding Remarks and Prolegomena to Future Rational Theology*, we provide an overview of the results reached in the first eight chapters, and argue that, properly understood, the concept of God is coherent. We emphasize that this result requires that we reject certain attributes that some traditional theologians have attributed to God. Nevertheless, the concept of God that emerges is, we argue, the one that is generated by the regulating idea of God as the greatest possible being. Finally, we indicate something of the philosophical context in which rational theology deals with the question of whether reason and experience can justify the belief that God exists.

NOTES

1   Søren Kierkegaard (1813–55) famously held that unreasoning faith in God is required of us and that we ought not to engage in rational theology. This is an extreme form of fideism, the view that our lack of knowledge should encourage us to have faith in God. On the other hand, Blaise Pascal (1623–62) and William James (1842–1910) argued that belief in God can be rationally justified on prudential or pragmatic grounds. These arguments are consistent with forms of fideism less extreme than Kierkegaard's. Saint Thomas Aquinas (1225–74) held a view that is incompatible with fideism. According to Aquinas, we can prove, and therefore we can know, that God exists; nevertheless, Aquinas maintains that there are many facts about God that we must accept on faith.

2   If a proposition, p, is self-evident for S, then p has intrinsic credibility for S. For example, the proposition that *if something is square, then it is square* may be self-evident for S. If a proposition, p, is self-evident for S, then p is acceptable for S even though S does not have evidence for p.

3   By the God of Judaism, Christianity, and Islam, we mean the God that is *common* to all three religions. Hence, any claim about God that is specific to any one of these religions, e.g., the doctrine of the Trinity, is beyond the scope of our inquiry.

4   Anselm literally put it this way: God is "a being than which nothing greater can be conceived." He utilized this definition as a premise in his famous ontological argument for the existence of God. In the interests of clarity, we have replaced the partly psychological phrase 'can be conceived' with the wholly nonpsychological term 'possible', and have replaced the indefinite article 'a' with the definite article 'the'. There is no reason to think that Anselm would have found either of these clarifications objectionable. See *Proslogium*, chap. II, in *Saint Anselm, Basic Writings*, trans. Sidney N. Deane (LaSalle, Ill.: Open Court Publishing Co., 1962).

BIBLIOGRAPHY

Anselm, *Monologium* and *Proslogium*, in *Saint Anselm, Basic Writings*, trans. Sidney N. Deane (La Salle, Ill.: Open Court Publishing Co., 1962).

Aquinas, T., *Basic Writings of Saint Thomas Aquinas*, 2 vols., ed. A. C. Pegis (New York: Random House, 1944).

Clifford, W. K. (1845–79), "The Ethics of Belief," in *Lectures and Essays* (London: Macmillan, 1879).

Hume, D., *Dialogues Concerning Natural Religion* (New York: Hafner Publishing Company, 1975).

Ibn Rushd (1126–98), *Fasl al-maqal* (*Decisive Treatise*), ed. G. Hourani, *Averroës on the Harmony of Religion and Philosophy* (London: Luzac, 1976).

James, W. (1842–1910), "The Will to Believe," in *The Will to Believe and Other Essays in Popular Philosophy* (New York: Dover, 1956).

Kierkegaard, S. (1813–55), *Concluding Unscientific Postscript*, trans. D. F. Swenson and W. Lowrie (Princeton, NJ: Princeton University Press, 1941).

Maimonides, *Guide for the Perplexed*, trans. M. Friedlander (London: George Routledge and Sons, 1904).

Pascal, B. (1623–62), *Pensées*, trans. A. Krailsheimer (Harmondsworth: Penguin, 1966).

Swinburne, R. T., *The Coherence of Theism* (Oxford: Oxford University Press, 1977).

Rowe, W. L., *Philosophy of Religion: An Introduction*, 2nd edition (Belmont, Calif.: Wadsworth, 1993).

1

The Idea of God

We will contrast various historical ideas of the divine with the idea of a maximally great being. The key great-making qualities of a maximally great being will be identified.

1.1 Historical Conceptions of the Divine

Historically, there have been various conceptions of the divine. Thales (ca. 625–ca. 545 BC), regarded by many as the first philosopher, is reputed to have said, "Everything is full of gods." Taken at face value, this statement implies that there are many gods. Thales also said, "The magnet has a soul." Still, Thales seems to have believed that only material things exist, since he is also reputed to have said, "Everything is from water." Thus, Thales apparently sought to explain things in terms of **natural** forces alone. On the other hand, many primitive religions are *hecastotheistic*, that is, they imply that every sort of object possesses **supernatural** powers. As the foregoing discussion suggests, while it was commonplace in ancient times to believe in a plurality of gods, there was no clear consensus about whether the gods are material or spiritual in nature.

The belief in, or worship of, a plurality of gods is known as *polytheism*. Thus, polytheism ranges from a belief in two gods (*ditheism*) to a belief in a countless number of gods (*myriotheism*). For example, according to Manichaeism, there are only two gods: a good god of light, and an evil god of darkness. At the other extreme, in certain primitive animistic religions it is supposed that every object in the universe contains a distinct divine being, implying there are indefinitely many gods. In the polytheistic religion of the ancient Greeks, a multitude of imperfect gods is acknowledged, each one of which has limited, specialized, superhuman powers: a god of thunder, a god of the oceans, a god of the sun, a god of the underworld, a god of love, a god of war, and so forth.

The polytheistic religion of the ancient Egyptians includes another element: the belief in, or worship of, animal gods (or beast gods), known as *zootheism* (or *theriotheism*). Three other forms of theism that have frequently been associated with polytheism are *anthropotheism*, the belief that the gods originated as men or are essentially human in nature; *herotheism*, the worship of deified men; and *autotheism*, the deification and worship of oneself. These three forms of theism are consistent with polytheism, as well as mutually consistent. Alexander the Great (356–323 BC) declared himself to be a god; his self-worship provides an illustration of herotheism, autotheism, and some elements of anthropotheism.

In contrast to the foregoing polytheistic pagan religious beliefs, *monotheism* is the belief that there is just one god. For instance, traditional forms of Judaism, Christianity, and Islam are monotheistic, subscribing to the belief that there is just one god, a god who is morally perfect and has unlimited, superhuman qualities.

Xenophanes (ca. 570–ca. 478 BC) is an early philosophical critic of pagan Greek polytheism, who apparently exhibits strongly monotheistic tendencies. The following striking observations are attributed to Xenophanes.[1]

> Homer and Hesiod ascribed to the gods whatever is infamy and reproach among men: theft and adultery and deceiving each other.
>
> Mortals suppose that the gods are born and have clothes and voices and shapes like their own. But if oxen, horses, and lions had hands or could paint with their hands and fashion works as men do, horses would paint horse-like images of gods and oxen oxen-like ones, and each would fashion bodies like their own. The Ethiopians consider the gods flat-nosed and black; the Thracians blue-eyed and red-haired.
>
> There is one god, among gods and men the greatest, not at all like mortals in body or mind. He sees as a whole, thinks as a whole, and hears as a whole. But without toil he moves everything by the thought of his mind. He always remains in the same place, not moving at all, nor is it fitting for him to change his position at different times.

As the foregoing quotations indicate, the usual sort of Greek paganism implies that the gods have bodies and minds like Greeks, and that the gods, like humans, are morally imperfect. Xenophanes provides two criticisms of anthropomorphic polytheism of this kind.

In the first quotation, Xenophanes ridicules the pagan belief that the gods are morally imperfect, on the ground that it is disgraceful to attribute morally imperfect actions such as theft, adultery, and deception to the gods. This may suggest that a divine being must be morally perfect.

The second quotation from Xenophanes suggests the following criticism of the belief that the gods have bodies like those of the Greeks.

(1) Different societies, e.g., Ethiopian society and Thracian society, accept incompatible propositions about the gods and their bodies.

(2) These incompatible propositions are equally likely to be true, e.g., the proposition that the gods have bodies which resemble those of the Ethiopians, and the proposition that the gods have bodies which resemble those of the Greeks, are equally likely to be true.

But the Law of Non-Contradiction implies that, necessarily, if there are two incompatible propositions, then one or both of those propositions is false. Therefore, (1) and (2) together entail that

(3) None of the incompatible propositions about the gods and their bodies referred to above is likely to be true.

In the third quotation, Xenophanes sets forth the alternative hypothesis that there is a unique greatest god, unlike mortals in body and mind: all-knowing, all-powerful, and unmoving.

While Xenophanes's alternative hypothesis strongly suggests monotheism, he does not deny that the greatest god is accompanied by a plurality of lesser gods. This is consistent with *henotheism*, the worship of a single god, without rejecting the existence of other gods. For instance, there is some reason to think that the ancient Hebrews were henotheists prior to the advent of Jewish monotheism.[2] Yet another possibility is *kathenotheism*, the worship of one god at a time as supreme, without rejecting the existence of other gods, and with the inclination to designate different gods as supreme in succession.

Monotheism may take a variety of forms, depending upon how God is conceived. First of all, God may be conceived of as either *personal* or *impersonal*. A personal god is a *person*, that is, a thing which can be aware of itself and of other things, and which can have a variety of mental **states**, including conscious beliefs, desires, and intentions. Traditional Judaism, Christianity, and Islam conceive of God as a personal being in this sense. On the other hand, certain traditional forms of Hinduism and Buddhism conceive of God as an impersonal, ultimate reality that transcends the illusion of plurality and change. Second, God may either be conceived of as a physical thing, or as a spiritual thing, or as a thing that is neither physical nor spiritual. A physical thing is a thing that is located in space; while a spiritual thing, or *nonphysical substance*, is a thing which is capable of consciousness, but which is not located in space.

Judaism, Christianity, and Islam have traditionally maintained that God is a spiritual thing that exists outside the realm of divinely created physical things. Thus, these three religions are forms of *psychotheism*, the belief in a wholly spiritual God or gods. The Irish philosopher Berkeley (1685–1753) proposed an interesting version of psychotheism. He argued that God is a spiritual thing that created a realm of non-divine spiritual things, but that no material, or even physical, things exist. According to Berkeley, everything that exists is either a spiritual thing or an idea, namely, an inner perception had by a spiritual thing. This view, a form of **idealism**, stands in sharp opposition to **physicalism** (or **materialism**), the view that everything that exists is physical (or material). The Hellenistic philosophy of Stoicism is committed both to materialism and to the reality of the divine. Stoic philosophers thought of the divine as a fluid material substance that permeates the universe and gives other material things their unity and purpose. Thus, Stoicism is a kind of *physitheism*, the belief in a God or gods that is physical in nature. Epicureanism provides another example of physitheism. Notice that each of the three conceptions of the divine discussed in this paragraph implies that any divine being is *not* **identical** *with* the universe, i.e., that a divine being is **diverse** from the universe.

On the other hand, *pantheism* is the view that God and the universe are *the very same thing*, i.e., that God is identical with the universe. A pantheist may hold that the universe, that is, the divine thing, is a material being. Such a materialistic version of pantheism seems to have been held by the early Greek philosopher Parmenides (ca. 504–ca. 456 BC), who was apparently influenced by Xenophanes. According to Parmenides, it is demonstrable *a priori* that change and plurality are an illusion, and that there is but one material thing, necessarily existing, eternal, indivisible, and immutable. This is a kind of *hylotheism*, the doctrine that identifies God with matter. Alternatively, a pantheist may hold that the universe, namely, God, is a spiritual being. The Prussian philosopher Hegel (1772–1831) seems to have held such an idealist version of pantheism. Finally, a pantheist may argue that the universe, that is to say, God, is neither a physical thing nor a spiritual thing. The Dutch philosopher Spinoza (1632–77) developed a notable example of this sort of pantheism. According to

Spinoza, the physical and spiritual realms are merely modes of God. Thus, God itself is neither physical nor spiritual in nature.[3]

1.2 God as a Maximally Great Being

According to the regulating notion of traditional Western theism, God is *the greatest being possible*. In other words, God is a possible being whose greatness cannot be surpassed, or even matched. During the Middle Ages, this notion of a maximally great being was developed in detail by theologians such as Anselm and Maimonides (1135–1204).

There are several reasons why this idea of God is worth exploring. First, it is of great historical importance and influence, and continues to play a vital role within the three great religious traditions of Judaism, Christianity, and Islam. Second, it is the idea of a *personal being*. For this reason, it is consistent with God's having a number of features which seem to be highly desirable from a religious perspective, for example, God's hearing our prayers, God's being purposeful, and so on. Third, this idea of God is the notion of a morally perfect being, implying that traditional Judaism, Christianity, and Islam are forms of *ethical monotheism*. Arguably, there are a number of respects in which ethical monotheism marks an intellectual advance over earlier beliefs in a plurality of morally imperfect gods. For one thing, on the assumption that there are **objective** moral values, the worship of a morally perfect God represents *moral progress* over the worship of morally imperfect gods. Furthermore, according to **Ockham's Razor**, an important principle of epistemic rationality, we should not multiply entities beyond necessity. Given this methodological principle, it follows that all other things being equal, monotheism, or a belief in *one* God, is *intellectually preferable* to polytheism, or a belief in *many* gods. Moreover, it seems that gods were often posited by polytheistic religions, at least in part, to explain various natural phenomena, for example, thunder, earthquakes, floods, and so on. Polytheistic religions of this sort attempt to provide theoretical explanations of these phenomena by means of the activities of a *variety* of divine beings. On the other hand, ethical monotheism attempts to provide a *unified* theoretical explanation of *the entire physical world*, namely, that the entire physical world was created and designed by a unique, supremely perfect being. Thus, as attempts at *theoretical explanation*, ethical monotheism is *far more ambitious* than any form of polytheism. Finally, the idea that God is *maximally* great or *infinitely* perfect generates many philosophically interesting problems about the great-making qualities or perfections of God. In what follows, we explore the logic of this important and fascinating idea.

Generally speaking, if a being has a certain degree of greatness, then that degree of greatness must be assessed relative to a particular *category* to which that being belongs. More specifically, the degree of greatness of a being, *x*, of a category, *C*, is determined by the extent to which *x* has the great-making qualities relevant for a being of category *C*. Great-making qualities typically vary from one category to another, and are a function of the nature of the category in question. For example, suppose *C* is the category, Car. Since a car is a humanly created artifact, the relevant great-making qualities pertain to the *purpose* or *function* of an artifact of this kind. Thus, relative to the category, Car, the relevant great-making qualities pertain to the worthiness and admirability of a car as a means of *automotive passenger transport*. In particular, these great-making qualities pertain to a car's design, materials, workmanship, performance, and so on. Given such criteria for grading a car, a Rolls Royce is a highly superior car. And, in particular, a Rolls Royce is a much greater, or better, car than a Yugo.

Presumably, in comparing two such cars, there are objective, **empirically** ascertainable facts about which one of them is more durable, reliable, efficient, and so forth. On the other hand, the contention that a particular set of qualities is relevant for assessing the greatness of a car is a value judgment, and is not obviously empirically ascertainable. The same is true of the contention that the qualities in such a set should be given certain weights.

Similarly, in conceiving of God as a maximally great being, traditional Western theism makes the value judgment that a certain set of qualities is relevant for assessing the greatness of such a being. This form of theism implies that God is a maximally great *substance*, rather than a maximally great *time, place, event, boundary, collection, number, property, **relation**, or proposition*. Yet, it seems that traditional Western theism is *also* committed to the idea that God is a maximally great *entity*, or being of any sort whatsoever, and hence to the idea that a maximally great *substance* is a greater *entity* than any possible insubstantial entity. This commitment reflects the influence of Aristotle (384–322 BC). Specifically, in his *Categories* Aristotle held that individual substances are the primary entities, and that entities of the other categories are dependent upon individual substances. Hence, if the aforementioned conception of God is intelligible, then a being's degree of greatness may be assessed relative to the category of Entity. It can be plausibly argued that Entity is a category on the ground that Entity is the *summum genus*, or most general kind, of all categories. Accordingly, the subdivisions of Entity include the categories of Concrete Entity and Abstract Entity; the subdivisions of Concrete Entity are categories such as Substance, Place, Time, Event, and Boundary; and the subdivisions of Abstract Entity are categories such as **Set**, Number, Property, Relation, and Proposition. Given such a taxonomy of categories, it seems that Entity qualifies as the limiting case of a category, since it is a category which applies *universally*.

Traditional Western theism implies that maximal greatness is determined by a particular set of great-making qualities or perfections, including maximal power (or *omnipotence*), maximal knowledge (or *omniscience*), maximal goodness and/or maximal virtue (or *omnibenevolence*), incorruptibility, and necessary existence. As we shall see, the possession of these *core* attributes entails or implies the possession of other attributes. According to traditional Western theism, God is the greatest being possible in virtue of possessing a *complete* set of great-making qualities or perfections.

Whether a particular quality should be included in such a set of great-making qualities depends upon the nature of the pertinent category. For instance, is *height* a great-making quality of the relevant kind? All other things being equal, if x is taller than y, then is x a greater being than y in the relevant sense? Anselm tried to answer this sort of question as follows.

> But I do not mean physically great, as a material object is great, but that which, the greater it is, the better or more worthy – wisdom, for instance. And since there can be nothing supremely great except what is supremely good, there must be a being that is greatest and best, i.e., the highest of all existing beings.[4]

Anselm's remarks may be taken to suggest that physical greatness cannot make a material object better or more worthy. But such a suggestion is mistaken. For example, it would seem that since mountains may be *graded* by how difficult they are to climb, Mt. Everest may be the *greatest* mountain at least partly *because* it is the *tallest* mountain. Nevertheless, Anselm's claim that physical greatness is not a great-making quality of *the sort* relevant to a supreme being can be defended along the following lines.

Although physical greatness may be a great-making quality relative to some categories of inanimate natural formations, for example, Mountain, it is not a great-making quality relative to the category relevant to the assessment of God's greatness, namely, the category of Entity. Since Entity is not a category of humanly created artifact, the great-making qualities relevant to this category do not pertain to the sort of function or purpose had by an artifact. Rather, the relevant great-making qualities pertain to an entity's *worthiness for worship and moral admiration*. Greatness of this kind is a function of a being's awesomeness and goodness (and/or virtue), and it is not difficult to see that God's core attributes are relevant to assessing his worthiness as an object of worship and moral admiration. In particular, perfect goodness and/or virtue are qualities that are morally admirable to a high degree. On the other hand, even though omnipotence, omniscience, and necessary existence are not morally admirable, they are awesome qualities that can make a morally admirable being worthy of worship. Yet, a being who is omnibenevolent and omniscient must be perfectly wise. Because of the epistemic and practical dimensions of perfect wisdom, perfect wisdom involves both omniscience and the morally admirable quality of being perfectly well-intentioned. Thus, perfect wisdom is *both* morally admirable and an awesome quality which can make an omnipotent being worthy of worship. Similar remarks also apply to divine incorruptibility. Indeed, it seems that a being can be *maximally* worthy of worship and moral admiration only if that being possesses all of the core attributes of God. Thus, it appears that physical greatness is a *relevant* great-making quality only if it ought to be included among these core attributes. However, these core attributes include omnipotence. And as we have said, we will argue later that being omnipotent entails being nonphysical. Since being nonphysical is incompatible with being physically great, such an argument implies that physical greatness is not a great-making quality of the relevant sort.

It seems that Anselm would accept the idea that the relevant great-making qualities pertain to a being's worthiness for worship and moral admiration. After all, he conceives of God as an object of worship and as an ideal moral agent. In any case, Anselm's assumption that wisdom and supreme goodness are great-making qualities of the relevant kind is quite consistent with the claim that if God exists, then God is a maximally great being with respect to his worthiness for worship and moral admiration.

But it has been alleged that maximal greatness is unintelligible. The charge is that maximal greatness can be shown to be self-contradictory, relying solely upon logical deductions from premises known *a priori*. If this charge is correct, then one or more of the divine attributes are either internally inconsistent or inconsistent with one another. This sort of *a priori* objection to the possibility of a maximally great being can take many different forms.

According to the first form of this *a priori* objection, it is impossible that there is a *greatest being*. In particular, it may be argued that there is no maximum degree of power, knowledge, or goodness; just as there is no largest number. In other words, for any degree of knowledge, power, or goodness, there is a greater degree; just as for any number, there is a larger number. Alternatively, it may be argued that, in general, greatness must be assessed relative to a restricted reference class, or to a category that does *not* apply *universally*. Yet, as we observed earlier, maximal greatness is to be assessed relative to Entity, a category that *does* apply universally. This second argument implies that it is a *category mistake* to speak of a maximally great *being*, as opposed to a maximally great thing of a less all-inclusive kind, for example, a greatest *car, diamond,* or *baseball player*. How weighty are these two arguments?

The first argument implies that there is no maximum degree of an attribute such as power, knowledge, or goodness; just as there is no largest number. But, on the other hand, there is a largest angle, namely, an angle of 360 degrees.[5] Thus, the question arises of whether power, knowledge, or goodness resembles *Number*, in *not* having a maximum degree, or resembles *Angle*, in *having* a maximum degree. The answer to this question is not evident. Thus, on first inspection, this attack upon the logical coherence of maximal greatness is inconclusive. It does not seem possible to resolve this matter definitively without an account of omnipotence, omniscience, or omnibenevolence. However, in later chapters, we attempt to provide accounts of these attributes. Based upon these accounts, we will generally seek to defend the notion that power, knowledge, and goodness *do* have a maximum degree.

The second argument maintains that greatness must be assessed relative to a nonuniversal category, a requirement which is not met by maximal greatness *per se*, for *it* is assessed relative to Entity, a universal category. We will answer this argument in the following fashion. First, although the category of Entity is universally applicable, the category of Substance is a nonuniversal category. Thus, if we can provide a coherent account of why a maximally great substance must also be a maximally great entity, then this attack upon the logical coherence of maximal greatness is unsuccessful. Below, we attempt to provide such an account.

To begin, every entity must be either a *necessary* being or a *contingent* being. Necessary beings do not depend upon contingent beings for their existence, but contingent beings do depend upon necessary beings for their existence. In other words, if x is a necessary being, and y is a contingent being, then x's existence does not entail y's existence, but y's existence entails x's existence. Equivalently, if x is a necessary being, and y is a contingent being, then x exists in *all* possible worlds, but y does *not*. In this sense, necessary beings are more *fundamental* than contingent beings. This may be taken to imply that, all other things being equal, a necessary being is a greater entity than a contingent being. However, since maximal greatness relates to an entity's *worthiness for worship and moral admiration*, all other things being equal, an entity which *intentionally creates good* is greater than an entity which does not. Moreover, necessarily, everything is either a concrete entity or an abstract entity, and an abstract entity, for example, the empty set, cannot have the power to create. Thus, only a concrete entity can have the power to create. It follows that a necessarily existing concrete entity that intentionally creates good is greater than either a contingent being or a necessary being that does not. Such a necessarily existing creative concrete entity must be a person, since only a person can intentionally create good. Because a person must be a substance, a necessarily existing concrete entity that intentionally creates good must be a substance.

It might be objected that a person need not be a substance, but could be a temporally extended event or process. Our reply is as follows. Necessarily, an event or process *occurs*; and necessarily, a substance *exists* but does *not* occur. Although it is coherent to say that a person *exists*, for instance, that Socrates exists, it is absurd to say that a person *occurs*, for instance, that Socrates occurs. We conclude that it is a category mistake to identify a person with a temporally extended event or process.

The creative potential of a necessarily existing substance that intentionally creates good is maximally enlarged and enhanced if, in addition, it has attributes such as omnipotence, omniscience, and omnibenevolence. Clearly, all else being equal, a necessary substance that is omnipotent, omniscient, and omnibenevolent is greater than any entity that is not. Furthermore, because a necessary substance exists in all possible worlds, and because it is hard to understand why what prevents a substance from *always existing* in a possible world would not prevent it from *ever existing* in some possible world, it would appear that a necessary substance is eternal at least in the sense of existing at all times. In any case, all else being equal, a maximally powerful, wise, and good being who is *temporally unlimited* and *exists at all times* is greater than such a being who is *temporally limited* or *fails to exist at some time*.[6] Finally, to say that a being is *incorruptible* is to say that it has its perfections *necessarily* or **essentially**. In other words, it has its perfections in every possible world in which it exists. Evidently, all other things being equal, such a being is greater than one which is *corruptible*, i.e., that could fail to have one or more of its perfections or great-making qualities. For instance, despite his superhuman powers and other virtues, Superman has an Achilles' heel: he can lose his super powers when he is exposed to kryptonite. This implies that Superman has those powers *contingently* or **accidentally**, rather than essentially. Since Superman is corruptible, he is not a maximally great being.

In the light of this reasoned derivation of the core attributes of a maximally great being, it appears that there is a coherent account of why God must be a maximally great *entity*. We conclude that the first attack upon the logical coherence of maximal greatness is unsuccessful.

As our derivation of the divine attributes illustrates, one or more of the core attributes of God, for instance, omnipotence and necessary existence, may entail or imply additional divine attributes, for example, substantiality and eternality. In later chapters, we will argue that God's possession of the core attributes, and in particular, his possession of omnipotence, entails that he has the additional attributes of substantiality, independence, personhood, spirituality, simplicity (being without parts), freedom, and uniqueness. On the other hand, we will argue that omnipresence, the attribute of being located at every place, is inconsistent with being a spiritual or nonphysical substance. In addition, we will try to show that atemporality and immutability are each inconsistent with God's exercising omnipotence. Based upon these arguments, we will argue that God is not omnipresent, atemporal, or immutable.

According to the second form of the *a priori* objection to the possibility of a greatest being, *too many* greatest beings are possible. In particular, it might be argued that maximal greatness can be **exemplified** either by two individuals at the same time, or by two individuals at different times, or by different individuals in alternative possible situations. If this is the case, then even though the greatness of a maximally great being could not be *surpassed*, it could be *matched*.

The following line of reasoning might be advanced to support the conclusion that the maximum degree of greatness is possibly exemplified by different beings. Historically, a variety of criteria for maximal greatness have been accepted, for example, a criterion which includes being omnipotent, being omniscient, and being nonphysical, and a criterion which includes maximal size, maximal mass, and maximal temporal duration. Since a nonphysical being cannot have size or mass, a single being cannot satisfy both of these criteria at once. But we may assume that each criterion is internally consistent. It can be argued that since such competing criteria for maximal greatness are equally justified, maximal

greatness is **subjective** in the sense of being inherently relative to those
who evaluate greatness. But if maximal greatness is subjective in this sense,
then it is possibly exemplified by different beings relative to different eval-
uators. If this line of reasoning is correct, then maximal greatness is possibly exemplified by *many* beings, and the notion of *the* greatest being
possible is incoherent.

In reply, we observe that even if there are many internally consistent,
mutually incompatible, equally justified criteria for maximal greatness, it
does not logically follow that maximal greatness is a subjective matter. The
most that logically follows is the skeptical conclusion that none of these
criteria for maximal greatness should be accepted.[7] Thus, this attack upon
the logical coherence of maximal greatness is based upon a logically
invalid inference. Moreover, the premise that the differing criteria for
maximal greatness are equally acceptable *and* mutually incompatible is
implausible. As we argued earlier, God's core attributes together entail that
he is most worthy of worship and moral admiration. But it is rather
implausible to suppose that if something has maximal size, mass, and duration, then it must also be most worthy of worship and moral admiration.
Thus, it seems that if the differing criteria for maximal greatness are relative to the *same* category, then they are *not* equally acceptable. The alternative is that the differing criteria for maximal greatness are relative to
different categories. But, then, the differing criteria for maximal greatness
are *not* mutually incompatible. For the foregoing reasons, this attack upon
the logical coherence of maximal greatness does not succeed. One may
fairly conclude, however, that if the notion of the greatest being possible
is intelligible, then a *nonsubjective* account of the relevant value judgments
is required. Even though maximal greatness is inherently relative to a *category*, it has not been shown to be inherently relative to *individual evalua-
tors* of greatness.

Still, the question remains, is maximal greatness possibly exemplified by
different beings? A definitive answer requires determining whether the
core set of divine attributes is possibly exemplified by different beings. A
determination of this kind requires an extensive analysis of the divine
attributes, in particular, of omnipotence. Such an analysis may be found
in subsequent chapters. Based upon this analysis, we will argue that the
core set of divine attributes is *not* possibly exemplified by different beings,
i.e., maximal greatness is not possibly exemplified by different beings.

According to the third form of the *a priori* objection, since every assessment of greatness is indeterminate, we cannot intelligibly ask whether a

maximally great being is possible. But is it true that all assessments of greatness are indeterminate? Surely not. For example, even if it is indeterminate whether a Rolls Royce is superior to a Jaguar, it remains clear that a Rolls Royce is superior to a Yugo. Since this attack on the logical coherence of maximal greatness is based upon a false assumption, it does not succeed.

There are other more specific objections to the internal consistency of maximal greatness. They attack the intelligibility of one or more of the divine attributes, taken either individually or in combination. A number of such objections will be considered and addressed as we proceed in our systematic examination of the divine attributes.

NOTES

1   Quoted in Baird and Kaufman, *Philosophical Classics, Volume 1: Ancient Philosophy*, 2nd edition (Upper Saddle River, NJ: Prentice-Hall, 1997), p. 16.
2   The ancient Hebrews were a group of tribes of the northern branch of the Semites that includes the Israelites, Ammonites, Moabites, and Edomites. A biblical passage that might be an echo of such early henotheistic attitudes can be found in Exodus, 15:11.

> Who is like you, O LORD, among the celestials;
> Who is like You, majestic in holiness,
> Awesome in splendor, working wonders!

In other translations, 'mighty' is used in place of 'celestials'. See *Tanakh, A New Translation of the Holy Scriptures according to the Traditional Hebrew Text* (Philadelphia and Jerusalem: The Jewish Publication Society, 1985), p. 108.
3   Spinoza's notion that God has infinitely many infinite modes that are ungraspable by us is of questionable coherence. Thus, this Spinozistic notion may violate the canons of rationality.
4   *Monologium*, chap. II, in *Saint Anselm, Basic Writings*, trans. Sidney N. Deane (LaSalle, Ill.: Open Court Publishing Co., 1962).
5   See William L. Rowe, *Philosophy of Religion: An Introduction*, 2nd edition (Belmont, Calif.: Wadsworth, 1993), p. 37.
6   The other alternative is to hold that a maximally great being is *atemporal*, but as we stated in the introduction, we will argue against the view that God is atemporal in chapter 5.
7   Compare Xenophanes's criticisms of anthropomorphic conceptions of the gods, discussed in section 1.1.

BIBLIOGRAPHY

Anselm, *Monologium* and *Proslogium*, in *Saint Anselm, Basic Writings*, trans. Sidney N. Deane (La Salle, Ill.: Open Court Publishing Co., 1962).

Cicero (106–43 BC), *De Natura Deorum* (*On the Nature of the Gods*), trans. H. Rackham (London: Heinemann, 1933).

Davis, S. T., *Logic and the Nature of God* (Grand Rapids, Mich.: Eerdmans, 1983).

Gale, R. M., *On the Nature and Existence of God* (New York: Cambridge University Press, 1991).

Levine, M., *Pantheism* (New York: Routledge, 1994).

Morris, T. V., *Anselmian Explorations: Essays in Philosophical Theology* (Notre Dame, Ind.: University of Notre Dame Press, 1987).

——(ed.), *The Concept of God* (New York: Oxford University Press, 1987).

——, *Our Idea of God* (Notre Dame, Ind.: University of Notre Dame Press, 1991).

Spinoza, B., *The Ethics*, in *The Ethics and Selected Letters*, ed. Seymour Feldman (Indianapolis, Ind.: Hackett Publishing Company, 1982).

Wierenga, E., *The Nature of God: An Inquiry into Divine Attributes* (Ithaca, NY: Cornell University Press, 1989).

2

Substantiality

The divine person is traditionally thought to be concrete and substantial (though not corporeal). We will elucidate these ideas by analyzing the concrete/abstract distinction and the concept of substance.

2.1 Substance Among Other Categories

As we have argued, God is conceived of as a concrete substance rather than as an abstract entity. But what is the relevant notion of a substance, and how is this notion to be defined or analyzed? And how is the relevant distinction between concrete and abstract entities to be understood?

Part of the problem is that terms such as 'concrete', 'abstract', and 'substance' have a number of different senses. To resolve this part of the problem we shall *specify* the concepts of "concreteness" and "substantiality" relevant to our categorization of God as a concrete entity and as substantial. After these concepts are specified, we shall attempt to *analyze* them.

There are three possible meanings of 'substance' that should be distinguished: (i) Aristotle's primary *ousia*, (ii) a quantity of material stuff of some kind, and (iii) an individual thing such as an inanimate physical object, a living organism, or a nonphysical soul.

There is considerable confusion surrounding Aristotle's use of the term 'primary *ousia*', which is often translated as *substance*. This translation can be misleading, since one ordinary meaning of 'substance' is an *individual thing* such as an inanimate physical object, or a living thing. But this is not what Aristotle means by the term 'primary *ousia*'. A more accurate

and less misleading translation of this term is *primary being* (or fundamental entity, or basic entity).[1] In the *Categories* Aristotle argued that individual things, e.g., living things, are the primary beings, and that essences are
secondary beings. However, in the later work, the *Metaphysics*, he changed
his view about primary beings, and seems to have concluded that forms,
rather than individual things, are the primary beings. At this point, Aristotle conceived of individual things as, in some sense, combinations of
form and matter. Although there may be a technical use of the term 'substance' in which it means *basic entity*, this is a different meaning than the
more ordinary sense, that of *individual thing*.

According to another ordinary sense of 'substance', a substance is a
quantity of material stuff of some kind, e.g., a quantity of gold, iron, oak,
or lamb. But it is one thing to say that there exists a quantity of material stuff of some kind, and quite another to say that there exists an *individual thing*, even if this individual thing is composed of a quantity of
stuff of the kind in question. For example, it is one thing to say that
Mary has *45 pounds of lamb*, and quite another to say that Mary *has a
lamb that weighs 45 pounds*. After all, a lamb must possess a certain *form*
and *unity* which a quantity of lamb need not possess. Furthermore, it is
possible for there to be an individual thing which has no proper parts,
e.g., a nonphysical soul, or a **point-particle** (which is a *physical* substance,
but is not *material* in any robust sense). And the existence of individual
things of these kinds does not entail the existence of a quantity of stuff
of any sort.

Since God is a nonphysical soul, and since a nonphysical soul is an individual thing, God is an individual thing or substance in the sense indicated. We have categorized substances in this sense as concrete entities
rather than as abstract ones.

But the terms 'concrete' and 'abstract' also have several different senses.
One way of understanding the concrete/abstract distinction equates being
concrete with being observable, and being abstract with being unobservable. However, since this understanding of the distinction is *epistemological*,
it is not directly relevant to our attempt to categorize the nature of God.

According to a second way of understanding the distinction, a concrete
entity is a physical object, e.g., an atomic particle, a rock, or a tree; and
an abstract entity is anything that is not a physical object, e.g., a time, a
place, or a boundary. On this understanding of 'abstract', since God is nonphysical, he is abstract. Thus, if we are to make sense of the notion that
God is a concrete individual thing, and *not* an abstract entity, then another
understanding of the concrete/abstract distinction is required.

Fortunately, a third understanding of the concrete/abstract distinction is available. This understanding of the distinction figures centrally in the contemporary debate between **realists** and **nominalists**. In the context of this debate, realists maintain that *abstracta* exist, whereas nominalists maintain that only *concreta* exist. Thus, for example, realism is compatible with the existence of abstract entities of the following kinds: properties (for example, redness, squareness), relations (for example, betweenness, diversity), propositions (for example, that all unicorns are vertebrates, that some vertebrates are horses), and sets (for example, the empty set, the set of Socrates, Plato, and Aristotle). On the other hand, the existence of concrete entities of the following kinds is compatible with nominalism: events (for example, storms and explosions), places (for example, **point-positions** and volumes of space), times (for example, instants and durations), boundaries (for example, surfaces and edges), **tropes** (for example, the particular wisdom of Socrates, *that* particular redness), substances (for example, physical objects and nonphysical souls), collections (for example, the **mereological sum** of the Earth, the Moon, and the Sun, and the mereological sum of the Statue of Liberty, the Great Wall of China, and the Leaning Tower of Pisa), and absences (for example, holes and shadows). This third understanding of the concrete/abstract distinction is the one that is relevant to our categorization of God as a concrete substantial entity.

Why is God thought to be such a concrete substance? As a being that is omniscient, omnipotent, and omnibenevolent, God has mental attributes such as believing, willing, and desiring. But only a concrete substance of the sort in question, that is, an individual thing, can have such mental attributes. Furthermore, it seems that if an entity is omniscient, omnipotent, and omnibenevolent, then that entity has intentions, beliefs, self-awareness, intelligence, and can perform actions. Such an entity is a person. But persons are a kind of concrete substantial entity. Finally, God is a nonphysical soul. Yet, it is also true that nonphysical souls are a kind of concrete substantial entity.

It follows that God is both a soul and a person. But to assert that a soul is a person, is not to imply that a soul is a *human* person: God is a *superhuman* or *divine* person. For example, Descartes (1595–1650) distinguishes between the human person and the soul, the former being formed from the "substantial union" of the human body and the soul.

As we have said, souls are a kind of concrete substantial entity. However, the relevant conception of the concrete/abstract distinction is not easy to analyze. For instance, an initial attempt that has some plausibility goes as follows. A concrete entity is something that enters into spatial or temporal relations, and an abstract entity is something that does not enter into relations of this kind.[2]

One objection to this proposal is that there could be a concrete entity that does *not* enter into spatial or temporal relations, namely, God. Since God is a nonspatial soul, he does not enter into spatial relations. In addition, if the traditional idea that God exists outside of time is correct, then God does not enter into temporal relations. But as we have indicated, we find the claim that God is atemporal to be problematic. So, we do not regard this objection as decisive.

Still, the proposed analysis is subject to another, more serious difficulty. It is that this account implies, falsely, that an abstract entity does not enter into temporal relations. Consider, for instance, an abstract entity such as wakefulness. Of course, this property cannot undergo **intrinsic change**, unlike, for example, Socrates, who intrinsically changes when he falls asleep. But an entity, *e*, can enter into temporal relations by undergoing **relational change**, even though *e* does *not* intrinsically change. Necessarily, if an entity, *e*, changes its relations to other entities, then *e* enters into temporal relations. For example, a basic particle which does *not* intrinsically change, but which is orbited by other particles over some interval of time, enters into temporal relations with these other particles. Similarly, since wakefulness is exemplified by Socrates at one time and not at another, this property undergoes relational change. Thus, wakefulness *does* enter into temporal relations.

We believe, however, that the foregoing attempt to analyze the concrete/abstract distinction can be improved by utilizing certain additional concepts of **ontology**. *Ontology* is the study of the more basic categories of existence, for example, Substance, Property, Relation, Place, Time, Event, and so on. We take the concept of an ontological category as undefined, and note that any comprehensive understanding of the world presupposes the use of such categories. A crucial component of our analysis of the concrete/abstract distinction is an intuitive notion of a class of ontological categories that are of a certain level of generality. Intuitively, the ontological categories on the following list, *L*, appear to be of the same level of generality.

List *L*: Event, Place, Time, Trope, Boundary, Collection, Absence, Property, Relation, and Proposition.

Examples of ontological categories which also seem to be at this level of generality but which we have not included on *L* are Substance and Set.

Consistent with what we said in the previous chapter, Entity is the most general ontological category. Entity subdivides into the ontological categories of Concrete Entity and Abstract Entity. Concrete Entity subdivides into the ontological categories of Substance, Place, Time, Event, Trope, Boundary, Absence, Collection, and so on. Abstract Entity subdivides into the ontological categories of Property, Relation, Proposition, Set, and so forth. Accordingly, we can say that Entity is at the highest level of generality (level A), Concrete Entity and Abstract Entity are at the next highest level of generality (level B), and the subdivisions of Concrete Entity and the subdivisions of Abstract Entity are at the next lower level of generality (level C). Furthermore, there are level D ontological categories which are subdivisions of level C ontological categories, and so on. For example, Physical Object and Nonphysical Soul are subdivisions of Substance; Surface, Edge, and Corner are subdivisions of Boundary; Shadow and Hole are subdivisions of Absence, and so forth.

Intuitively speaking, to say that an ontological category is at level C is to say that it is of the same level of generality as the categories on L. This idea can be explained in a simplified fashion as follows. Assume for the sake of argument that there could be entities belonging to each of the ontological categories on L. In that case, an ontological category is at level C if and only if either (i) that category neither subsumes nor is subsumed by a category on L, and (ii) that category is not subsumed by an ontological category which is not on L and which satisfies (i). (The relevant notion of category subsumption can be understood in terms of this example: Boundary *subsumes* Surface just because, first, necessarily, a surface is a boundary, and second, possibly, some boundary is not a surface.)[3] As we shall see, the notion of an ontological category at level C can be used to analyze both the concrete/abstract distinction and the notion of a substance.

The concrete/abstract distinction can now be analyzed as follows. An entity, x, is concrete if and only if x is an instance of a level C category which could be **instantiated** by some entity, y, which has spatial or temporal parts; and an entity, z, is abstract if and only if z is not concrete. We take the general concept of parthood as undefined. Examples of *spatial* parts are the right and left halves of a physical object, and examples of *temporal* parts are the first and second halves of a hour. Proper parts of these kinds are concrete. Perhaps there are also *logical* parts, for instance, the properties that are the conjuncts of the compound property of being a man *and* being unmarried. Any such proper parts are abstract.

This account of the concrete/abstract distinction gives the correct result in the two problem cases discussed earlier. First, even if God lacks spatial and temporal parts, he is an instance of a level C category, namely, Substance, which could have some (other) instance with spatial parts, for example, a tree. Hence, our analysis of the concrete/abstract distinction has the desired implication that God is a concrete entity. Our analysis also has the desired consequence that wakefulness, an instance of the level C category Property, is an abstract entity. This follows from the fact that there could not be an abstract property that has spatial or temporal *parts*, logically consistent with our earlier argument that an abstract property such as wakefulness enters into temporal *relations*.

2.2 Substance and Independence

An important view in the history of metaphysics is that a substance is *autonomous* or *independent* in a way in which an insubstantial entity is not. Three important historical figures who seek to defend independence theories of substance are Aristotle, Descartes, and Spinoza. Aristotle and Descartes attempt to develop independence theories of substance that are compatible with the apparent possibility of both a single uncreated divine substance and a plurality of non-divine created substances.[4] In contrast, Spinoza develops an independence theory of substance that entails that there can be only one substance, uncreated and divine. Thus, Spinoza's theory precludes any possibility of a plurality of substances of any kind. These and other implications of Spinoza's theory of substance are critically examined in section 2.3.

According to a first attempt to analyze substance in terms of independence, a substance has a very strong sort of ontological independence. According to this attempt, x is a substance if and only if x can exist without *any other entity* existing. This proposed analysis implies that a substance is a basic entity in a very strong sense. Unfortunately for this proposal, it does not seem necessary for a substance to be a basic entity in this sense. Indeed, there appear to be individual substances whose existence entails the existence of other entities. For example, the existence of a compound physical object entails the existence of its *parts*; the existence of any material object entails the existence of *places* or *boundaries*; and the existence of a substance of any sort entails the existence of *properties* had by that substance. For these reasons, this first attempt to analyze substance in terms of independence does not succeed. Nevertheless, as we have argued at length elsewhere, substance can be analyzed in terms of a weaker sort of independence by using the notion of an ontological category at level C.[5]

To begin, a substance is an entity of a particular level C ontological category. According to our analysis, the instances of this category of Substance must meet certain independence conditions *qua* being instances of that category. In other words, we shall argue that the concept of substance can be analyzed in terms of independence conditions derived from an entity's belonging to a level C ontological category. Our analysis can be stated in terms of the **conjunction** of three independence conditions as follows.

> **(D1)** *x* **is a substance = df. *x* is an instance of a level *C* category, *C1*, such that: (i) *C1* could have a *single* instance throughout an interval of time, (ii) *C1*'s instantiation does *not* entail the instantiation of *another* level *C* category which satisfies (i), and (iii) it is impossible that something belonging to *C1* has a *part* belonging to *another* level *C* category (other than the categories of Concrete Proper Part and Abstract Proper Part).**[6]

Although clause (i) of *D1* implies that there could be a substance that is independent of any other substance, it does not imply that *every* substance could be independent of any other substance. For example, clause (i) of *D1* is logically consistent with there being a compound substance that is dependent upon its substantial parts. Hence, according to clause (i) of *D1*, an entity, *x* (regardless of whether *x* is simple or compound), is a substance in virtue of *x*'s belonging to a level C category which could have a single instance throughout an interval of time. Clause (i) of *D1* characterizes a substance in terms of an independence condition implied by the instantiability of a certain level C category.

Clause (ii) of *D1* implies that an entity, *x*, is a substance only if *x*'s instantiation of a level C category is independent of the instantiation of another level C category which could have a single instance throughout an interval of time. However, although the existence of a substance may entail the existence of entities of another level C category, for example, properties, in no case is this *other* category such that *it* could have a single instance throughout an interval of time. We conclude that the category of Substance satisfies clause (ii) of *D1*.

Clause (iii) of *D1* implies that an entity, *x*, is a substance only if *x* belongs to a level C category whose instantiation by an item is independent of any other level C category being instantiated by a *part* of that item. In general, a part of a physical substance could only be a physical substance or a portion of physical stuff, and a nonphysical soul has no parts. Hence, it appears to be impossible for a substance to have a part that belongs to another level C category of the sort in question, for instance, a place, a time, a boundary, an event, a trope, an absence, a property, a relation, a proposition, and so on.[7] Thus, the category of Substance seems to satisfy clause (iii) of *D1*.

D1 is compatible with either of two assumptions. On the first, all individual substances have contingent existence: each substance could fail to exist. On the second assumption, there is a single necessarily existing substance, G, such as God, a substance which could not fail to exist. On either of these assumptions, it is possible for there to be a substance, s, which exists throughout some interval of time, t, without any other substance existing within t. On the first assumption there could exist throughout t but a single contingent substance. On the second assumption, if G exists in time, then there could exist throughout t but a single necessary substance; and if G exists outside of time, then there could exist throughout t but a single contingent substance.

We shall question the traditional theological claim that God is essentially atemporal, and question the intelligibility of there being both something that is in time and some substance that is outside of time. Nevertheless, *D1* allows for this possibility.

However, it might be objected that *D1* is incompatible with divine creativity. It might be reasoned that since God is perfectly good, he necessarily creates good things. If God necessarily creates, then for every time t, he necessarily creates something at t. Since an interval of time must contain more than one time, and since God has necessary existence, one might conclude that it is not possible that there is just one thing throughout an interval of time.

But if the claim that God necessarily creates is taken to imply that for every time t, he necessarily creates something at t, then this claim is implausible. Of course, it is true that God necessarily has *the power* to create. But this does not entail that God necessarily exercises this power. It might be assumed that God necessarily creates something at *some* time. However, this does not imply that for every time t, God necessarily creates something at t, as the objection to *D1* under discussion requires. For example, it is plausible to suppose that, possibly, God creates the first contingent substance, then he does not create anything for a time, then God creates the second contingent substance, then he does not create anything for a time, and so on. It seems possible that a pattern of *varying* divine creative activity of this sort is at least as good as a pattern of *constant* divine creative activity. Moreover, God can bring it about that a *substance* undergoes *change* throughout some interval of time, for example, that a soul undergoes mental changes throughout the interval of time in question. But this entails that God creates a *nonsubstantial* entity at *every* time in that interval, namely, some *change* or *event*. Hence, even if for *every* time *t*, God necessarily creates *something* at *t*, it does not follow that it is impossible that there is just one *substance* throughout some interval of time. Thus, we conclude that *D1* is compatible with divine creativity.

Yet another possible objection to *D1* is that if there is an individual substance, then there must be other substances, namely, the [spatial] parts of the individual substance in question. But it is only true that a *compound* substance must be composed of other substances. It is possible for there to be a *simple* substance that has no other substance as a [spatial] part, for instance, a nonspatial soul, a point-particle, or an indivisible, spatially extended, particle.[8] Furthermore, possibly, there is an *enduring substance* that does not have another shorter-lived substance as a [temporal] part or sub-stage. (In contrast, necessarily, a *temporally extended event* has other shorter-lived events as temporal parts or sub-stages.) Still, arguably, there could be a temporally extended substance that *does have* other shorter-lived substances as temporal parts, e.g., a four-dimensional physical object in a four-dimensional **space–time continuum**. But, possibly, there is an enduring, indivisible, physical particle in three-dimensional space (*not* four-dimensional space-time) which *does not have* another shorter-lived, indivisible, physical particle as a [temporal] part or sub-stage; and possibly, there is an enduring nonspatial soul which does not have another shorter-lived soul as a [temporal] part or sub-stage. Thus, it *is* possible that throughout an interval of time, *t*, there exists an indivisible substance and no other substance, for example, just one enduring indivisible particle, or just one enduring nonspatial soul.

On the basis of the preceding discussion, we conclude that the category of substance satisfies the three clauses of *D1*. On the other hand, it appears that the categories of Event, Time, Place, Trope, Boundary, Collection, Property, Relation, Proposition, and Set could *not* have a single instance over an interval of time. Let us briefly explore the nature of these categories in order to give some indication of how this observation can be supported.

Consider first the categories of Property and Trope. Necessarily, either an abstract property, or a concrete trope, is an entity that stands in lawful logical or causal relations to *others* of its kind. For example, the existence of squareness (or of a particular squareness) entails the existence of straightness (or of a particular straightness). Similar arguments apply to the categories of Relation, Proposition, Set, and so on.

With respect to the category of Place, necessarily, if space exists, then it has an intrinsic structure that is compatible with the occurrence of motion. This implies that, necessarily, if space exists, then space contains at least *two* places.

In the case of the category of Time, necessarily, if time exists, then it has an intrinsic structure that is compatible with creation, destruction, **qualitative change**, or relational change. It follows that, necessarily, if time exists, then there are at least *two* times.

With regard to the category of Boundary, necessarily, every boundary is spatial or temporal in character. The existence of a boundary entails the existence of an extended, continuous, space or time which contains infinitely many extended places or times. Moreover, necessarily, whatever is *bounded* has a dimension lacked by its *boundary*, e.g., a dimension of thickness, area, length, or duration. Thus, necessarily, if there is one (spatial or temporal) boundary, then there are infinitely many *other* spatial or temporal boundaries.

Consider next the category of Event. Necessarily, an event that occurs over an interval of time is a process. Necessarily, a process involves other sub-processes that are themselves events. Hence, necessarily, if an event occurs over an interval of time, then there is *another* event that occurs within that temporal interval.

Finally, let us consider the category of Collection. Necessarily, if a concrete collection, c_1, exists throughout an interval of time, t, then c_1 has at least two parts, x and y, both of which exist throughout t. In that case, there must be a shorter time, $t^\star$, which is a sub-time of t and which is a part of another concrete collection, c_2, for example, a shorter-lived collection either composed of $t^\star$ and x, or composed of $t^\star$ and y. Hence, necessarily, if a concrete collection exists throughout an interval of time, then there is *another* concrete collection that exists within that interval of time.[9]

In sum, there could not be just *one* entity of any of the foregoing level C categories [throughout an interval of time.] Moreover, in each case there is no *other* level C category which could be instantiated by an entity belonging to that category, and which could have a single instance throughout an interval of time. Hence, [clause (i) of] $D1$ has the desirable consequence that an entity that belongs to any of these categories is insubstantial. Clauses (ii) and (iii) of *D1* enable our analysis to deal with insubstantial entities of various other kinds.

For example, suppose for the sake of argument that a yellow after-image is an insubstantial mental entity of the irreducible category **Sense-Datum**. On this supposition, a sense-datum is not an event, a property, a trope, a boundary, and so on. If so, then an after-image belongs to the level *C* category of Sense-Datum. But the instantiation of this category entails the instantiation of *another* category that satisfies clause (i) of *D1*, namely, the category of Substance. After all, there cannot be a sense-datum unless there is a perceiving substance. It follows that the category of Sense-Datum does not satisfy clause (ii) of *D1*. Moreover, there is no *other* level *C* category which satisfies *D1* and which could be instantiated by a sense-datum. Thus, clause (ii) of *D1* has the desirable implication that a sense-datum is an insubstantial entity.

Finally, consider the level *C* category of Absence. An absence is an insubstantial concrete entity consisting of a *lack* of one or more concrete entities. An absence is either wholly extended between parts of a bounding concrete entity or wholly extended between bounding concrete entities. One possible example of an absence is a hole in a bagel. But if a hole, *h*, exists, then *h* has as *parts* certain extended *places* or *volumes of space* that are inside of that hole.[10] But Place is a level *C* category which is *other than* the category of Absence. It follows that the category of Absence fails to satisfy clause (iii) of *D1*. In addition, there is no *other* level *C* category which satisfies *D1* and which could be instantiated by an absence. Hence, clause (iii) of *D1* has the desired consequence that an absence is not a substantial entity.[11]

2.3 Spinoza's Divine Substance

As we have seen, according to traditional Western theism, God is a person. A conflicting viewpoint is provided by Spinoza's philosophical system. In particular, Spinoza's system implies that a maximally great being is an impersonal substance. So, while Spinoza accepts the idea that God is a maximally great individual thing, he rejects the idea that God is a person.

Spinoza's system is based in part on his definition of substance in terms of independence. But as we shall see, Spinoza's definition has rather extreme implications about what qualifies as a substance. Spinoza's famous definition of substance is as follows.

> By substance I mean that which is in itself and is conceived through itself;
> that is, that the conception of which does not require the conception of
> another thing from which it has to be formed.[12]

The interpretation of this definition is a matter of dispute. It is clear,
however, that Spinoza believed that for something to be an individual substance, it had to possess a very strong sort of independence. It had to be
both causally and conceptually independent of any entity of the same sort.
Thus, Spinoza's substance cannot be caused to exist; nor can it be sustained by any entity. Moreover, Spinoza maintains that a substance cannot
share its nature with any other entity, since if it did, one could not conceive of one without conceiving of the other. Based partly on the premise
that a substance cannot share its nature with any other entity, Spinoza
reaches the remarkable conclusion that, necessarily, there is but *one* substance, namely, the entire universe, and that the nature of the universe is,
in part, to be extended and conscious. Spinoza identifies this one substance with God, and therefore accepts the pantheistic view that God is
identical with the entire universe.

All of this follows from Spinoza's definition of substance, a definition
that he treats as **axiomatic**, for Spinoza makes no effort to argue for it.
But a definition of substance should be adequate to the intuitive data
regarding substances. And one of the most powerful of these data is the
belief that each one of us has, namely, that one is an individual substance.
It is also part of the commonsense ontology that many substances exist,
including other people, animals, plants, and inanimate material objects.
Spinoza gives no good reason for his rejection of these data, so his definition of substance is unmotivated and merely stipulative. And while we
have defended the idea that substance is *somehow* to be understood in
terms of independence, we do think that Spinoza's definition of substance
attributes to a substance the wrong sort of independence, a sort that it
does not possess. Unlike Spinoza's definition, our independence criterion
of substance [D1] is consistent with the existence of a plurality of
substances.[13]

Like traditional Western theists, Spinoza claims that God is both substantial and maximally great. But there are profound differences between
the God of traditional Western theism and Spinoza's God. According to
Spinoza, infinite thought and infinite spatial extension are two of the essential attributes of God. But in Spinoza's view, God has no center of awareness. More specifically, God's thought is divided among an infinity of
separate minds, corresponding to an infinity of separate bodies. Spinoza

regards these bodies and minds as finite modes of an infinite God. Such a God is impersonal in the sense that it *necessarily lacks a unitary personality*.

The following line of reasoning shows why Spinoza's God is also impersonal in the stronger sense of not qualifying *as a person*. First of all, something is a person only if it possibly has self-awareness, and something possibly has self-awareness only if it possibly has a unitary personality. Thus, any person possibly has a unitary personality. Since Spinoza's God necessarily lacks a unitary personality, his God does not qualify as a person. Spinoza's system implies that persons are mere insubstantial modes of God.

However, it can be plausibly argued that a being that is impersonal in either of the two foregoing senses is not maximally worthy of worship and moral admiration. To begin, it seems that a being is maximally worthy of worship and moral admiration only if that being is both maximally worthy of worship and maximally worthy of moral admiration. It also seems that a morally admirable being is *maximally worthy* of worship only if that being possibly understands acts of worship, for example, prayers for good health, or requests for divine forgiveness. Yet, because Spinoza's God necessarily lacks a unitary personality, it necessarily fails to understand or respond to an act of worship. Furthermore, in the sense in which it may be said that Spinoza's God is responsible for every *good* act, it may also be said that Spinoza's God is responsible for every *evil* act. This sense of *responsibility* is *causal* rather than *moral*. Thus, an impersonal being of this kind is *amoral*, and does not seem to be as worthy of moral admiration as human sages such as Socrates (470–399 BC), Hillel (ca. 50 BC–ca. 10 AD), and Buddha (ca. 563–ca. 483 BC). For the foregoing reasons, we conclude that Spinoza's God is not maximally worthy of worship and moral admiration. Thus, it would appear that Spinoza's claim that his God is a maximally great being is mistaken.

Spinoza acknowledges that his God is impersonal and amoral, and by implication, not worthy of moral admiration. Still, Spinoza might reply that worship can be merely an expression of feelings such as wonderment and awe, and that God is a maximally great being simply because it is maximally worthy of such worship. The claim that Spinoza's God, or the universe, may inspire feelings of great wonderment and awe is plausible enough. Indeed, according to Aristotle, serious philosophical or scientific reflection begins with feelings of awe and wonderment inspired in some such manner. On the other hand, Spinoza would admit that certain qualities are worthy of moral admiration. So, the foregoing Spinozistic reply presupposes both (i) that the wondrous and awesome qualities of Spinoza's God are relevant great-making qualities, and (ii) that morally admirable qualities are *not* relevant great-making qualities. Since it is intuitively plausible that morally admirable qualities *are* relevant great-making qualities, their exclusion from this system of values seems arbitrary and unjustified. Thus, the Spinozistic reply in question is unconvincing. One may fairly conclude that Spinoza's conception of God is *not* a conception of a maximally great being. Moreover, since Spinoza maintains that his God lacks certain qualities that are worthy of moral admiration, Spinoza is seemingly inconsistent in asserting that his God is the greatest being possible.

NOTES

1   This is recognized, for instance, in Richard Hope's translation of Aristotle's *Metaphysics* (Ann Arbor, Mich.: University of Michigan Press, 1968).

2   For an account of the concrete/abstract distinction basically along these lines see Bertrand Russell, *The Problems of Philosophy* (London: Oxford University Press, 1950), pp. 89–100.

3   For a more detailed and formal account of the notion of an ontological category's being at level C, see Joshua Hoffman and Gary S. Rosenkrantz, *Substance Among Other Categories* (Cambridge: Cambridge University Press, 1994), pp. 182–7. This account does not depend upon the simplifying assumption that there could be entities of each of the categories on L and implies that an ontological category is at level C only if there could be an entity belonging to that category.

4   For criticisms of Aristotle's and Descartes's theories of substance see *Substance Among Other Categories*, chap. 2, and Joshua Hoffman and Gary S. Rosenkrantz, *Substance: Its Nature and Existence* (London: Routledge, 1997), chap. 1.

5   See *Substance Among Other Categories*, pp. 89–143, and *Substance: Its Nature and Existence*, pp. 43–72. In addition, we criticize four historical accounts of substance: (1) a substance is that which can undergo intrinsic qualitative change; (2) a substance is that in which properties inhere; (3) a substance is, or presupposes, a "bare particular" which lacks properties, or could lack properties; (4) a substance is a bundle or collection of features. There are two problems for (1). First, it appears that there could be a fundamental particle that is substantial, but incapable of undergoing intrinsic qualitative change. Second, it seems that the surface of a rubber ball is insubstantial, but is capable of undergoing intrinsic qualitative change. (2) is flawed because properties can inhere in an insubstantial entity, e.g., an event. The difficulty with (3) is that the notion of a propertyless entity appears to be incoherent. Finally, (4) is criticized on the ground that the way in which a substance unites its qualities cannot be analyzed in terms of a bundle or collection of those quali-

ties; and on the ground that a bundle or collection of qualities would have
essential properties that a substance would lack. See *Substance Among Other
Categories*, chaps. 2 and 3, and *Substance: Its Nature and Existence*, pp. 9–42.

6   By an interval of time we mean a nonminimal time. And by *C1*'s having a
single instance throughout such an interval, *i*, we mean that something instan-
tiates *C1* throughout *i*, and there is no other instance of *C1* in *i*. Finally,
when a category, *C1*, is said be *other* than a category, *C2*, we mean that *C1*
and *C2* are not necessarily **coextensive**.

7   For a further defense of this claim see *Substance: Its Nature and Existence*,
pp. 65–9.

8   Note that an indivisible, spatially extended particle has spatially extended
parts. However, these parts cannot exist independently of the whole of which
they are parts. Yet, necessarily, a substance, *s*, is *autonomous* in this sense: *s* can
exist independently of any other contingently existing substance, *s**, unless
*s** is a proper part of *s* or *s** helped generate *s*. Since a spatially extended
proper part of an indivisible particle fails to satisfy this autonomy requirement, it does not qualify as a substance. Rather, it is just a *concrete proper part*
[of a substance.] Such an insubstantial portion of physical stuff would be an
instance of an additional, special, level *C* category, namely, Concrete Proper
Part. The wording in clause (iii) of *D1* that excludes the category of Concrete Proper Part from consideration accommodates this possibility of an indivisible substance that has an entity of another level *C* category as a part.

9   This implies that the category of Collection fails to satisfy clause (i) of *D1*.
But note that *D1* also implies that concrete collections are not substances in
virtue of clause (iii), a clause that basically requires that it is impossible that
an entity of a level *C* category has as a part an entity of another level *C* category. After all, something that belongs to a concrete collection is a *part* of
that collection, and it is evidently *possible* for something that belongs to a
collection to be an entity of a level *C* category *other than* the category of
Collection, e.g., an entity such as a substance, an event, or a place.

10 For a defense of this intuitive claim see *Substance: Its Nature and Existence*, pp.
66–7.

11 Note that the category of Absence satisfies clause (i) of *D1*. Consider, for
example, the possibility of there being nothing but two temporally separated
flashes and a period of darkness, *d*, between them. We may assume that in
this possible situation *d* is the only absence throughout the interval of time
in question. On the other hand, it can be argued that the category of Absence
fails to satisfy clause (ii) of *D1* on the following grounds. First, the category
of Substance satisfies clause (i) of *D1* and this category is other than the category of Absence. Second, necessarily, if there is an absence, then there is a
substance, e.g., a substance which flashes, a substance which is perforated, a
substance which is shadowed or which casts a shadow, and so on. (Though,
clearly, there could be a substance without an absence.) Still, some have

claimed that there could be a flash without there being a substance that flashes, and thus it is controversial whether the existence of an absence requires the existence of a substance. But since clause (iii) of *D1* implies that absences are not substances, we can remain neutral with respect to this controversy. For a general discussion of this controversy see *Substance: Its Nature and Existence*, pp. 64–5.

12   *The Ethics*, part I, definition 3. This quotation is from the Samuel Shirley translation, *The Ethics and Selected Letters*, ed. Seymour Feldman (Indianapolis, Ind.: Hackett Publishing Company, 1982), p. 31.

13   However, it is also true that *D1* is consistent with the claim that, necessarily, there is one and only one substance. Thus, *D1* is *neutral* about whether there could be a plurality of substances. This sort of neutrality has some theoretical advantages.

BIBLIOGRAPHY

Aristotle, *Categories*, trans. J. Ackrill, in *The Complete Works of Aristotle*, ed. Jonathan Barnes, 2 vols. (Princeton, NJ: Princeton University Press, 1984), 1:7.

——, *Metaphysics*, trans. Richard Hope (Ann Arbor, Mich.: University of Michigan Press, 1968).

Hoffman, J. and Rosenkrantz, G. S., *Substance Among Other Categories* (Cambridge: Cambridge University Press, 1994).

—— and ——, *Substance: Its Nature and Existence* (London: Routledge, 1997).

Lowe, E. J., *Kinds of Being: A Study of Individuation, Identity and the Logic of Sortal Terms* (Oxford: Blackwell, 1989).

——, *The Possibility of Metaphysics: Substance, Identity, and Time* (Oxford: Oxford University Press, 1998).

Rosenkrantz, G. S. and Hoffman, J., "The Independence Criterion of Substance," reprinted in *Metaphysics: Contemporary Readings*, ed. S. D. Hales (Belmont, Calif.: Wadsworth, 1999), pp. 384–96.

Simons, P., "Particulars in Particular Clothing: Three Trope Theories of Substance," reprinted in *Metaphysics: Contemporary Readings*, ed. S. D. Hales (Belmont, Calif.: Wadsworth, 1999), pp. 397–411.

Spinoza, B., *The Ethics*, in *The Ethics and Selected Letters*, ed. Seymour Feldman (Indianapolis, Ind.: Hackett Publishing Company, 1982).

3

Incorporeality

According to traditional theology, God is soul (a purely spiritual being). We will clarify the notion of a soul, and argue that a soul cannot literally be omnipresent. It has been charged that the notion of a soul is unintelligible, and similarly, that body–soul interaction is impossible. We will answer these charges. Finally, we will argue that there is a sense in which a soul must be simple.

3.1 Spirituality and Omnipresence

In asserting the existence of God, traditional Western theism asserts the existence of a purely spiritual being. According to this form of theism, God is a nonphysical spirit, or soul, with the power to affect physical things. In addition, many theists are committed to the existence of other souls that have this power, for example, angels, demons, or souls of human beings.

The notion of a soul can be explicated in terms of the concept of substance, the concept analyzed in the previous chapter. It appears that, broadly speaking, at least two kinds of substance are possible: (i) physical objects (typically, *bodies*), and (ii) [nonphysical] souls. A physical object is a *spatial substance*: a substance that is located in space. A soul is a *nonspatial substance that has mental properties*; it is a substance which is not located in space and which is conscious, or at least capable of consciousness.[1] Because God is a nonspatial conscious substance, God is a soul.

On the other hand, a "ghost" that literally has shape, size, and spatial location does not count as a soul. It would be either an "exotic" physical entity, or else a kind of "subtle" physical stuff. (A massless particle is an example of an exotic physical entity, whereas a gas or plasma is an example of a kind of subtle physical stuff.) However, it might be thought that there could be a soul that is spatially located provided that it occupies only a *point* of space. But it is far from clear that such a spiritual substance is a genuine possibility. But even if there could be a spiritual substance of this kind it would not be a *purely* spiritual being. That is, it would not be *wholly* outside of the physical world, since it would occupy a point of space. When traditional Western theism affirms the existence of God, angels, and so forth, it is affirming the existence of purely spiritual beings, and this is what the authors mean by the term 'soul' or 'spirit'. For these reasons, we regard *not being spatially located* as a logically necessary condition of being a soul.

Another aspect of traditional Western theism is the omnipresence of God. However, as we have seen, since God is a soul, he is not spatially located. But then how can God be omnipresent? To say that a thing is, literally speaking, omnipresent, is to say that it is located, either wholly or partly, in *every* place. But there are two very different conceptions of this literal sort of omnipresence.

According to the first conception, an omnipresent thing has infinite, or at least maximum, spatial extension, and has spatially extended proper parts.[2] Such a being would be spread out, as it were, throughout the entirety of space, i.e., would have spatially extended parts. But since God is a nonphysical soul, it is clear that he cannot be omnipresent in this sense.

According to the second conception, an omnipresent thing is *wholly* located at *each point* in space. On this conception, an omnipresent thing has locations, but no size or extension. Perhaps there could be a thing that, as on the first conception, has infinite or maximal spatial extension. But it is difficult to understand how there could be a *substance* that is wholly located at each of a number of different places (or points) at once. It might be thought that there is an *abstract property*, e.g., *Punctitude*, which is wholly located at a number of different points at once in virtue of its being exemplified simultaneously at each one of those points.[3] But God is a *concrete entity*, and a concrete entity could not be wholly located at a multiplicity of places (or points) at once.

Realizing this, Augustine (354–430) defends the claim that God is wholly located at each point in space in another sense.[4] He does so by arguing that space is *in* God. Augustine's defense of divine omnipresence attributes location to God only in a *nonliteral* sense, since space cannot literally be *in* a nonspatial soul (though it appears that an *idea* of space can literally be *in* a soul). It seems, therefore, that Augustine confuses an *idea* of a spatial entity with a *spatial entity*.

As Aquinas (1225–74) seems to have recognized, there is a different nonliteral sense in which God can be said to be omnipresent in virtue of being omniscient.[5] Aquinas's idea seems to be that God's knowledge of the physical world is such that it is *as if* God were literally omnipresent. That is, since God has knowledge of what exists at every place, God can *metaphorically* be said to be "present" at every place, even though he is *literally nowhere*. Similarly, since God has power over what exists at every place, he also can metaphorically be said to be "present" at every place in virtue of being omnipotent. We conclude that since God is *not spatially located*, there is no *literal* sense in which he could be omnipresent.

3.2 Are Souls Unintelligible?

The possibilities of souls, and of the interaction between souls and bodies, are and have been highly controversial. For example, in the idealist tradition, some idealists have argued that *physical* substances are impossible, and that interaction between substances is possible only in the case of souls. On the other hand, some philosophical materialists have argued that *spiritual* substances are impossible, and that interaction between substances is possible only in the case of bodies. We estimate that the great majority of philosophers nowadays hold the latter view.

Varieties of philosophical objections to the intelligibility of both the notion of a soul and the notion of a soul affecting a body have been raised. Since traditional Western theism presupposes the intelligibility of these notions, the **soundness** of any of these objections entails the unintelligibility of this form of theism. (Recall that by a soul we mean any non-spatial substance that has mental properties, whether human or divine, contingent or necessary.) We shall defend traditional Western theism against the objections in question. In this section, we defend the claim that souls are possible. This claim is a conceptual one and, therefore, can be defended by purely philosophical, *a priori* arguments. Here we remain neutral on the issue of whether souls, or even bodies, actually exist, an issue that cannot be settled by reason alone. The other important conceptual issue concerning souls and bodies which we address in this chapter is that of the possibility of *interaction* between them. We defend this possibility in the next section.

   In his *Meditations On First Philosophy*, Descartes plausibly argues that the
existence of a soul is conceivable. He does so by raising rational doubts
about the existence of a physical world. One of these doubts is based upon
the fallibility of sense-perception. Human sense-perception is a belief-
forming faculty which sometimes forms false beliefs, for example, in
certain cases of perceptual illusions. If a belief-forming faculty sometimes
forms false beliefs, then a belief acquired *via* that faculty is not *completely*
certain. Thus, a belief acquired *via* sense-perception is not completely
certain. Now, Descartes's belief in a physical reality is acquired *via* sense-
perception. Therefore, Descartes's belief in a physical reality is not completely certain. Another of Descartes's rational doubts about the existence
of a physical world is based upon the possibility of dreams, and the lack
of a conclusive criterion for distinguishing between dreams and waking
experiences. For any waking experiences, there could be dream experiences that are indistinguishable from those waking experiences in their
sensory content. If so, then he is not completely certain whether he is
awake or dreaming. But if he is not completely certain whether he is
awake or dreaming, then his belief in a physical reality is not completely
certain. Hence, his belief in a physical reality is, in fact, not completely
certain.
   So, Descartes has two plausible arguments that imply that his belief in
a physical reality is not completely certain. Yet, Descartes plausibly argues
that he *does* have an infallible and completely certain awareness of his own
existence through self-consciousness. Therefore, relative to Descartes's very
high standard of complete certainty, there could be a thinking thing who
rationally doubts the existence of a physical world, while remaining certain
of its own existence. Thus Descartes persuasively argues that he can conceive of his own existence together with the nonexistence of the physical world. Conceivably, then, there exists a nonphysical thinking thing, that
is, a soul. Despite arguments like those of Descartes, it has been frequently
held that the notion of a soul is unintelligible. What are the reasons that
have been put forward in support of this claim?
   A first argument protests that the nature of a soul cannot be fully
explained without describing it in *negative terms*, i.e., as *unlocated*.[6] We reply
that there are intelligible *physical* entities whose nature cannot be fully
explained unless they are described in negative terms. For example, to
fully explain the nature of a photon, a photon must be described as having
zero rest mass (i.e., as *not* having rest mass). Of course, the basic nature of
a photon includes certain other, *positive* attributes. But the same is true of
the basic nature of a soul. It includes such positive attributes as *being a*

substance and *being conscious* (or *being capable of consciousness*). So, if it is argued that souls are unintelligible because their basic nature is *wholly* negative, then such an argument is **unsound**.

A second kind of challenge to the intelligibility of the concept of a soul is based on the premise that for any intelligible ontological category, there must be an adequate *principle of individuation* for entities of that category. (A principle of individuation provides an analysis of the *diversity at a time* of entities of some category.) For instance, Leibniz (1648–1716) argued that any two entities must possess different qualities.[7] Most philosophers now reject "Leibniz's Law," and allow for the possibility of two **qualitatively indistinguishable** concrete entities. In the case of *physical objects*, such a possibility (or possible world) consists of there being a number of objects which exactly resemble one another throughout their history and which are symmetrically arranged in space throughout their history, for example, a static world consisting of an infinitely long row of exactly similar, evenly spaced, spheres whose centers lie on the same straight line. Nevertheless, philosophers who allow for the possibility of such worlds nevertheless often accept the premise that for such entities, there must be a principle of individuation. If they are correct, then it follows that the principle of individuation for these entities is not solely in terms of **qualitative universals**, that is, the principle is at least partly in terms of *non-qualitative* properties or *relations* to other specific concrete entities.

Let us assume that if there could be a soul, then there could be two souls, each of which has the same qualitative properties as the other. Two such souls would exist at the same times and, at any given time of their existence, would be qualitatively indistinguishable in their thoughts, experiences, and so forth. Keith Campbell is representative of those philosophers who argue that since two souls of this kind would *lack* a principle of individuation, the concept of a soul is unintelligible. Entities that are intelligible, Campbell assumes, do not lack such a principle of individuation. Campbell holds that bodies, which are intelligible, are individuated by their different locations (i.e., by their relations to places).

Note that Campbell is referring to individuation at a moment in time. He says that

> Atoms, and material things generally, are individuated and counted by their positions. Non-spatial spirits cannot, of course, be individuated and counted in this way. But then, in what way can they be individuated and counted? If there really is no difference between one spirit and two spirits of exactly similar history and contents, then spirits are a very suspect sort of thing indeed.[8]

The problem with this argument is its presupposition that with respect to Campbell's demand for a principle of individuation, bodies are *better off* than souls. Two bodies, he thinks, even if qualitatively indistinguishable, can be individuated at a time by their different places. On the other hand, souls, when qualitatively indistinguishable, lack location, and therefore cannot be individuated at a time.

Suppose that we have two qualitatively indistinguishable bodies, x and y, that x occupies place p_1, and that y occupies place p_2. Campbell thinks that x differs from y in that x occupies place p_1 while y does not.

But, if two qualitatively indistinguishable *bodies* must have a principle of individuation, then *so* must two qualitatively indistinguishable *places*, that is, p_1 and p_2. Thus, let us ask: what is the principle of individuation for two qualitatively indistinguishable places?[9]

The answer to this question will depend on whether space is relational or absolute. If space is relational, then the existence of places depends on the existence of spatially located entities, and the individuation of places must involve their relations to such entities. Since Campbell assumes a substance ontology, so shall we.

If space is relational, and p_1 and p_2 are different places, then one of these places has a relation to a body that the other lacks, and it might be said that it is this that individuates that place. This will not do for the purposes of Campbell's argument, since it is viciously circular to individuate bodies in terms of places, and places in terms of bodies. And more generally, for any two ontological categories, F and G, it is viciously circular to individuate Fs in terms of Gs, *and* to individuate Gs in terms of Fs.

The alternative that remains to be considered is that bodies are individuated by their places and that such places are regions of an absolute space. Since absolute space can exist without bodies, *absolute* places are *not* individuated by their relations to bodies. Thus, if space is absolute, and if bodies are individuated by their places, then what individuates places? The only replies to this question that need to be considered are the following four.

First, it might be claimed that places are individuated by their *locations*, i.e., by the places they *occupy*. But this is impossible, since a place does not occupy (or is not *in*) a place.[10] Hence, places are no better off than souls in this respect.

Second, it might be said that a place is individuated by relating it to *some other place*, via a relation *that nothing can bear to itself*, e.g., the relation of proper parthood. But the exemplification of such a[n] [*irreflexive*] relation presupposes the *diversity* (and therefore the *individuation*) of the entities it relates. Thus, any attempt to individuate a place by relating it to some *other* place in this way is viciously circular. And in general, any attempt to individuate entities of some ontological category by [irreflexively] relating them to other entities of the same category is viciously circular.

Third, it might be maintained that *nothing* individuates places. If this is the reply, then places have no principle of individuation. But if this is so, then why suppose that souls need a principle of individuation? On the other hand, if places need a principle of individuation, but do not have one, then places are unintelligible. Hence, if bodies need a principle of individuation, but have no such principle unless it is in terms of their locations, and places are unintelligible, then bodies are unintelligible as well. Once again, souls are no worse off than are bodies.

Finally, it might be argued that places are individuated either by their exemplification of different *nonqualitative* abstract properties or by their possession of different concrete tropes. An example of a nonqualitative property would be *being identical with that* (where *that* = the place in question). Such a nonqualitative property is known as a **haecceity** or "**thisness**."[11] On the other hand, an example of a trope would be *a particular shape* (of the place in question). Tropes cannot inhere in more than one substance at a time. But in either of these cases, we may assume that souls are individuated by the same sorts of properties or tropes, for instance, by the nonqualitative property, *being identical with that* (where *that* = the soul under discussion), or by a trope, for example, *a particular consciousness* (of the soul in question).

In sum, whether space is relational or absolute, the attempt to individuate bodies in terms of places does not yield any result that makes bodies any better off than souls with respect to individuation. Therefore, if bodies or places are intelligible, then arguments like Campbell's do not establish any unintelligibility in the concept of a soul.

This might elicit the response that while bodies are *separated* from one another at a time by their *spatial apartness*, nothing *separates* unlocated souls from one another at a time.[12] In a similar vein, Ernest Sosa argues against the possibility of souls by appealing to the idea that if x is diverse from y, then there must be a relation holding between x and y which is *other* than diversity but which, like diversity, nothing can bear to itself. Sosa calls this idea the principle *that Diversity Cannot Stand Alone* (*DCSA*). He argues that it is necessarily true that a body coincides in space with itself, and that there could not be two bodies which coincide in space. As Sosa observes, this implies that diverse bodies satisfy *DCSA* in virtue of their spatial apartness. However, he argues that diverse souls do *not* satisfy *DCSA*, since there is *not* an additional relation of the sort required which holds between diverse souls.

Our response to such arguments is that if bodies are separated by their spatial apartness, then souls are separated by their *epistemic apartness*, i.e., their incapacity to be directly aware of one another's mental states. In other words, if bodies satisfy *DCSA* in virtue of their spatial apartness, then souls satisfy *DCSA* in virtue of their epistemic apartness. This notion of epistemic apartness presupposes an account of a soul's being *directly aware* of a state. To say that a soul, S, is *directly aware* of a state, s_1, is to say that (i) S is aware of s_1, and (ii) S is not aware of s_1 *by means of* S's being aware of *another* state s_2. It may be assumed that God, an omniscient soul, is aware of the mental states of other souls. For example, suppose that Jane is a sad soul. Then God is aware of Jane's being sad. But, necessarily, if God is aware of Jane's being sad, then he is aware of this state of Jane by means of his being [directly] aware of *another* state, namely, a state of himself which is *his experiencing* Jane's being sad.[13] Thus, although *Jane* can be directly aware of Jane's being sad, *God* cannot be. In general, it is a necessary truth that if x is other than y, then x cannot directly experience a mental state of y. Thus, necessarily, a soul is *incapable* of being directly aware of the mental states of *another* soul, and God could not be directly aware of the mental states of another soul.[14] Moreover, it is necessarily true that a soul is capable of being directly aware of its *own* mental states. It follows that souls satisfy *DCSA* in virtue of their epistemic apartness. We conclude that souls are no worse off than bodies with respect to there being a[n] [irreflexive] relation [other than diversity] that separates them from one another.

However, it should be emphasized that neither the spatial apartness of bodies nor the epistemic apartness of souls can serve as a *principle of individuation* for bodies or souls, respectively. After all, spatial apartness and epistemic apartness are both [irreflexive] relations which nothing can bear to itself, and as we argued earlier, any attempt to individuate entities of some category by [irreflexively] relating them to other entities of the same category is viciously circular.

Finally, it has been argued that souls are unintelligible because they lack a *principle of persistence*.[15] (For an entity to *persist* is for it to exist at two different times, t_1 and t_2, and a principle of persistence provides an analysis of the *identity over time* of entities of some category.) This argument is based on the idea that if there could be a persisting entity of some category, then there must be a principle of persistence for entities of that category. Let us make the obvious assumption that if souls are possible, then there could be souls that persist. What, then, is the principle of persistence for souls? It has been argued that souls are unintelligible because souls, not occupying places, lack a principle of persistence. It has also been argued that since bodies occupy places, they *do* have a principle of persistence, one in terms of their spatiotemporal continuity.[16] A spatial entity, e, which exists from times t_1 to t_2, is *spatiotemporally continuous* if and only if the spatiotemporal coordinates which e occupies from t_1 to t_2 form a [mathematically] continuous sequence [without a gap]. It is widely held that spatiotemporal continuity is the principle of persistence for bodies; or at least, that spatiotemporal continuity is the principle of persistence for *basic* bodies, namely, fundamental particles.[17] The claim is that, necessarily, a body (or, at least, a *basic* body) persists if and only if it is spatiotemporally continuous.

Of course, souls, not occupying places, do not persist in virtue of their being spatiotemporally continuous. However, if there is a spatiotemporally continuous body, then there must be *persisting places*. What, then, is the principle of persistence for places? As in the case of the individuation of places at a time, the answer to this question will depend on whether space is relational or absolute. If space is relational, then the existence of places depends on the existence of bodies, and the persistence of places must involve their relations to persisting bodies. Thus, if space is relational, and p_1 at t_1 is the same place as p_2 at t_2, then p_1 and p_2 must bear the same relations at the same times to bodies that persist from t_1 to t_2. Hence, if space is relational, then the principle of persistence for places involves the persistence of bodies. As we have seen, however, if the principle of persistence for bodies involves spatiotemporal continuity, then this principle *presupposes* the persistence of places. But it is viciously circular to propose *both* a principle of persistence for bodies in terms of the persistence of places, and a principle of persistence for places in terms of the persistence of bodies. And in general, for any two ontological categories F and G, it is viciously circular to account for the persistence of Fs in terms of the persistence of Gs, *and* to account for the persistence of Gs in terms of the persistence of Fs.

Even if space is absolute, it is viciously circular to account for the persistence of bodies in terms of the persistence of places, and the persistence of places in terms of the persistence of bodies. So, if space is absolute and the persistence of bodies is accounted for in terms of the persistence of places, then what accounts for the persistence of places? The only replies to this question that need to be considered are the following.

A first reply is that the principle of persistence for places is their spatiotemporal continuity. However, an entity can be said to be spatiotemporally continuous only if that entity *occupies* places over time. But, as we
pointed out in our discussion of the individuation of places at a time, a
place does not *occupy* (and is not *in*) a place. Thus, persisting places are not
spatiotemporally continuous in the relevant sense, and this first reply
cannot be correct.

A second reply is that places persist, but have no principle of persistence. But this implies that persisting entities of some categories have
no need of a principle of persistence! Why suppose, then, that persisting
souls need a principle of persistence?[18] Moreover, suppose that if an entity
of a certain category can persist, then there must be a principle of persistence for entities of that category. In that case, since places lack a principle of persistence, places are unintelligible (assuming that if it is possible
for there to be places, then it is possible for places to persist). In addition,
given that bodies have no principle of persistence unless they have one
in terms of spatiotemporal continuity, and given that spatiotemporal continuity requires the persistence of places, it follows also that bodies are
unintelligible.

A third reply is that the persistence of a place can be accounted for in
terms of a principle involving either a nonqualitative haecceity or a trope
that a place possesses at different times. In this context, an example of a
nonqualitative haecceity would be the property of *being identical with that*
(where *that* = the place in question), and an example of a trope would be
that particular shape (of the place in question). In this case, the persistence
of a soul *also* can be accounted for in terms of a principle presupposing
the same kind of property or trope, for example, by the nonqualitative
haecceity, *being identical with that* (where *that* = the soul under discussion),
or by the trope *that particular consciousness* (of the soul under discussion).

In conclusion, whether space is relational or absolute, the attempt to
provide a principle of persistence for bodies in terms of spatiotemporal
continuity does not yield any result that makes bodies any better off than
souls with respect to such an attempt. Therefore, if bodies or places are
intelligible, the argument under discussion does not establish any unintelligibility in the concept of a soul.

As we have observed, since souls are nonspatial, souls lack a principle
of persistence in terms of spatiotemporal continuity. We shall now argue
that *bodies* also lack a principle of persistence in terms of spatiotemporal
continuity, and hence that bodies are no better off than souls in this
respect.

Since the following case seems possible, spatiotemporal continuity does not appear to be a *logically necessary* condition of the persistence of a body. First, suppose that body, b, occupies place, p_1, at time, t_1. Next, suppose that there is another place, p_2, such that at every time between t_1 and a later time, t_2, b occupies p_2. In this sort of case, b instantaneously "jumps" in space. That is, b persists, and although b's history is *temporally* continuous, b's history is *spatially* discontinuous.

It also seems possible for b to persist, and for b's history to be *temporally* discontinuous. In such a case an object "jumps" in time, for example as follows. A body, b, occupies place, p_1, at a moment of time, t_1. At every time between t_1 and a later moment of time, t_2, b (and each of its parts) fails to exist. At t_2, b occupies p_1. This case presupposes that, possibly, a body is totally annihilated and then comes back into existence.[19] The possibility of such a case also implies that spatiotemporal continuity is not a logically necessary condition of the persistence of a body.

The possibility of a body making a spatial or temporal "jump" might be attacked as follows. This possibility presupposes that in some possible world someone has conclusive evidence (or at least justification) for believing that such a "jump" occurred. But, there is no such possible world.

Our reply is this. For an observer to reidentify even a spatiotemporally continuous body (other than himself), an **inductive** or *nonconclusive* justification is needed (at least implicitly).[20] Such a justification is ultimately based on successive perceptions of that body that reveal a similarity in that body's sensory properties at different times.[21] An inductive justification for such a reidentification may involve inference to the best explanation, causal reasoning, testimony, and so forth.[22]

The need for such inductive justifications of reidentification claims can be illustrated as follows. Suppose that person, S, has a physical object, x, under observation at time, t, in ordinary conditions. It seems to S that from t to a later time, t', she has observed x continuously. On the basis of this evidence, S identifies the object she sees at t' with the object she saw at t. But it may be that while S was watching x, x had zoomed away too fast for S to notice, and that another object, y, indistinguishable from x in its intrinsic qualitative properties, had zoomed in, again too fast for S to notice. It is possible for S to be in a situation like this, and thus, to have the very best evidence she can have for reidentifying a material object. Nevertheless, S may be mistaken in her reidentification of x. True, S may anticipate a possibility such as the one described and endeavor to rule it out, but there are others she cannot anticipate. Furthermore, there are possibilities that S can anticipate but cannot rule out, because of the inherent limitation of the accuracy of the observations she can make. Finally, there are some possibilities S can rule out only by presupposing other reidentifications that are themselves uncertain. In the light of the fact that the possibilities of such failures to observe are endless, it is clear that none of us can reidentify a physical object other than himself or herself without relying (at least implicitly) upon an inductive or nonconclusive justification for the reidentification in question.

An inductive justification for reidentifying a body need not involve the premise that this body is spatiotemporally continuous. Hence, given that an inductive justification is possible when an observer seeks to reidentify an external body that is spatiotemporally continuous, an inductive justification is possible also when an observer seeks to reidentify an external body that "jumps" in space or time. For example, take a possible case of an apparent spatial "jump." Suppose that while you are staring at a ball of distinctive appearance, it disappears from its spot on the left side of your desk, and a ball that is indistinguishable in its sensible qualities instantly appears on the right side.[23] Alternatively, in a possible case of an apparent temporal "jump," the ball vanishes from its spot, and two minutes later a ball that is indistinguishable in its sensible qualities appears in the same spot. In either of these cases, the following circumstances could obtain. First, the most sophisticated and exhaustive empirical tests give no indication that the "prejump" ball (or any of its parts) is spatiotemporally continuous with the "postjump" ball (or any of its parts). Second, the "prejump" ball and the "postjump" ball appear to be indistinguishable in their intrinsic qualitative properties and velocities when examined with our most accurate instruments, within the limits of experimental error. Third, such an apparent "jump" invariably occurs under replicable conditions of a certain kind. In these circumstances, all other things being equal, one would possess an inductive justification for believing that the ball had made a "jump" in space or time.

Since objects do not ordinarily appear to "jump" in space or time, if there were an isolated case in which one seemed to observe an object to "jump" in space or time, then perhaps the most reasonable hypothesis would be that one has experienced an illusion. But since in possible scenarios like those just envisioned objects *do* ordinarily appear to "jump" in space or time, in such scenarios the hypothesis that one has experienced an illusion would not be a reasonable one. Alternatively, in scenarios of this kind it can be hypothesized that the first object one observes has been totally destroyed and that the perceptually indistinguishable object one observes later is a newly created twin. It can be further supposed that this twinning phenomenon is a sheer coincidence, or that it is the work of some unobservable agent or mechanism. Other, more implausible hypotheses are also available. Clearly, however, the simplest and best explanation, and the one we are therefore justified in accepting in the possible situations under discussion, is the hypothesis of a spatial or temporal "jump."[24]

Enough has now been said to make it plausible that spatiotemporal continuity is not a logically necessary condition for the persistence of a body (or of a basic body). Hence, although souls lack a principle of persistence in terms of spatiotemporal continuity, so do bodies. Once again, souls turn out to be no worse off than bodies in this respect.

Nevertheless, it may be the case that souls are impossible without our being able to rationally conclude that they are impossible. Thus, we do not claim to have *demonstrated* here, or to know with certainty, that souls are possible. We only claim that since there are at present no conclusive reasons to think that souls are impossible, and since the concept of a soul is *prima facie* intelligible, we are justified in believing that souls are possible.

3.3 Is Body–Soul Interaction Unintelligible?

Ernest Sosa and others have challenged the intelligibility of causal interaction between bodies and souls, on the grounds that it violates the **supervenience** of causal properties upon noncausal properties.[25] In this argument, we are invited to consider the possibility of a world, W_1, in which there are two qualitatively indistinguishable souls, s_1 and s_2, and two qualitatively indistinguishable bodies, b_1 and b_2, such that: s_1 and b_1 causally interact, s_2 and b_2 causally interact, but s_1 does not interact with b_2, and s_2 does not interact with b_1. Sosa defends the fairly plausible thesis that an object's causal properties supervene upon its noncausal properties. Sosa means by this that no single possible world, such as W_1, could contain two pairs of entities exactly alike noncausally but each differently interrelated causally. That is to say, causal relations supervene upon *qualitative noncausal factors*. Could there then be a world such as W_1 in which s_1 interacts with b_1 but not with b_2, while s_2 interacts with b_2 but not with b_1? Well, in order for s_1, s_2, b_1, and b_2 to interact as described in W_1, there must be some *noncausal* relation between s_1 and b_1 which does not hold between s_1 and b_2, and there must be some *noncausal* relation between s_2 and b_2 which does *not* hold between s_2 and b_1. However, because s_1 and s_2 are unlocated, this relation cannot be a *spatial* one, and, Sosa argues, we have absolutely no idea of what relation it might be. Accordingly, Sosa infers that it is "a great mystery how souls could interact causally with bodies."[26] He would have us conclude that since there is no such possible world as W_1, body–soul interaction is impossible.

Sosa's argument has the following key presupposition:

(*Premise 1*) If body–soul interaction is possible, then there is a possible world such as W_1.

It might be claimed that *Premise 1* is *intuitively* plausible. Be that as it may, it is not clear why a defender of the intelligibility of **dualistic** interaction should grant *Premise 1*, *all things considered*. After all, such a defender might reason as follows. Take a world, W_2, in which there is a pair of qualitatively indistinguishable souls, s_1 and s_2, and a pair of qualitatively indistinguishable bodies, b_1 and b_2, such that: s_1 and b_1 causally interact, and s_2 and b_2 causally interact. Let it be assumed that no single world could contain two pairs of entities exactly alike noncausally but each differently interrelated causally. We have no hint of any relation holding between s_1 and b_1 (or between s_2 and b_2) which does not also hold between s_1 and b_2 (or between s_2 and b_1), respectively. Hence, it is plausible that in W_2, s_1 must interact causally with *both* b_1 and b_2, and s_2 must interact causally with *both* b_1 and b_2. In other words, the situation in W_2 is one in which the effects of interaction in the respective bodies and souls are *causally overdetermined*. Admittedly, such a situation would be strange, but then so would be a symmetrical world containing a pair of qualitatively indistinguishable bodies and a pair of qualitatively indistinguishable souls! Nor does it seem to be *impossible* for a soul to causally interact with two bodies, and for a body to causally interact with two souls. The foregoing argument seems to us to entail the falsity of *Premise 1*.

On the other hand, suppose that there is a convincing argument that implies that it is impossible for a soul to interact causally with two bodies or for a body to interact causally with two souls. Suppose, too, that no single world could contain two pairs of entities exactly alike noncausally but each differently interrelated causally. Now, consider a world, W_3, containing two qualitatively indistinguishable souls, s_1 and s_2, and two qualitatively indistinguishable bodies, b_1 and b_2. Again, we do not have the slightest hint of any relation holding between s_1 and b_1 (or between s_2 and b_2) that does not hold as well between s_1 and b_2 (or between s_2 and b_1), respectively. In the light of this, and the foregoing two suppositions, it is plausible to conclude that in a world such as W_3, there simply *could not be* any causal interaction between either s_1 and b_1 or b_2, or s_2 and b_1 or b_2. And once again, we arrive at a conclusion incompatible with *Premise 1*.[27]

Since each of the foregoing lines of argument seems no less plausible than Sosa's argument against the intelligibility of dualistic interaction, we conclude that if Sosa's argument is to be convincing, then further substantive support for his key assumption, *Premise 1*, is needed. At present, we have no idea of how such support could be provided. On the other hand, if no support of this kind is available, our reply to Sosa's argument reveals an interesting and generally unnoticed implication of dualistic interactionism, namely, that if it is true that all causal relations supervene on purely qualitative, noncausal facts, then there are no possible worlds such as W_1, but only ones such as W_2 or W_3.

The classical attack on the intelligibility of causal interaction between souls and bodies is based on the following argument.

Argument A

(*Premise A1*) Necessarily, a body, but not a soul, has spatial location.
(*Premise A2*) Necessarily, a soul and a body interact only if *they both have spatial location*.

Therefore, it is impossible for a soul and a body to interact.

Premise A1 is unquestionably true. However, it is not clear that *Premise A2* is true. Sosa's argument, based in part on the supervenience of causal properties upon noncausal properties, is an example of an attempt to defend *Premise A2*. We have rejected that argument. However, there is another, more traditional, argument for *Premise A2*. In what follows, we try to show that this traditional argument and certain related ones are unsuccessful.

According to this traditional argument, the production of motion in a body can only be understood in terms of the *transference* of motion from one object to another. (Typically, this transference is characterized in terms of the collision of bodies and the transference of motion by impact.) This argument's assumption that the production of motion in a body can only be understood in terms of the transference of motion might be defended by appeal to the following *transference principle*:

(*TP*) Necessarily, if *a* brings it about that *b* is *F*, then *a* does so in virtue of the transference of *F*-ness from *a* to *b*.

Let *b* be a body, and let *F* be motion. In that case, the transference principle implies that *a* could not bring it about that *b* is in motion unless *a* is in motion and transfers that motion to *b*. However, body–soul interaction is possible only if it is possible for a soul to produce motion in a body. Hence, body–soul interaction is possible only if motion can be transferred from a soul to a body. Since the transference of motion from *a* to *b* requires that both *a* and *b* have spatial location, it follows that, necessarily, a soul and a body interact only if they both have spatial location.

TP presupposes the necessity of what Jonathan Barnes has called the *synonymy principle*:

(*SP*) If *a* brings it about that *b* is Ø, then *a* is Ø.[28]

However, as Barnes points out, *SP* is false.[29] For example, a piece of clay can be caused to be triangular by an object that is not triangular, say, a rolling pin. It follows that *TP* is false as well. Thus, neither the transference principle nor the synonymy principle can be used to provide a plausible defense of the crucial assumption that the production of motion in a body must be understood in terms of the transference of motion.[30] Nor is it obvious that a persuasive defense of this assumption can be provided in terms of some narrower principle regarding motion. Must motion be produced by motion? We shall argue that it need not be.

It is extremely plausible that causal interaction can be understood in terms of universally **quantified** general laws. If causal interaction is to be understood in terms of such general laws, then there can be functional or correlational causal relationships that *do not* involve the production of motion by the transference of motion. (This seems to be true whether or not David Hume [1711–76] and his followers are correct to deny that these laws express some kind of objective necessary connection.) For instance, consider the Law of Gravitation. According to this law, there is mutual gravitational attraction between any two pieces of matter. As a result, two such pieces of matter accelerate toward each other. It is a law that each acquires a motion, but it is not the case that motion is *transferred* from one to the other. Must there be a deeper explanation of the accelerations in question in terms of transference of motion? Not necessarily. In a domain of causal activity, one could eventually arrive at laws or causal principles which are basic or fundamental, and which therefore describe interactions unexplainable in terms of any more general laws or principles. As far as we know, the Law of Gravitation is a *basic* principle or law, correlating one physical phenomenon with another, a principle or law that is *itself* physically inexplicable.[31] Therefore, it seems that the aforementioned accelerations are causally related to one another in virtue of some functional law, but this causal interaction is neither a transference of motion, nor explainable in terms of other transferals of motion. Hence, production of motion in a body need not be understood in terms of the transference of motion.

Since the argument under consideration for *Premise A2* makes the key assumption that the production of motion in a body must be understood in terms of the transference of motion, this argument is unsuccessful. We have conceded that if a soul interacts with a body, then this entails that there is a psycho–physical correlation law that cannot be explained in terms of any more general or more basic physical law. However, it appears that a correlation law of this kind is unintelligible only if a physically inexplicable *physical*–physical correlation law is unintelligible. But, as we argued, a correlation law of the latter kind is *not* unintelligible. In particular, it seems both that universal gravitation is such a law, and that universal gravitation is intelligible. Since a physically inexplicable physical–physical correlation law is not unintelligible, there seems to be no reason to reject the intelligibility of a physically inexplicable psycho–physical correlation law.[32]

Another attempt to justify *Premise A2* is based upon the following two principles. The first is a *restricted* version of the transference principle:

(RTP) Necessarily, if *a* brings it about that *b* is Ø, then *a* does so in virtue of the transference of *some* property from *a* to *b*.

The second is a principle of the nontransferability of causally relevant properties between bodies and souls:

(NTP) There *could not* be a property, *P*, had by *both* a physical object, *x*, and an unlocated soul, *y*, such that *P* is transferred between *x* and *y*, and it is in virtue of this transference that *x* and *y* interact.

The conjunction of RTP and NTP entails *Premise A2*. But both *RTP* and *NTP* are problematic.

First, if *RTP* were true, then the Law of Gravitation could not be a *basic* physical law, *and* there could be no [deeper] *basic* physical law that explains the Law of Gravitation, either in terms of how bodies affect the geometry of space-time, or in terms of the transmission or propagation of particles or waves. *RTP* would entail this because none of these laws involve the transference of some property from one body to another in explaining how gravitation results in the motions of bodies. But since either the Law of Gravitation or some such deeper physical law may well be, and seems likely to be, a basic physical law, *RTP* may well be false.

Second, in any case, there appear to be two kinds of possible cases that refute *NTP*. (1) It seems that, *possibly*, a physical object and a soul *both* have the property of consciousness, and interaction between them occurs in virtue of a transfer of consciousness from a soul to a physical substance, followed by a transfer of consciousness in the opposite direction.[33] (It could happen that a transfer of consciousness from a soul to *a physical object* is the first link in a causal chain that results in the motion of that physical object, and that a transfer of consciousness to *a soul* from a physical object results in a change in the state of consciousness of that soul.) Thus, for example, a human's soul could interact in this manner with certain living parts or cells of a human body, or a soul of another kind, for instance, an angel, could interact in this way with a conscious, living organism, for example, a human or some other creature. As a result, a soul would produce motion in a body, and a body would produce a change of consciousness in a soul. (2) It seems possible for both a body and a soul to have the property of having energy or the ability to do work, and for interaction between them to occur in the form of transfers of energy. In this context, the ability to do work can be taken to mean *either* the ability to produce some physical effect or a more general ability, namely, *the ability to do something*. There are many things souls have the ability to do, for instance, solve mathematical problems, which a body could enhance by interaction with a soul. Clearly, the same holds for the enhancement of bodily abilities by souls.

For these reasons, *NTP* seems to be false. Thus, *Premise A2* cannot be justified by deriving it from the conjunction of *RTP* and *NTP*. Is there another way to justify *Premise A2* that is more plausible than the arguments we have criticized? We cannot think of one. As far as we can tell, there is no good reason to accept *Premise A2*. Since the classical attack on the intelligibility of body–soul interaction is based on *Premise A2*, we conclude that this attack is ineffective.

A final argument against the intelligibility of body–soul interaction can be formulated as follows.

Argument B

(*Premise B1*) If it is possible that there is body–soul interaction, then it is possible that a physical law is violated.

(*Premise B2*) It is not possible that a physical law is *violated*.

Therefore, it is impossible that there is body–soul interaction.

It appears that *Premise B2* is entailed by a plausible account of lawfulness. Necessarily, if L is a law, then L is a true universally quantified **conditional**. Necessarily, a universally quantified conditional is *violated* just when there exists a counter-instance to that conditional. For example, the conditional $(\forall x)(Fx \rightarrow Gx)$ is violated if and only if $(\exists x)(Fx \ \& \ {\sim}Gx)$. Necessarily, there does not exist a counter-instance to a *true* universally quantified conditional. It follows that it is not possible for a law to be violated. It appears, then, that *Premise B2* is true, and we shall not question it.

It might also appear that *Premise B1* is true; nevertheless, we shall argue that it is false. To begin, consider a fundamental physical law such as the Law of Conservation of Energy. According to this law, the total amount of energy in a *closed* system, S, remains constant. This law is compatible with the possibility that the total amount of energy in S increases as a result of energy introduced from *outside S*. Thus, if S = the physical world, then the Law of Conservation of Energy is compatible with the possibility that the total amount of energy in the physical world increases as a result of energy introduced from a supernatural entity which exists outside of the physical world. In other words, the introduction of such energy into the physical world would not violate the Law of Conservation of Energy.

And more generally, consider a typical physical law, L, of the form: for any physical object, x, if x is F, then x is G. Unless the defender of *Argument B* is simply begging the question, he must concede that L says implicitly that for any physical object, x, if Fx then Gx, *provided that there is no true conjunction of a nonphysical law and initial conditions which implies that x is both F and not-G*. Since L describes only interaction between physical states, it is appropriate to classify it as a *physical* law. An implicit *ceteris paribus* provision of the kind indicated guarantees the inviolability of a physical law of the form in question, even if there are interventions by supernatural influences.[34] Such a provision accomplishes this by limiting the scope of such a physical law to physical interactions, and functions similarly to the closure provision in the Law of Conservation of Energy we discussed earlier. Parallel remarks apply to physical laws of any kind.

Suppose that a physical state, P_1, is produced by a soul-state, S_1, and that if S_1 were to fail to exist, then there would be a true conjunction of a physical law, L, and physical initial conditions which implies that P_1 fails to exist. Although, as we have argued, L is not *violated* in such a case, it is accurate to say that L is *superseded* or *overruled*. A soul-state supersedes or overrules a physical law if and only if a soul-state produces a physical state that is contrary to the physical state that would have existed if *only natural causes* were operative. Observe that a law's being superseded in this sense *does not* have the implication that a law is false. On the other hand, a law's being violated *does* have this apparently absurd implication. Hence, a law's being superseded does not imply that a law is violated, and it is a mistake to conflate the superseding of a law with the violating of a law. If the superseding of a law is assimilated to the violation of a law, a deceptive appearance is created that certain kinds of supernatural interventions would violate a physical law.[35]

We believe that the foregoing considerations imply that *Premise B1* is false. Hence, the argument for the unintelligibility of body–soul interaction based on *Premise B1* is unsound.[36]

Our reply to *Premise B1* puts us in a position to understand why God would necessarily be a soul, or a nonphysical substance, rather than a body, or physical substance. To begin, God would be an omnipotent substance. Yet, an omnipotent substance necessarily has the power to supersede or overrule *any* physical law. So, God would have the power to supersede or overrule any physical law. For example, God would have the power to cause a mountain to float miraculously in midair. Were God to exercise such a power, he would overrule a physical law, since the mountain would not have floated unless God had willed it to do so and the mountain did not float due to any natural cause, e.g., magnetic forces. But a physical substance is necessarily subject to *some* physical laws. Thus, a physical substance *cannot* have the power to supersede or overrule *every* physical law. Consequently, it is impossible for God to be a physical substance. Thus, God must be a nonphysical substance. In other words, God must be a soul. In sum, God is necessarily a soul, because he is necessarily omnipotent.

3.4 Divine Simplicity

Most, if not all, familiar substances have parts. But God is a simple substance, and to be simple is to be without parts. Let us see why God must be a simple substance.

To begin with, God is a concrete entity. Because it is impossible for a concrete entity to have *abstract* parts, we conclude that it is not possible for God to have abstract parts. Thus, the abstract properties of omnipotence, omniscience, and omnibenevolence are not *parts* of God. (In general, one should distinguish between a thing's *properties* and its *parts*.) If a part is not abstract, then it is concrete. Does God have *concrete* parts? There are three sorts of concrete parts that need to be considered. First, there are spatial parts, for instance, the parts of a table. Second, there are temporal parts, for example, the innings of a baseball game. Third, it seems possible that there are concrete parts that are neither spatial nor temporal. For example, it appears possible that there is a collection of nonspatial concrete entities such as nonspatial tropes (say, coexisting, concrete conscious tropes of a soul). These tropes are concrete parts of a collection of this kind, but they are neither spatial nor temporal parts of it.

As we have seen, God is a nonspatial substance. Therefore, God does not have *spatial parts*. But does God have temporal parts? Any substance which has spatial or temporal extension and which is in *space-time* has parts that have spatial *and* temporal dimensions, and in that sense, has spatial and temporal parts. But this in no way suggests that God has temporal parts. After all, since God is nonspatial, he is *not* in space-time.

On the other hand, many traditional theologians hold that God is *atemporal*. If they are correct, then it also follows straightforwardly that God does not have temporal parts.

However, there is a third possibility, namely, that God is in time, but not in space-time. Assume for the sake of argument that God is temporal in this sense. In that case, it can be plausibly argued that God undergoes intrinsic qualitative change as a consequence of being omniscient. Suppose that at time, t_1, Mt. Etna is erupting, at t_2 (five years later than t_1), Mt. Etna is quiet, and at t_3 (five years later than t_2), Mt. Etna is erupting once again. Because God is omniscient, if he is in time, then at t_1, *God believes that Etna is erupting and that in five years Etna will be quiet.* But if God is in time, then at t_2 he does *not* have this belief about Etna. Rather, at t_2, *God believes that Etna is quiet and that in five years Etna will be erupting.* Thus, if God is in time, then he undergoes an intrinsic qualitative change with respect to these beliefs about Mt. Etna.[37]

So, if God is in time, then he is a persisting substance that undergoes intrinsic qualitative change. However, there are two important views about the nature of persisting substances. According to the *endurance* view, because persisting substances wholly and completely exist at every moment of their existence, they do not have temporal parts. According to the *perdurance* view, persisting substances only exist in part at each moment of their existence. That is, persisting substances consist of a sequence of temporal parts, much like events do. There is a sense in which a perduring substance that had temporal parts with different intrinsic qualities would not undergo intrinsic qualitative change – it would merely have temporal parts that have different properties.[38] In other words, there is a sense in which such a perduring substance would be a static, temporally expansive entity that displays qualitative variegation over its temporal expanse from one time to another. The perdurance view is often motivated by a commitment to the existence of space-time. Since God is not in space-time, and since the main reason for thinking that a persisting substance perdures rather than endures is that it is in space-time, there is little reason to think that God perdures.[39] Thus, it can be plausibly argued that the idea of a nonspatial, persisting, substantial God is the idea of an *enduring* soul, that is, of a persisting spiritual substance without temporal parts.[40]

In sum, it seems that whether God is inside of time or outside of it, he lacks temporal parts. Thus, we conclude that God does not have temporal parts.

Does God have concrete parts that are neither spatial nor temporal? We can envision God's having concrete parts of this kind only if he is a collection or **complex** of nonspatial, concrete attributes, or tropes. Yet, it may be thought that if the *bundle theory of substance* is correct, then God *is* such a complex or collection.

There are two fundamentally different sorts of bundle theories about substance. The **eliminative** bundle theory holds that there are no substances. Instead, there are collections of nonsubstances, which collections are *not* to be identified with substances. This view usually maintains that what are *thought* to be substances are really collections of insubstantial entities.

However, the eliminative bundle theory does not shed any light on the nature of God. After all, a maximally great being is a *substance*, and the eliminative theory does not offer an account of substance. For this reason, we shall not consider the eliminative bundle theory any further here.

A second sort of bundle theory is **reductionist** rather than eliminative. In its most plausible form this theory *identifies* a substance with a complex of tropes. Such a theory attempts to provide an analysis or definition of the concept of substance by maintaining that, necessarily, for any x, x is a substance if and only if x is a complex of tropes that enter into an appropriate unifying relation. It aims to achieve a measure of ontological parsimony by identifying *substances* with collections or complexes of *nonsubstantial concrete entities*, namely, tropes. It is sometimes thought that such collections or complexes have tropes as parts.

However, there is a fundamental difficulty for the reductionist bundle theory that arises from the very idea of a trope. A trope, for example, the particular wisdom of Socrates, is a concrete entity of a certain kind. Yet, intuitively, a concrete entity of this kind can only exist as a trope *of* something, for instance, Socrates, and this something seems to be a *substance* in which the trope inheres. But, surely, if such a trope *depends* upon a substance as a subject of inherence, then a substance cannot be *reduced* to a collection or complex of tropes.

There are also problems with the argument that the reductionist bundle theory is ontologically more parsimonious than an ontology of irreducible substances. An ontology of tropes, *plus* collections or complexes of them, is no more economical than an ontology which rejects the existence of collections or complexes and accepts the existence of [irreducible] substances, plus tropes. This is because in each case there is a commitment to just *two* basic kinds of entities, *tropes* plus *collections or complexes* of them, on the one hand, and *tropes* and *substances*, on the other. Still, the reductionist bundle theorist finds the notion of a substance to be considerably more mysterious than the notion of a collection or complex. So, a reductionist bundle theorist defends her account by arguing that the notion of a substance stands in need of analysis, but that *all* attempts to analyze this notion are inadequate. One of these attempts is our analysis of this notion in terms of independence. Accordingly, if our proposed analysis is correct, then this argument in support of the bundle theory is not a good one.

Moreover, our analysis of substance implies that God does *not* have tropes as parts. God is a substance, and Trope and Substance are different level C categories. According to our analysis, a substance does not have parts belonging to *another* level C category. Nevertheless, in what follows, we will provide a further argument against the contention that God has tropes as parts, that is, without appealing to our analysis of substance.

To begin, in order to identify a soul with a complex of nonspatial tropes, there must be a relation that unites this spiritual complex of tropes into a single "substantial" complex. It surely won't do to say that *any* collection of spiritual tropes is a soul. Consider a collection of different spiritual tropes belonging to diverse souls, S_1, S_2, S_3, S_4, S_5, etc., for example, the collection of S_1's belief that grass is green, S_2's feeling of sadness, S_3's sensation of red, S_4's fear of snakes, S_5's feeling of envy, etc. Collections of this kind are evidently *not* souls, but it is not clear how the bundle theorist can avoid implying that they are. Since a soul is nonspatial, a spiritual complex of tropes cannot be unified by the spatiotemporal coincidence of these tropes, that is, by their completely coinciding in space at some time. That leaves the following three possibilities. (*P1*) A spiritual complex of tropes is unified by each of those tropes standing in some causal connection to the others. (*P2*) A spiritual complex of tropes is unified by each of those tropes standing in some logical or modal connection to the others. (*P3*) There is some other sort of relation that unifies a spiritual complex of tropes.

What causal relation could unite the tropes in a spiritual complex of nonspatial tropes? Perhaps such a causal connection is analogous to the causal connection in a human body between the heart, the lungs, the kidneys, the brain, the liver, the blood, and so on. If any of these organs ceases to function then this would cause all of the other organs to cease to function. There are two proposals for a causal principle of unity that need to be considered. The first is given by the following definition:

(D1) *a*, *b*, *c*, . . . are the tropes which belong to a spiritual complex of nonspatial tropes ⇔ in *every* causally possible situation, if any one of the nonspatial tropes *a*, *b*, *c*, . . . ceases to exist, then its ceasing to exist causes all of the rest of these nonspatial tropes to cease to exist.

D1 is subject to the following decisive objection. To begin with, it is possible for a soul to lose one of its intrinsic qualities without losing all of them. For example, possibly, a soul loses a certain feeling of jealousy without losing its capacity for consciousness; and possibly, a soul loses a particular feeling of anger without losing a particular feeling of disappointment, and *vice versa*. Moreover, every soul possesses some particular intrinsic quality essentially, for example, its capacity for consciousness. However, *D1* entails that if *one* intrinsic quality of a soul, x, ceases to exist, then *all* of the intrinsic qualities of x cease to exist, including those essential to x, implying that x ceases to exist. Hence, *D1* rules out the possibility of a soul's undergoing a change in an intrinsic quality (while that soul continues to exist). Since this is an unacceptable conception of a soul, it follows that the **analysans** of *D1* does not provide a logically **necessary condition** for the unity of a spiritual complex of tropes.

Does the following less demanding alternative proposal for a causal principle of unity fare any better?

> **(D2)** *a, b, c,* . . . are the tropes which belong to a spiritual complex of nonspatial tropes ⇔ at least one of the nonspatial tropes *a, b, c,* . . . is such that in *some* causally possible situation, if that nonspatial trope ceases to exist, then its ceasing to exist causes all of the rest of these nonspatial tropes to cease to exist.

D2 avoids the objections to *D1*, since *D2* requires only that in *some* circumstances the going out of existence of some trope of a soul causes all of the other tropes of that soul to go out of existence. This is compatible with the possibility, in other circumstances, of the persistence of a soul through change. Thus, the defender of *D2* would assert that any case in which a soul is annihilated is a case in which one trope's ceasing to exist, for example, an essential trope of a soul such as its being capable of consciousness, causes all of its other tropes to cease to exist. It seems that the *analysans* of *D2* provides a logically *necessary* condition for a complex of nonspatial tropes to be a soul. But trouble arises when we ask whether this *analysans* provides a logically **sufficient condition** for a complex of nonspatial tropes being a soul. Given an appropriate notion of spiritual causal connections, it certainly appears that there could be a pair of souls s_1 and s_2 such that it is causally necessary that s_1's capacity for consciousness exists at a time if and only if s_2's capacity for consciousness exists at that time. After all, it is common for one thing's existence to depend upon another thing's existence, for example, a child's existence depends upon its mother's existence; and there can be circumstances in which there are two coexisting things such that the existence of each of them depends upon the existence of the other, for example, a pair of living things which are conjoined twins. Moreover, at least on some readings, quantum mechanics implies that there are far-flung pairs of micro-particles that are causally coordinated or "entangled." Such readings imply, for example, that there is a far-flung pair of micro-particles, p_1 and p_2, such that it is causally necessary that p_1 is spin-up at a time if and only if p_2 is spin-down at that time. So, we may assume that in some possible world, W, there is a pair of causally coordinated souls, s_1 and s_2, such that it is causally necessary that s_1's capacity for consciousness exists at a time if and only if s_2's capacity for consciousness exists at that time. Since a soul's capacity for consciousness is essential to it, if a soul's capacity for consciousness ceases to exist, then this entails that all of that soul's tropes cease to exist. Hence, s_1 and s_2 are causally dependent upon one another for their existence, that is, either one of them ceasing to exist would cause the other one to cease to exist. Thus, in W, it is causally necessary that if s_1's capacity for consciousness ceases to exist, then all of the rest of s_1's and s_2's tropes cease to exist. Hence, *D2* implies that in W, the complex of the tropes of the *two* souls, s_1 and s_2, comprises a *third* soul. But it is evident that the complex of the tropes of a pair of souls would *not* comprise a third soul.[41] Therefore, the *analysans* of *D2* does not provide a logically sufficient condition for the unity of a spiritual complex of tropes. We conclude that the possibility of two causally interdependent souls generates a counter-example to any attempt to analyze the unity of qualities of a soul *via* causal dependence among spiritual tropes as in *D2*.

According to strategy *P2*, the notion of a spiritual complex of tropes should be understood in terms of *logical* or *modal* connections holding among the tropes which belong to the complex. An important and ingenious recent instance of *P2* is the bundle theory of Peter Simons.[42] Simons utilizes a complex of logical or modal relations in order to analyze the concept of a substantial complex of tropes. He distinguishes between the *core* or essential tropes belonging to such a substance and the *peripheral* or accidental tropes of such a substance. We apply Simons's account of the core of a substantial complex of tropes to souls as follows:

> **(D3)** *a*, *b*, *c*, . . . **are the tropes which belong to a soul's** *core* **complex, *C*, of nonspatial tropes ⇔ each one of the nonspatial tropes *a*, *b*, *c*, . . . is such that its existence necessitates the existence of all of the rest of these nonspatial tropes.**

Next, we apply Simons's analysis of the periphery of a substantial complex of tropes in the following manner:

> **(D4)** *a*, *b*, *c*, . . . **are the tropes which belong to the** *periphery* **of a soul's core complex, *C*, of nonspatial tropes ⇔ (i) each one of the nonspatial tropes *a*, *b*, *c*, . . . is such that its existence necessitates the existence of the tropes in *C*, and (ii) each one of *a*, *b*, *c*, . . . is such that the tropes in *C* could exist without it existing.**

Finally,

(D5) x is a soul = df. x is a complex of nonspatial tropes which consists of a core of nonspatial tropes and a periphery of nonspatial tropes which belongs to that core.

For example, God's core would include tropes of omnipotence and omniscience, while his periphery includes tropes of God's knowledge of various contingent matters of fact, for example, his knowledge that Jane is sad. Each of the latter entails each of the former, but not *vice versa*, and all of the former entail one another.[43] Thus, the omniscience of God entails the omnipotence of God, and *vice versa*. God's knowledge that Jane is sad entails God's omniscience, but not *vice versa*: God could exist even if it were false that Jane is sad. On the other hand, Jane, a contingent soul, has a core that includes Jane's capacity for consciousness, and, we may assume, a periphery including Jane's pleasures and pains. Jane's capacity for consciousness can exist without those particular pleasures and pains existing, but those pleasures and pains cannot exist without Jane's capacity for consciousness existing.

The following argument implies that if God exists along with contingent souls, then the foregoing theory implies a contradiction. God by definition is a *necessary* being. If God exists, and if a contingent soul, *s*, exists, then the existence of any one of the tropes belonging to *s* necessitates the existence of the core tropes belonging to God, but not *vice versa*. Furthermore, because both God and *s* are souls, the tropes belonging to God and *s* are nonspatial. Hence, given our application of Simons's theory to souls, the tropes belonging to *s* meet all of the conditions for being in the periphery of God's core tropes! Thus, on the theory in question, God has accidentally all of the tropes belonging to any contingent soul, for instance, tropes of non-omnipotence and non-omniscience. Of course, this is impossible. As we have observed, in God's *core* are to be found tropes of omnipotence and omniscience, among other tropes. From *D5*, it follows that God would be, for example, both essentially omnipotent and accidentally non-omnipotent, and essentially omniscient and accidentally non-omniscient.

Hence, given the possible existence of God and contingent souls, *D5* implies a contradiction, and its *analysans* does not provide an acceptable logically sufficient condition for something's being a soul. Our diagnosis of what has gone wrong in this account is that the kind of connections postulated to hold among tropes of the same substantial complex, namely, ones seemingly both necessary and **synthetic**, could also hold between the core of a necessary substance and the tropes of certain contingent substances.

Another related difficulty for this account arises as follows. Consider a concrete spiritual event, e, for example, a sensation of a yellowish flash. e has a core of tropes which are essential to its existence. And it may be assumed that e has a periphery of inessential tropes containing (at least) certain relational tropes, for example, e's particular coexistence with a sensation of a loud sound. Hence, the existence of a core of tropes, and of a periphery of tropes that are connected in an appropriate way to that core, is not a logically sufficient condition for those tropes to belong to a substantial complex. Consequently, the difference between a complex of tropes that belong to a *spiritual event* and a complex of tropes that belong to a *substantial soul* cannot be explained by D5. This seems to be a fatal objection to D5.

A final approach to solving the problem of unity for the collectionist theory falls under P3, that the unity of a substantial complex of nonspatial tropes is provided by some hitherto as yet unspecified relation. What might this nonspatial, noncausal, nonmodal relation be? The contemporary metaphysicians, Bertrand Russell (1872–1970) and Hector Neri-Castañeda (1924–91), give one sort of answer.[44] According to each of them, there is an *undefined* relation that does the job, a relation which Russell calls "compresence," and a relation which Castañeda calls "consubstantiation." Such an undefined relation is supposed to account for the unity of the constituents of substantial complexes at a time.[45] But adopting this relation as undefined is unsatisfactory, since it would seem that without an account of this relation we have no notion of what this relation is. For instance (Castañeda):

> We take physical objects to be very special systems of guises intimately related to one another by just one very special relation that cannot receive a better name than *consubstantiation*.[46]

Of course, it won't do to say that, for example, sad and jealous are consubstantiated just when a thing is sad and jealous, inasmuch as this presupposes the ordinary concept of an individual substance, and an account of this ordinary concept cannot appeal to this same ordinary concept. Nor will it do to say the following (Russell):

> Two events are 'compresent' when they are related in the way in which two simultaneous parts of one experience are related. At any given moment,

I am seeing certain things, hearing others, touching others, remembering others, and expecting yet others. All these percepts, recollections, and expectations are happening to me now; I shall say that they are mutually 'compresent'.[47]

In this passage, Russell explicitly appeals to the *self* as that to which various mental particulars are related. But a reduction of substances to complexes of nonsubstantial items cannot rely on a unifying relation that has no intuitive content other than a relation of mutual inherence in a substance. Thus, it would seem that neither Russell nor Castañeda has provided a unifying relation for substantial complexes.

It would appear, then, that the bundle theory of substance cannot explain what unifies the qualities of a soul. Hence, one cannot appeal to the bundle theory of substance to show that God (or any other soul) has tropes as parts.[48] On the other hand, we have defended an independence theory of substance, a theory which implies that a soul does not have tropes as parts. If this theory of substance is correct, then God (or any other soul) is not a complex entity having tropes as parts.

In sum, it seems that God does not have abstract parts, spatial parts, temporal parts, or concrete parts of any other kind. We conclude that in this sense, simplicity *is* an attribute of God.

However, according to traditional theology, divine simplicity should be understood in ways that seem rather incredible from a commonsense point of view. The first of these understandings is that God is essentially atemporal. The second is that God literally does not have qualities.

If God were essentially atemporal (outside of time), then for God there would be no earlier or later, past or future, but only an "everlasting present." Since an essentially atemporal being is necessarily incapable of entering into temporal relations, such a being could not either change its intrinsic qualities or change its relations to other things.[49] Thus, an essentially atemporal God is immutable in a very strong sense.[50]

Divine simplicity might be thought to entail divine atemporality on the grounds that (i) if God exists in time, then he exists *over time*, and (ii) if a thing exists over time, then this entails that it has *temporal parts*. However, we have already argued that the persistence of a soul does *not* entail that it possesses temporal parts. Thus, we do not accept that divine simplicity should be understood as entailing divine atemporality.

The second way that divine simplicity has sometimes been understood is as implying that God has only one quality, which quality is identical with God. If this were so, then all of the so-called divine attributes would be identical with one another and with God. For instance, God's

omnipotence = God's omniscience = God's omnibenevolence = God. The
ideas behind this view are: (1) if God were a different entity than a quality
of his, then God would consist of a substance + a quality, and God would
not be simple; (2) if God is identical with a quality of his, and if God
were to possess *another* quality, then God could not be identical as well
with that second quality.

Understanding divine simplicity as implying that God is atemporal
and without qualities is seemingly incoherent. For example, how can God
be outside of time when he interacts with things that are in time, and
when his relationships with temporal things are constantly changing? The
traditional doctrine that God is identical with the sole property of God
is also unacceptable. Divine simplicity might be thought to entail that God
does not have more than one quality on the ground that a thing's qualities are *parts* of it. But as we have argued, a thing's qualities are *not* parts
of it. Furthermore, how can a *substance*, namely, God, be identical with a
quality, for example, omnipotence? Does not any attempt to identify a substance with a quality involve the commission of a fundamental category
mistake?

As we shall see in the chapters to follow, questions of these sorts pose
profound problems for the traditional doctrine of divine simplicity.
However, our treatment of divine simplicity shows how the doctrine of
divine simplicity can be given a coherent formulation. God is simple in
the way that any soul is simple.

NOTES

1   According to Descartes, a soul is essentially or necessarily conscious. An alternative view is that a soul is essentially or necessarily *capable* of consciousness.
It is not altogether clear which of these views is correct. We remain neutral
on this point.

2   If space is infinite, then such a being would have infinite spatial extension;
if space is finite, then such a being would have finite spatial extension, but
would occupy the whole of this finite space.

3   Some scholars have attributed this view of properties to Aristotle.

4   Letter 187, in *Letters*, trans. W. Parsons, The Fathers of the Church, Volume
30, ed. J. De Ferrari (New York: Fathers of the Church, Inc., 1955), pp.
165–203.

5   *Summa Theologiae* (New York: Benziger Brothers, 1948), Ia, 8, 3.

6   For example, see Douglas Long, "Disembodied Existence, Physicalism, and
the Mind–Body Problem," *Philosophical Studies* 31 (1977), pp. 307–16. Long

seems to assume that any sort of entity whose nature cannot be explained without negative terms is unintelligible.

7 According to "Leibniz's Law," necessarily, for any x and y, $x = y$ if and only if for any property P, x has $P \leftrightarrow y$ has P. 'P' ranges over all properties, either intrinsic or relational, provided that they are qualitative, i.e., can be expressed without naming a specific concrete entity. See **qualitative universal** and **relational quality** in the glossary.

8 Keith Campbell, *Body and Mind* (Garden City, NY: Anchor Books, 1970), pp. 44–5.

9 Campbell and others who give this sort of argument never seem to pose this crucial question.

10 Of course, every place is either a proper or improper *part* of some place, and enters into spatial relations with itself and other places, e.g., relations of distance. Similarly, although a place is *identical with* a place, namely, itself, this is not at all the same thing as a place's *occupying* (or being *in*) a place.

11 For an account of the concept of haecceity as well as a defense of the existence of haecceities, see Gary S. Rosenkrantz, *Haecceity: An Ontological Essay* (Dordrecht: Kluwer, 1993).

12 See Ernest Sosa, "Subjects Among Other Things," in *Philosophical Perspectives, 1, Metaphysics* (Atascadero, Calif.: Ridgeview, 1987), pp. 155–87 (esp. pp. 160–4).

13 But suppose that it is impossible for God to be sad (and impossible for him to be in pain). [See section 5.3 for considerations that favor these suppositions.] Does this entail that it is impossible for God to *experience* Jane's being sad (and impossible for God to *experience* Jane's being in pain)? We do not think so. After all, even though it is *impossible* for God to be four-sided, it is *possible* for him to experience a square's being four-sided. Admittedly, it is much easier for us to understand *what it would be like* for God to experience a square's being four-sided than it is for us to understand *what it would be like* for God to experience Jane's being in pain. But this asymmetry can be explained by the fact that we are *familiar* with experiences of a square's being four-sided, and *unfamiliar* with an experience of another's being in pain. (Similarly, even if a congenitally blind individual, S, understands what it is like for one to *tactually experience* a square's being four-sided, because S is unfamiliar with a visual experience, S is unable to understand what it would be like for one to *visually experience* a square's being four-sided.) Thus, we see no reason to deny the possibility of God's experiencing Jane's being in pain (or of God's experiencing Jane's being sad).

14 This is another instance of how rationality circumscribes what can be attributed to God. Rationality requires that any description of God be consistent with every apparent necessary truth. Anything inconsistent with a necessary truth is *impossible*.

15 For example, John Perry, "A Dialogue on Personal Identity and Immortality," in *Reason and Responsibility*, 7th edition, ed. Joel Feinberg (Belmont, Calif.: Wadsworth, 1989), pp. 323–41.

16 For example, Richard Swinburne, *Space and Time* (New York: St. Martin's Press, 1968), chap. 1; C. D. Broad, *Scientific Thought* (Paterson, NJ: Littlefield, Adams, 1959), p. 393; Robert Coburn, "Identity and Spatiotemporal Continuity," in *Identity and Individuation*, ed. M. Munitz (New York: New York University Press, 1971), pp. 51–101; Sydney Shoemaker, *Self-Knowledge and Self-Identity* (Ithaca, NY: Cornell University Press, 1967), pp. 4–5; and David Wiggins, *Identity and Spatiotemporal Continuity* (Oxford: Blackwell, 1971).

17 Compound bodies, it seems, can exist intermittently through disassembly and reassembly. This is why it is suggested that the requirement of spatiotemporal continuity be restricted to simple or basic bodies.

18 It might be objected that souls stand in need of a principle of persistence, even though places do not, because souls, unlike places, can undergo intrinsic change. This objection does not succeed because it implies that, for example, physical objects that can undergo intrinsic change require a principle of persistence, whereas indivisible physical objects that cannot undergo intrinsic change do not require such a principle. However, possibly, at a time t_1, there is an immutable physical atom, a_1, and at a later time t_2, a_1 coexists with another qualitatively indistinguishable atom a_2. In the light of this possibility, immutable physical atoms stand no less in need of a principle of persistence than mutable compounds of them.

19 The denial of this possibility is often attributed to John Locke (1632–1704) on the basis of the following quotation: "one thing cannot have two beginnings of existence" (*An Essay Concerning Human Understanding*, ed. John Yolton [London: Everyman, 1974], book 2, chap. 27, "Of Identity and Diversity"). However, we believe that this is a misreading of Locke, and that he never meant to deny the possibility of intermittent existence. For an argument to this effect, see Joshua Hoffman, "Locke on Whether a Thing Can Have Two Beginnings of Existence," *Ratio* 22 (1980), pp. 106–11.

20 We leave open the possibility that each of us is a physical object and can reidentify himself or herself on wholly deductive grounds. For an argument that implies that each of us can reidentify himself or herself on wholly deductive grounds in virtue of grasping his or her own nonqualitative haecceity, see *Haecceity: An Ontological Essay*.

21 For an argument in support of this claim, see John Pollock, *Knowledge and Justification* (Princeton, NJ: Princeton University Press, 1974), chap. 6.

22 Ibid.

23 By a sensible quality in this context what is meant is an intrinsic qualitative sensible property, where a qualitative property is one which can be expressed

without naming a specific concrete entity. By two objects being indistinguishable in sensible qualities, what is meant in this context is that they are indistinguishable relative to inspection by means of the senses.

24 The conclusion that it is possible for a physical object to "jump" in space receives further support from contemporary quantum physics – at least on some interpretations. Baruch Brody, for example, invokes the authority of contemporary quantum physics in support of the claim that spatial jumping is possible. See Brody's *Identity and Essence* (Princeton, NJ: Princeton University Press, 1980), chap. 3. From a historical point of view, Leibniz (as well as Hume) allowed for the logical possibility of spatial jumping. See *Gottfried Wilhelm Leibniz: Philosophical Papers and Letters*, ed. Leroy E. Loemker (Dordrecht: Reidel, 1969), pp. 515–16.

25 Sosa, "Subjects Among Other Things," pp. 166–7. John Foster appears to have originated this sort of argument against the intelligibility of interaction. See his "Psychophysical Causal Relations," *American Philosophical Quarterly* 5 (1968), pp. 64–70. But Foster introduced the argument only to refute it. We will cite his replies to the argument.

26 Sosa, "Subjects Among Other Things," p. 166.

27 Foster also has two replies to this sort of anti-interactionist argument. See Foster, "Psychophysical Causal Relations" and "In *Self*-Defense," in *Perception and Identity*, ed. G. F. MacDonald (London: Macmillan, 1979), pp. 168–70. The two replies are summarized in Foster, "A Defense of Dualism," in *The Case for Dualism*, ed. John Smythies and John Beloff (Charlottesville, Va.: University Press of Virginia, 1989), pp. 1–23. Both of Foster's replies, however, involve the rejection of Sosa's premise that all causal relations supervene on purely qualitative noncausal facts. But we do not reject this premise in making our two replies to Sosa.

28 Jonathan Barnes, *The Presocratics, Volume 1* (Boston, Mass.: Routledge and Kegan Paul, 1979), p. 119.

29 Ibid.

30 It should be noted that, unlike the transference principle, the synonymy principle says nothing about the transference of properties. The transference principle is based on the intuition that if a brings it about that b is F, then there is a transfer of F-ness from a to b, a transfer in which F-ness is *conserved*. It is logically consistent to reject this intuition, and yet accept the synonymy principle based upon another intuition, namely, that *like can only be produced by like*. Rather than appealing to the transference principle to defend *Premise A2*, one can appeal *instead* to the necessity of the synonymy principle. Such a defense of *Premise A2* begins with the following observation. If the synonymy principle is necessarily true, then motion in a body can only be brought about by something that is in motion. But, if something is not located in space, then it cannot be in motion. Hence, motion in a body can only be brought about by something that is located in space. However,

body–soul interaction is possible only if it is possible for a soul to produce motion in a body. Therefore, *Premise A2* is true.

Yet, since the synonymy principle is false, the foregoing defense of *Premise A2* is unsound. The defender of *Premise A2* might retreat to the following *restricted* synonymy principle:

> **If *a* brings it about that *b* is Ø, then there is some property that *a* and *b* have in common.**

Although this restricted principle is a necessary truth, it is *trivial*. Any two entities must have *some* property in common, e.g., *being self-identical*. Since a soul and a body have a property in common, e.g., *concreteness, substantiality*, the restricted synonymy principle cannot be used to support *Premise A2*.

31 Since a circle of explanatory laws is a *vicious* circle, the alternative to there being an inexplicable [basic] law is an *infinite regress* of explanatory laws. But it is doubtful that there is such an infinite regress of explanatory laws (though such an infinite regress may be possible).

32 Although there *is* a sense in which a fundamental psycho–physical correlation law is mysterious, namely, in the sense that nothing explains this law, a fundamental physical–physical correlation law is mysterious in the same sense.

33 John Locke famously held that he saw no impossibility *either* in consciousness being "superadded" to a body, *or* in the existence of a conscious soul. Many contemporary physicalists agree with Locke that some bodies are conscious, namely, ourselves. And we have already argued that souls are possible.

34 To suppose otherwise is to hold that science is metaphysically committed to materialism, and is inconsistent with any other metaphysics. We think this is an incorrect understanding of the status of science and its laws. In any case, if science *were* committed to materialism, it could not justifiably be so committed for conceptual reasons. All we are arguing here is that it is *conceivable* for there to be body–soul interaction, which *is* a conceptual claim, and science has no good reason to oppose this claim.

35 Of course, if there are no supernatural causes, then no physical law is ever superseded, and the sort of implicit *ceteris paribus* clauses upon which we have been insisting would be redundant. But this has no bearing on the validity of the distinction between a law's being violated and its being superseded.

36 Compare Joshua Hoffman's "Comments on 'Miracles and the Laws of Nature' by George Mavrodes," *Faith and Philosophy* 4 (1985), pp. 347–52. It should be emphasized that *Argument B* and the other arguments we criticize in this section are *conceptual* objections to the *intelligibility* of dualistic interaction. We have not considered (perhaps more plausible) *empirical* objections to dualistic interaction such as those based upon appeals to a verifiable principle of the causal closure of the physical world, or to the explanatory completeness of physics, together with the empirical implausibility of systematic causal overdetermination.

37 This sort of argument dates back to the Middle Ages. However, a revival of interest in such arguments in contemporary times was prompted by Norman Kretzmann's paper, "Omniscience and Immutability," *Journal of Philosophy* 63 (1966), pp. 409–21.

38 Compare P. T. Geach, *Logic Matters* (Berkeley, Calif.: University of California Press, 1972), pp. 302–18, and D. H. Mellor, *Real Time* (Cambridge: Cambridge University Press, 1981), chaps. 7 and 8.

39 It is also sometimes argued that a persisting substance perdures on the ground that a persisting substance can be identified with a temporal sequence of complexes of tropes. However, such an argument presupposes the bundle theory of substance, a theory that we criticize in the text below. It should also be noted that an enduring substance's undergoing qualitative change is consistent with the logical Law of the Indiscernibility of Identicals insofar as this law can be taken to assert that, necessarily, for any x and y, if $x = y$, then for any property P, and for any time t, x has P at $t \leftrightarrow y$ has P at t.

40 We discuss the possibility of an enduring soul in relation to our analysis of the concept of substance in section 2.2.

41 Similarly, the complex of the tropes of a pair of living organisms would not comprise a third living organism.

42 See Peter Simons, "Particulars in Particular Clothing: Three Trope Theories of Substance," reprinted in *Metaphysics: Contemporary Readings*, ed. S. D. Hales (Belmont, Calif.: Wadsworth, 1999), pp. 397–411.

43 By saying that a trope *T1* 'entails' a trope *T2* we mean that the existence of *T1* necessitates the existence of *T2*.

44 Bertrand Russell, *Human Knowledge: Its Scope and Limits* (New York: Simon and Schuster, 1948), chaps. 7–8; H. N. Castañeda, "Thinking and the Structure of the World," *Critica* 6, no. 18 (1972), pp. 43–81, and "Perception, Belief, and the Structure of Physical Objects and Consciousness," *Synthese* 35 (1977), pp. 285–351.

45 Castañeda's and Russell's substantial complexes do not contain tropes, but rather other kinds of nonsubstantial entities. Still, the trope bundle theorist can adapt the basic strategy that Castañeda and Russell propose for unifying these complexes.

46 In "Perception, Belief, and the Structure of Physical Objects and Consciousness," Castañeda offers a set of axioms for the consubstantiation relation (the "Law of Communion," the "Law of Conditional Reflexivity," etc.). However, these axioms do not explicitly *define* consubstantiation, since that notion occurs within them. Nor do we accept the idea that they provide a so-called implicit definition of consubstantiation, since more than one relation could satisfy the axioms. In our view, without an intended interpretation, axioms are mere uninterpreted **schemata**. For a defense of this view, see Gary Rosenkrantz, "The Nature of Geometry," *American Philosophical Quarterly* 18 (1981), pp. 101–10.

47 *Human Knowledge: Its Scope and Limits*, p. 329.

48 To be fair, the bundle theorist might take the position that the tropes which
    constitute a substance are not literally *parts* of that substance. Actually, this is
    Peter Simons's position. ["Particulars in Particular Clothing: Three Trope
    Theories of Substance," pp. 403–4.] But in that case, the bundle theory does
    not support the conclusion that God has tropes as parts, and so does not
    threaten the doctrine of divine simplicity.

49 See section 2.1.

50 Note that there is also a very strong sense in which God's existence would
    not be *accidental*, namely, that if God exists, then God is a necessary being
    who is not temporally limited. Thus, it is impossible for God to undergo *sub-
    stantial* change, i.e., to come into being or pass away.

BIBLIOGRAPHY

Campbell, K., *Body and Mind* (Garden City, NY: Anchor Books, 1970).

Descartes, R., *Meditations on First Philosophy*, trans. John Cottingham, Robert
    Stoothoff, and Dugald Murdoch, in *The Philosophical Writings of Descartes,
    Volume 2* (Cambridge: Cambridge University Press, 1984).

Foster, J., *The Immaterial Self: A Defence of the Cartesian Dualist Conception of the
    Mind* (London: Routledge, 1991).

Hoffman, J. and Rosenkrantz, G. S., "Are Souls Unintelligible?," in *Philosophical
    Perspectives, 5, Philosophy of Religion* (Atascadero, Calif.: Ridgeview, 1991), pp.
    183–212.

Long, D., "Disembodied Existence, Physicalism, and the Mind–Body Problem,"
    Philosophical Studies 31 (1977), pp. 307–16.

Perry, J., "A Dialogue on Personal Identity and Immortality," in *Reason and Respon-
    sibility*, 7th edition, ed. Joel Feinberg (Belmont, Calif.: Wadsworth, 1989), pp.
    323–41.

Rosenkrantz, G. S., *Haecceity: An Ontological Essay* (Dordrecht: Kluwer, 1993).

Sosa, E., "Subjects Among Other Things," in *Philosophical Perspectives, 1, Metaphysics*
    (Atascadero, Calif.: Ridgeview, 1987), pp. 155–87.

Taliaferro, C., *Consciousness and the Mind of God* (Cambridge: Cambridge Univer-
    sity Press, 1994).

Wierenga, E., "Anselm on Omnipresence," *New Scholasticism* 52 (1988), pp. 30–41.

4

Necessary Existence

God is said to be a "necessary being," that is, a being that exists in every possible world. We will elucidate the notion of a necessary being and in so doing will assess competing accounts of possible worlds. It is sometimes thought that God is a "self-existent being," that is, a being whose existence is explained by itself. We will argue that this notion of self-existence is incoherent.

4.1 Necessity and Contingency

According to traditional Western theism, God has *necessary* existence, has the core attributes of omnipotence, omniscience, and omnibenevolence *necessarily*, and has certain other attributes merely *contingently*. The study of *logical modalities* such as necessity, contingency, impossibility, and possibility is known as **modal logic**. In this chapter we examine the nature of these logical modalities and their application to God.

The logical or metaphysical modalities of necessity and contingency can be variously predicated of the *existence of beings*, the *properties of beings*, and the **truth-values** *of propositions*. Let us consider examples of each of the three types of predications.

We begin with propositions. Every proposition has a *truth-value*. According to classical logic, there are just two truth-values: truth and falsehood. Thus, assuming classical logic, every proposition is either true or false.

Compare the following two lists of propositions.

List 1	List 2
It is raining	*Either it is raining somewhere or it is not*
All crows are black	*If something is red, then it is colored*

There is a red thing over there	*If something is red, then it is red*
Squares exist	*If something is square, then it has four sides*
John has two pairs of socks	*2 + 2 = 4*

List 1 consists of *contingent* propositions. A contingent proposition is a proposition that is capable of truth *and* capable of falsehood. For example, at one time it is true that it is raining, and at another time it is not; it is possibly true that all crows are black, yet it is also possibly true that there are non-black, albino crows; and so on. The concept of a contingent proposition can be understood in terms of the notion of a *possible world*. In particular, it can be said that a proposition is contingent if and only if it is true in at least one possible world, and false in at least one possible world. List 2 consists of *necessary* (or *necessarily true*) propositions. A necessary proposition is a proposition that must be true; it is incapable of falsehood. For instance, no matter what happens, it is true that it is either raining somewhere or it is not; in any possible situation, it is true that if something is red, then it is colored; and so forth. It can be said that a proposition is necessary if and only if there is no possible world in which it is false. Thus, a necessary proposition is true in all possible worlds.

These and related notions can be understood in terms of the *a priori* logical law that nothing can both be and not be, known as the *Law of Non-Contradiction*. A proposition is a *contradiction* or is *formally inconsistent* when it both asserts something and denies that very thing. For example, the proposition that *there exists a red thing that is not red* is formally inconsistent, as is the proposition that *it is raining somewhere and it is not*. According to the Law of Non-Contradiction, any proposition which is formally inconsistent, or which entails a contradiction, is *impossible* (or *necessarily false*). Such a proposition must be false; it is incapable of truth. Thus, the proposition that *there exists a red thing that is not red* is impossible, as is the proposition that *there exists a colorless red thing*. These impossible propositions are patently absurd. Clearly, to deny a necessary proposition is to entail a contradiction. For instance, denying that *every red thing is colored* entails the absurdity that *there is a colorless red thing*, and thereby entails the contradiction that there exists a red thing that is not red. However, in the case of a contingent proposition, neither it nor its denial entails a contradiction. For example, *all crows are black* is such that neither it nor its denial, namely, *some crow is non-black*, entails a contradiction. Thus, *all crows are black* and *some crow is non-black* are each *possible* propositions (propositions which are capable of truth). Hence, a possible proposition is any proposition that *is not impossible*, that is, any contingent or necessary proposition.

In logic, the denial or negation of a proposition can be expressed by prefixing an indicative sentence with the negation sign '~'. The negation sign means *it is false that*. Denying or negating a proposition reverses its truth-value. Thus, if the proposition that *horses exist* is true, then the proposition that *~(horses exist)* is false; and if the proposition that *unicorns exist* is false, then the proposition that *~(unicorns exist)* is true. It follows that the negation of a necessary proposition is an impossible proposition, for example, the negation of the necessity *2 + 2 = 4* is the impossibility *~(2 + 2 = 4)*; the negation of an impossible proposition is a necessary proposition, for instance, the negation of the impossibility *a spherical cube exists* is the necessity *~(a spherical cube exists)*; and the negation of a contingent proposition is another contingent proposition, for example, the negation of the contingency *it is raining somewhere* is the contingency *~(it is raining somewhere)*, one of which is a *contingently true proposition* and the other of which is a *contingently false proposition*.

Attributions of necessity, contingency, impossibility, or possibility to propositions are *de dicto*; they pertain to *dicta*, that is, to *propositional* or statement-like units. On the other hand, any *property* of a *thing* can be characterized as either *necessary* to *that thing* or *contingent* to *that thing*. An attribution of this kind is *de re*; it pertains to a *res*, that is, to a *thing*, rather than to a *dictum* or propositional entity.

A thing's contingent or accidental properties are those that are merely incidental to its existence. That is, the thing in question could exist without those properties. For example, suppose Jane is blond. Evidently, Jane can cease to be blond while continuing to exist. Thus, blondness is an accidental property of Jane. In other words, Jane is *contingently* blond. (It should be noted that this is *compatible* with the fact that the *proposition* that *all blonds are blonds* is *necessary*.) On the other hand, a thing's necessary properties are those that belong to its essential nature. In other words, the thing in question could not exist without those properties. For instance, consider a rock. It cannot exist unless it has spatial location. Thus, spatial location is an essential property of that rock. That is, the rock *necessarily* has spatial location.

The notions of a thing's contingent and necessary properties are often understood in terms of possible worlds. First, a thing, x, has a property, P, necessarily if and only if (i) x has P, and (ii) x has P in every possible world in which x exists. For example, if God exists, then he has the property of omnipotence necessarily, implying that God is omnipotent in every possible world in which he exists. Second, a thing, x, has a property, P, contingently if and only if (i) x has P, and (ii) x lacks P in some possible world in which x exists. If God exists, then he has certain properties contingently, for instance, a property such as believing that in five years Mt. Etna will be erupting, implying that in some possible world God does not believe that in five years Mt. Etna will be erupting.

Finally, every *entity* must either be a *contingent being* or a *necessary being*. (A contingent being is said to have *contingent existence*, and a necessary being is said to have *necessary existence*.) To say that a being is contingent is to say that it is possible for it not to exist. Thus, a contingent being exists in at least one possible world and fails to exist in at least one possible world. For example, an oak tree is a contingent being. To say that a being is necessary is to say that it is necessary for it to exist. Hence, a necessary being exists in all possible worlds. For instance, if God exists, then he is a *concrete* necessary being; and it seems that a necessary proposition such as $2 + 2 = 4$ is an *abstract* necessary being.

A necessary proposition cannot imply the existence of a contingent being. Hence, if every concrete entity is a contingent being, then no necessary proposition implies the existence of a concrete entity. On the other hand, if some concrete entity is a necessary being, for example, God, then there are necessary propositions that imply the existence of a concrete entity.

As we have seen, the logical modalities of necessity and contingency can be predicated of the *existence of beings*, the *properties of beings*, and the *truth-values of propositions*. There are two approaches for providing a *unitary account* of these three kinds of attributions. The first approach takes the *de dicto* locution 'it is necessary that p' as undefined and attempts to explicate attributions of *necessary properties* to *things* and *necessary existence* to *things* in terms of this locution.[1] Most advocates of this approach find the notion expressed by *de dicto* locution 'it is necessary that p' to be more intuitive than the one expressed by the *de re* locution 'x is necessarily F'. The second approach takes the *de re* locution 'x is necessarily F' as undefined and attempts to explicate attributions of *necessity* to *the truth of propositions* and of *necessary existence* to *things* in terms of that locution.[2] Proponents of this approach usually argue that it has more explanatory power than the first approach. It is controversial whether either of these two approaches is entirely successful.

In any case, we shall argue that due to God's special nature, attributions to *God* of necessary existence, necessary properties, and contingent properties can be explicated in terms of the *de dicto* locution 'it is necessary that p'. To see this, suppose for the sake of argument that God exists. This entails that God is maximally great, in other words, that his greatness is not possibly surpassed or matched. Indeed, since maximal greatness requires necessary existence, it is necessarily true that God is maximally great. In that case, both God and maximal greatness have necessary existence, implying that they exist in all possible worlds. Moreover, maximal greatness is essential to God, and is necessarily not had by anything other than God. In other words, maximal greatness is an **individual essence** of God. (An individual essence of a thing, x, is a property which x has essentially and which is necessarily not had by anything other than x.) In the light of these implications of the existence of God, we propose the following definitions.

(**D1**) **God is a necessary being = df. necessarily, the maximally great being exists.**
(**D2**) **God is necessarily F = df. necessarily, the maximally great being is F.**[3]
(**D3**) **God is contingently F = df. (i) the maximally great being is F, and (ii) ~(necessarily, the maximally great being is F).**[4]

It should be noted that *D1–D3* do not provide a *general* account of the attribution of necessary existence, necessary properties, and contingent properties, but only a more modest account of such attributions to *God*.[5] But this more modest account helps us to better understand the nature of God.

4.2 Necessary Beings and Contingent Beings

A maximally great being's perfections include noncontingency, not being temporally limited, and incorruptibility. Thus, if God exists, then he is a necessary being who cannot be created or destroyed. It can be argued that every non-divine substance is a contingent being, and hence that no non-divine entity is a necessary substance. Compound physical objects such as gold atoms, water molecules, and cats are contingent substances that can be created or destroyed by assembly or disassembly. Of course, an *indivisible* physical object cannot be created or destroyed in this way. So it might be thought that indivisible basic particles are necessary substances. Although theoretical physics seems to imply that there *are* indivisible basic or fundamental particles, for instance, electrons, it also implies that these basic particles can be created or destroyed, though of course not by means of assembly or disassembly. According to theoretical physics, for each kind of indivisible basic particle there is a corresponding kind of indivisible basic anti-particle. For example, the anti-particle corresponding to the electron is the positron. The collision of an electron and a positron results in their *mutual destruction*, though photons are created as a byproduct. Conversely, the energy of photons can *create* long-lasting electron–positron pairs, though the photons are thereby destroyed. It is also theorized that transitory electron–positron pairs **randomly** pop in and out of existence within the quantum vacuum (independently of the creation or destruction of photons). These so-called *virtual particles* are created *ex nihilo* and very shortly thereafter undergo total destruction.[6] It seems, then, that the theories of empirical science do not provide any ground for believing that there is a concrete substance that is a necessary being. So, it can be argued that every concrete substance is a contingent being, unless there is a divine substance, for example, God. If God exists, then he is both a concrete substance and a necessary being.

In David Hume's *Dialogues Concerning Natural Religion* the character of Cleanthes argues that it is unintelligible to say that God is a necessary being.

> Nothing is demonstrable unless the contrary implies a contradiction. Nothing that is distinctly conceivable implies a contradiction. Whatever we conceive as existent, we can also conceive as non-existent. Consequently there is no being whose existence is demonstrable. . . . The words, therefore, *necessary existence* have no meaning or, which is the same thing; none which is consistent.[7]

Cleanthes's remarks suggest the following *a priori* argument for atheism. Necessarily, whatever is conceivable is possible. For any concrete thing x, x's nonexistence is conceivable to us. Therefore, the nonexistence of any concrete thing is possible. Hence, there is not a concrete thing that is a necessary being. Necessarily, if God exists, then he is a concrete thing that is a necessary being. Consequently, it is impossible that God exists.

We object to the premise that, necessarily, whatever is conceivable is possible. After all, people can sometimes conceive of things that are actually impossible. The fact that a proposition has the *psychological* property of *conceivability* is no guarantee that it has the *logical* property of *possibility*. For instance, according to the Goldbach Conjecture, every even number greater than 4 is the sum of two odd primes. It is both conceivable that the Goldbach Conjecture is provable, and conceivable that the Goldbach

Conjecture is unprovable. But one of these two conceivable alternatives is impossible. Therefore, it is false that whatever is conceivable is possible, contrary to what the foregoing *a priori* argument for atheism assumes.

It may be replied that even if conceivability does not entail possibility, it is still true that whatever is *distinctly* conceivable must be possible.[8] Here it is assumed that the distinct conception of something is a superlative cognitive achievement. This suggests a second *a priori* Humean argument for atheism. Necessarily, whatever is distinctly conceivable is possible. For any concrete thing x, x's nonexistence is distinctly conceivable to us. Consequently, the nonexistence of any concrete thing is possible. Therefore, there is not a concrete thing that is a necessary being. Necessarily, if God exists, then he is a concrete thing that is a necessary being. Thus, it is impossible that God exists. The trouble with this argument is that there seems to be no good reason to accept the assumption that for *any* concrete thing its nonexistence is *distinctly* conceivable to us. Thus, even if we can *conceive* of the nonexistence of any concrete thing, there might still be a concrete necessary being the nonexistence of which is not *distinctly conceivable* to us. We conclude that both of the foregoing Humean arguments for atheism are unsound. Thus, Hume has not shown that the existence of God is impossible.

4.3 Modalities and Possible Worlds

As we have described, attributions of necessity and contingency can be understood in terms of possible worlds. We shall argue that an adequate conception of the ontological status of possible worlds implies that there are *abstract* necessary beings such as propositions. There are four general positions on the ontological status of possible worlds that need to be considered: the **conceptualist** model, the *combinatorial model*, the *abstract worlds model*, and the *concrete worlds model*.

According to the conceptualist model, possible worlds are *mental constructions*, for instance, complexes of thoughts or concepts.[9] The conceptualist model implies that for any x, if x is possible, then x is possible *because* there are one or more thinkers who have an idea of x. But then the thinkers *themselves* are possible *because* they have *reflective ideas*, that is, ideas of *themselves*. This seems to get things backwards: it appears that reflective ideas are possible *because* thinkers are possible. Thus, it seems that there is an explanatory incoherence at the very heart of the conceptualist model.[10] If this is correct, then the conceptualist model is unacceptable.

Furthermore, the conceptualist model implies that if there are never any reflective thinkers, then there are never any possibilities at all. Thus, if it is *possible* that there are never any reflective thinkers, then the conceptualist model has the absurd consequence that *it is possible that there are never any possibilities at all.* The conceptualist model can avoid this absurdity only by presupposing that it is *necessary* that there is reflective being, for example, God. But it is not clear to us that there is sufficient epistemic justification for accepting this controversial presupposition. (A practitioner of rational theology should accept the presupposition in question only if he or she has sufficient epistemic justification for accepting it.) Thus, we have doubts about any model of possible worlds that depends upon such a presupposition.

According to the combinatorial model, the actual world is the set or collection of everything there is, and the other possible worlds consist of all of the possible combinations of the basic entities that exist in the actual world.[11] Unfortunately, though, this model cannot accommodate possible worlds containing fundamental particles or souls that do not exist in the actual world. We assume that a model of possible worlds should allow for such worlds. However, since fundamental particles and souls are not compound things, possible fundamental particles or souls which do not exist in the actual world cannot be understood in terms of possible combinations of basic entities that exist in the actual world. We regard this as a rather serious shortcoming of the combinatorial model.

According to the abstract worlds model (AWM), a possible world is an *abstract entity*, for instance, a very large conjunction of propositions, a conjunction which is *maximal* or *suitably complete*, and which does not imply a contradiction. Such an infinite conjunction of propositions is itself a possible proposition. AWM is associated with Alvin Plantinga.[12] AWM presupposes the classic logical Law of Excluded Middle, i.e., that every proposition is either true or false, and also that every proposition has necessary existence. According to AWM, the actual world includes only *true* propositions.[13] There are infinitely many other possible worlds, and each of them includes one or more *false* propositions. In the light of *D1*, we can see that on AWM, God exists *in* every possible world if and only if the *true proposition* that *the maximally great being exists* is included in every abstract possible world. Given AWM, if God exists in the actual world, then he exists in every possible world in this sense, and the proposition that *the maximally great being exists* is itself a necessary being, though an abstract one.

On the other hand, according to the concrete worlds model (CWM), a possible world is a *concrete entity*, for example, a causally isolated collection of concrete things. This model is associated with David Lewis.[14] According to CWM, each of the infinitely many concrete worlds is causally inaccessible to all of the others. *The actual world* is the collection of concrete things of which *we* are a part. Some *other* possible worlds are collections of concrete things of which *we* are *not* a part. It follows that no single thing exists in more than one possible world, though each thing has *counter-parts* in other worlds that resemble it. *Transworld identity* is rejected on the ground that no formal criterion of transworld identity is available.

It might be argued that CWM is unacceptable because it implies that *all* of a concrete entity's *dated properties* are essential to it. On this model concrete entities are "world-bound"; each of them exists in just *one* possible world. Moreover, necessarily, if an entity, *e*, has a property at some time, *t*, then at *every* time it is true that *e* has that property at *t*. Hence, CWM implies that for any concrete entity, *x*, any property *F*, and any time *t*, if *x* has *F* at *t*, then it is literally impossible for *x* to lack *F* at *t*. For example, if Jones is sitting at *t*, then CWM implies that it is literally impossible that *Jones* is not sitting at *t*. Thus, CWM appears to imply that Jones is *essentially* sitting at *t*. But this implication of CWM is extremely unintuitive: it certainly seems literally possible for *Jones* to be standing at *t* rather than sitting at *t*. It follows that there is an intuitive sense in which Jones appears to be *accidentally* sitting at *t*. So, it seems that by implying that Jones is essentially sitting at *t*, CWM is guilty of a kind of *excessive essentialism*. Lewis seeks to escape this charge of excessive essentialism by *redefining* an essential property of a concrete entity as a property of a concrete entity which *every* counter-part of that concrete entity possesses; and by *redefining* an accidental property of a concrete entity as a property of a concrete entity which *some* counter-part of that concrete entity lacks. In particular, Lewis would argue that since there is a possible world in which a counter-part of Jones is standing at *t*, Jones is accidentally sitting at *t*. Still, because a counter-part of Jones is someone *other than* Jones, this alleged sense of Jones's accidentally sitting at *t* is a rather unintuitive one. Moreover, AWM sustains a much more intuitive understanding of Jones's accidentally sitting at *t*, an understanding which implies that in some possible world *Jones* is not sitting at *t*. Is there a good reason why we should settle for CWM and the unintuitive understanding of Jones's accidentally sitting at *t* that it requires?

Ontological parsimony is often given as a reason for preferring CWM to AWM. The contention is that CWM posits only concrete entities, whereas AWM posits both concrete entities and abstract entities.[15] It is

claimed that by positing abstract entities AWM multiplies entities unnecessarily. Since one should not multiply entities unnecessarily, it can be
argued that CWM is preferable to AWM.

Nevertheless, ontological parsimony is a good reason for preferring
CWM to AWM only if CWM accommodates the data. Indeed, if a theory
T_1 accommodates the data, and another theory T_2 does not, then T_1 is
preferable to T_2 even if T_2 is ontologically more parsimonious than T_1.
AWM accommodates the intuitive datum that it is literally possible for
Jones to be standing at t rather than sitting at t, but it seems that CWM
does not. Thus, it appears that *even if* CWM is ontologically more parsimonious than AWM, AWM is preferable to CWM.

In any case there are good reasons to deny that ontological parsimony
favors CWM over AWM. To begin with, Lewis accepts the existence of
sets. In particular, according to Lewis, properties are reducible to sets. But
sets are abstract entities.[16] Thus, it seems that AWM does not enable us to
avoid postulating abstract entities after all.

Indeed, it can even be argued plausibly that ontological parsimony
favors AWM over CWM. To see this, notice that there are two relevant
ways in which entities can be multiplied unnecessarily: (i) by multiplying
unnecessarily the number of *explanatory categories*, and (ii) by multiplying
unnecessarily the number of entities *within* an explanatory category. When
nominalists argue that their ontology of concrete entities is more parsimonious than the realist's ontology of concrete and abstract entities
their argument is that realism multiplies entities unnecessarily in the *first*
of these two ways. On the other hand, when Copernicus (1473–1543)
argues that his heliocentric theory of the solar system is more parsimonious than Ptolemy's geocentric theory on the ground that it utilizes
far fewer epicycles, Copernicus's argument is that Ptolemy's theory of the
solar system multiplies entities unnecessarily in the *second* of the two ways.
Since the proponents of CWM postulate the existence of abstract sets,
and since there are an uncountable infinity of abstract sets, it seems that
CWM is just as committed as AWM to an uncountable infinity of abstract
entities. But unlike AWM, CWM is also committed to an uncountable
infinity of concrete individual things. Hence, proponents of AWM can
argue plausibly that CWM multiplies *concrete entities* unnecessarily. This is
to multiply entities unnecessarily in the second of the two ways specified
earlier.

But there are two replies that might be offered on behalf of Lewis.
First, it might be argued that if propositions are abstract entities of an
irreducible category, then there are abstract entities of *another* irreducible

category, for example, properties or sets.[17] However, such a reply presupposes that sets are abstract entities of an irreducible category and that *their* existence does *not* imply that there are abstract entities of another irreducible category. But then it cannot be assumed that the existence of irreducible propositions (or properties) implies that there are irreducible abstract entities of another category, e.g., sets.[18] So, it does not seem to be true that AWM must reduce properties or propositions to sets in order to avoid being committed to abstract entities of more irreducible categories than CWM. We conclude that this first reply is problematic.

Second, it might be argued that abstract properties and propositions are suspect because they lack a formal criterion of identity, while abstract sets are *not* suspect in this respect. Sets, it is argued, have a formal criterion of identity in terms of their membership: a set S_1 = a set S_2 if and only if S_1 and S_2 have the same members. This reply presupposes that a category of entity that lacks a formal criterion of identity is suspect. But we shall argue that this presupposition is false. If there is a formal criterion of identity for entities of some category, then this criterion must refer to entities that belong to one or more *other* categories. For instance, sets cannot be identified unless there is reference to entities which belong to other categories and which are members of sets; and arguably, substances are identified by reference to attributes, places are identified by reference to bodies, times are identified by reference to events, and so on. Hence, in each such case either (i) there is an *infinite regress* of these references, (ii) there is a *circle* of these references, or (iii) there is a *stopping place*: a reference to an entity which has *primitive* identity, namely, which lacks a formal criterion of identity and which is therefore not identified by reference to anything else. Of these three alternatives it is the third and final one that is by far the most plausible. Thus, it is very likely that there are entities that have primitive identity. And propositions (or properties) are as good a candidate as any for entities with primitive identity. Therefore, the lack of a formal criterion of identity for propositions (or properties) should not place them under suspicion. Consequently, the second reply on behalf of Lewis does not succeed.

In a related vein, it may be noted that skepticism about transworld identity is fueled by doubts about the possibility of a formal criterion of transworld identity for concrete entities.[19] But the demand for a formal criterion of *transworld identity* for concrete entities is no more reasonable than the demand for a formal criterion of *identity* for propositions (or properties). Primitive identities are acceptable in both of these cases.

Further criticisms of CWM raise doubts about the intelligibility and intuitiveness of its ontological presuppositions. First, CWM postulates the existence of infinitely many, causally isolated concrete worlds. That is, according to CWM, no entity in one possible concrete world can interact with, or even be located within the same space-time continuum as, an entity in another possible concrete world. But the intelligibility of radically isolated, spatiotemporally discontinuous physical systems of this kind is questionable.[20] Second, even if CWM is intelligible, the ontology it postulates is wildly unintuitive. No ordinary language-user who understands modal discourse has the faintest idea that by using such terms she is thereby committed to the existence of infinitely many causally isolated concrete universes. Such an ordinary language-user would be astonished to hear that her modal discourse implies the existence of infinitely many "counter-parts" to herself and to every other actual object. Lewis might reply that the same language-user would be as astonished to learn that her modal discourse implied the existence of infinitely many, causally inaccessible abstract entities, as AWM implies. But there are a great many terms in ordinary language that certainly appear to be the names of abstract entities, abstract singular terms such as 'bravery', 'redness', 'squareness', and so forth. On the other hand, there are no terms in ordinary language that appear to name one's counter-parts! Moreover, as discussed earlier, CWM itself postulates the existence of infinitely many, causally inaccessible abstract entities, namely, sets. For these reasons, it certainly looks as though CWM's ontological presuppositions are less intuitive than AWM's.

Based upon the foregoing considerations, we conclude that AWM is preferable to CWM.[21] Moreover, since AWM provides an account of possible worlds that is objective, AWM is free of the defects of the conceptualist model. In addition, unlike the combinatorial model, AWM allows for the possibility of fundamental particles and/or souls that do not exist in the actual world. AWM allows for the possibility of these simple substances because AWM implies that for any possible substance, actual or nonactual, simple or compound, there is a proposition of the form 'a exists' which is necessarily such that it is true (false) just in case the possible substance in question exists (does not exist). It can be argued that a singular proposition of this kind involves a haecceity or individual essence that is either exemplified (when the possible substance exists) or unexemplified (when the possible substance does not exist). So, AWM identifies a possible world in which there is a simple substance that does not exist in the actual world with a maximal conjunctive proposition that has as a conjunct an appropriate contingently *false* singular contingent proposition of the aforementioned sort. Hence, AWM does not have the drawback of the combinatorial model (of ruling out nonactual possible simple substances).

Thus, of the four models of possible worlds considered, AWM appears to be the best. Since AWM implies that there are abstract propositions or properties that are necessary beings, there are reasons for accepting the existence of abstract necessary beings of at least one of these kinds.

The debate over these models of possible worlds has interesting implications for theism, for God is conceived differently within the context of AWM than within the context of CWM. On the one hand, God may be conceived as a being whose greatness could not be *surpassed*. On the other hand, God may be conceived as a being whose greatness could neither be *surpassed* nor *matched*. This is the conception we originally introduced.[22] The second conception precludes the possibility of a being *other than* God who is unsurpassably great, but the first conception does not. Thus, the second conception is more robust than the first. Still, both of these conceptions seem to be consistent with an Anselmian characterization of God as *a being than which nothing greater can be conceived*. As we shall see, AWM is consistent with *the more robust conception*. But we shall argue that although CWM is consistent with *the less robust conception*, CWM is *not* consistent with the more robust one.

To begin, suppose for the sake of argument that CWM is correct, and that God exists in the actual world. In that case, God has counter-parts in other possible worlds. For one thing, God has both essential properties, for example, God's core property of omnipotence, and accidental properties, for example, incidental ones such as believing that in five years Mt. Etna will be erupting. It follows that God has counter-parts in other possible worlds. All of these counter-parts share God's essential properties, but some of these counter-parts do not share his accidental properties. In addition, God is a necessary being. Of course, the notions of a necessary being and a contingent being need to be redefined for the purposes of CWM. In particular, CWM implies that for any concrete entity, x, in the actual world, if x is a *necessary being*, then x has a counter-part in *every* other possible world, and that if x is a *contingent being*, then x lacks a counter-part in *some* other possible world. It follows that God has a counter-part in every non-actual possible world. But since God and his counter-parts share the core essential properties of God, God and his counter-parts are *equally great*. Thus, it seems that CWM is *not* consistent with the idea that divine greatness is not possibly matched.

It might be thought that Lewis is able to avoid this conclusion, since Lewis is willing to allow for the possibility that there are *abstract entities*

that exist outside of *all* of the concrete possible worlds.[23] Can CWM
accommodate the idea that the greatness of God is unmatchable by
identifying God with an abstract entity that exists outside of all possible
worlds? Because God *interacts* with concrete entities, and is a *person*, with
beliefs, preferences, and intentions, he is a concrete entity. So, such a way
of accommodating this idea is unavailable for CWM.

Why cannot Lewis say that God is a concrete entity that exists outside
of all possible worlds? Saying this would seriously compromise CWM:
it would imply that CWM does not provide a model that covers all
concrete possibilities.

We conclude that CWM is inconsistent with God's having *unmatchable
greatness*. On the other hand, CWM seems to be consistent with God and
each of his counter-parts having *unsurpassable greatness*. AWM also appears
to be consistent with God's having unsurpassable greatness. In addition,
on either CWM or AWM it may be assumed that if a being has unsurpassable greatness, then in *any* possible world in which it exists its
greatness is *unmatched in that world*. But in contrast to CWM, AWM
accommodates the stronger claim that divine greatness is *unmatched in any
possible world*. After all, AWM implies that God does *not* have equally great
counter-parts, implying instead that God exists in *every* possible world. So
within the context of AWM, God's greatness being unsurpassed and
unmatched in *the actual world* entails that his greatness is unsurpassed and
unmatched in *any* possible world.

We conclude that CWM does not allow us to conceive of God in the
robust manner of AWM. In other words, while CWM allows us to conceive of God as a being whose greatness could not be *surpassed*, CWM
does not allow us to conceive of him more robustly as a being whose
greatness could not be surpassed or *matched*. But as we have argued there
are good reasons for preferring AWM to CWM. We infer that the more
robust of these two conceptions of God is preferable.

Finally, the construction of *theoretical* models of possible worlds is basically a twentieth-century development. Traditional Western theologians
rely instead upon an *intuitive* understanding of logical modalities. Thus,
it is preferable to understand the *historical* notion of God in terms of a
model of possible worlds that accommodates the *intuitive* data, that is, in
terms of AWM rather than CWM. But AWM implies that if God exists,
then he is a being of unsurpassable and unmatchable greatness. We conclude that the historical notion of God should be understood in terms of
the idea that he is a being whose greatness could neither be surpassed
nor matched.

4.4 Necessary Beings versus Self-Existent Beings

Assuming that God exists, is there an *explanation* of his existence? Typically, the existence of a *contingent being* can be explained by describing how it was created. For example, we can explain the existence of the Statue of Liberty by describing how its parts were made and then assembled. But God's existence cannot be explained by describing how he was created. After all, God could not be a created being. Could there be an explanation of his existence?

If God exists, then his existence is a necessary fact. A fact, *F1*, explains a necessary fact, *F2*, only if *F1* is necessary and *F1* entails *F2*. There are such explanations of necessary facts in mathematics. For example, in Euclidean geometry we can explain **theorems** about *triangles* and their *angles* by logically deriving these theorems from *axioms*. In particular, the theorem that the sum of the interior angles of a triangle is equal to a straight angle can be explained in this way. The axioms in question concern *straight lines* rather than *triangles* and *angles*, and straight lines are geometrically more fundamental than triangles and angles. Since the axioms are *necessary*, and since the axioms *logically entail* the theorems, the theorems are *necessary* too. Nevertheless, because the axioms express more *fundamental* geometrical relationships than the theorems,[24] the logical derivation of the theorems from the axioms *explains* the theorems. If a necessary mathematical fact can be explained, then conceivably the necessary fact that God exists can also be explained. On the other hand, it is also conceivable that God's existence has no explanation whatsoever. A fact that has no explanation whatsoever is known as a **brute fact**. Thus, conceivably, the necessary fact that God exists is simply a brute fact. Does God's existence have an explanation or is his existence a brute fact?

Historically, discussion of this question has occurred within the context of philosophical principles about explanation. A seminal figure is the early scholastic philosopher Saint Anselm.[25] He makes use of two principles about explanation, both of which he claimed to know *a priori*. First, *for any x, either x is explained by another, or x is explained by itself, or there is nothing which explains x.* Second, that *whatever exists must have an explanation of its existence.* Anselm's second principle is his version of what is known as the principle of sufficient reason; let us call Anselm's second principle *PSR* for short. Taken in a strict and literal sense Anselm's *first* principle is an incontrovertible necessary truth, but his *second* principle has proved to be controversial.

Anselm uses his *second principle* to infer that God's existence is not a brute fact. In other words, by applying *PSR* to God's existence, Anselm infers that there must be an explanation of God's existence. However, by applying the *first principle* to God's existence, Anselm concludes that either (i) God's existence is explained by *another*, or (ii) God's existence is explained by *itself*, or (iii) there is *nothing* that explains God's existence. Since Anselm has already concluded that God's existence has an explanation, Anselm infers that God's existence is either explained by *another* or explained by *itself*. Anselm then argues that *another* cannot explain God's existence. He reasons that if God's existence were explained by *another*, then his existence would *depend* upon that other thing and, therefore, God would not be supremely great. In Anselm's view, the supremely great being cannot be dependent for its existence upon any *other* being. So, Anselm concludes that God's existence must be explained by *itself*, in other words, that God must be a *self-existent* being.[26] Anselm takes this to imply that *God's existence* is explained by his *nature* or *essence*.

However, Anselm's notion of a self-existent or self-explanatory being is rather obscure. For example, Anselm takes it to be an implication of divine self-existence that (i) God's existence is *not* explained by anything *else*, (ii) God's existence *is* explained by his *essence*, and hence that (iii) God is a necessary being. Unhappily, (i) and (ii) are incompatible *unless* God is identical with his essence. Anselm accepts the doctrine that God is identical with his essence; among traditional theologians such as Anselm this doctrine is commonly thought to be an implication of divine simplicity. But as we have argued, it is a category mistake to suppose that God, a *substance*, is identical with his essence, a *quality*. Moreover, necessarily, any quality of a concrete entity [of any sort] *inheres* in that concrete entity. But God's essence is a quality of God, and God is a concrete entity. So, *God's essence* inheres in *God*. Since it is impossible for a concrete entity to *inhere* in *itself*, it follows that *God* cannot inhere in *himself*. Because *God's essence* inheres in God, but *God* does not, God and his essence are diverse. For all of these reasons, God and his essence *cannot* be identical.[27] Hence, (i) and (ii) *are* incompatible. Thus, if God's existence is explained by his essence, then strictly speaking God's existence is explained by something *else*. However, God's existence being explained by his essence seems compatible with God's being maximally great. There is no reason to accept without qualification Anselm's assumption that God's existence cannot depend upon something else.

Still, there are *qualified* versions of Anselm's assumption that are acceptable. For example, since God is a *necessary being*, it is clear that his existence cannot depend upon any *contingent being*. In addition, since it seems that all *substances* other than God are contingent beings, it appears that his existence cannot depend upon the existence of any other *substance*.

Given the foregoing discussion of problematical features of Anselm's notion of self-existence, it is reasonable to distinguish at least three different senses of *self-existence*. According to the first sense, an entity, x, is self-existent if and only if x's existence is explained by x's existence. But the notion that there is an x such that x's existence is explained by x's existence is viciously circular. It is absurd to suppose that something is *explanatorily prior* to *itself*. (An obviously absurd case of something's being explanatorily prior to itself is *something's creating itself*.) Thus, it is not possible for anything, including God, to be self-existent in this first sense. In other words, this first sense of self-existence is incoherent. According to the second sense, to say that something is self-existent is just to say that it is a necessary being. But to assert that God is self-existent in this sense adds nothing to the core idea of God, an idea that already includes the notion that God is a necessary being. So, this second sense of self-existence is redundant in this context. Finally, according to the third sense, an entity, x, is self-existent if and only if x's *existence* is *explained* by x's *essence*. This sense of self-existence does not seem to be either incoherent or redundant. It seems to be an open question whether God can be said to be self-existent in this third sense. This is the sense of self-existence that we focus on below.

As we have seen, Anselm's argument that God is self-existent depends upon *PSR*. Anselm finds himself unable to conceive of the possibility of something that lacks an explanation. David Hume, on other hand, maintains that there could be something that lacks an explanation, for example, an object that spontaneously pops into existence without any explanation. Hume finds himself perfectly well able to conceive of such a possibility; whereas Anselm finds the notion of such a possibility to be utterly absurd and unintelligible. Because intuitions about these matters vary widely among individuals, there does not seem to be any way conclusively to settle the disagreement in question. We are inclined to side with Hume and to admit the abstract possibility of spontaneously generated objects. So we are inclined to reject *PSR*.

Another problem with *PSR* can be brought out as follows. If everything that exists must have an explanation of its existence, and nothing that exists can be explained by *itself*, then everything that exists must be explained by *another*. But if everything that exists must be explained by another, then for everything that exists there must be either an *infinite regress of explanations*, i.e., x_1 is explained by x_2, x_2 is explained by x_3, x_3 is explained by x_4, . . . , or a *circle of explanations*, e.g., x_1 is explained by x_2, x_2 is explained by x_3, and x_3 is explained by x_1. Since nothing can be explained by itself, *PSR* has the untoward consequence that for everything that exists there must be either an infinite explanatory regress or a circular system of explanations. But it is not at all plausible to think that God's existence is explained by his essence, his essence is explained by the essence of his essence, the essence of his essence is explained by the essence of the essence of his essence, and so on *ad infinitum*. Nor is it at all plausible to think that God's existence is explained by his essence, his essence is explained by the essence of his essence, and the essence of his essence is explained by his existence. More generally, the consequence that infinite explanatory regresses or circular explanations are *ubiquitous* is problematic. Since *PSR* has this consequence, *PSR* is problematic.

Of course, if Anselm is mistaken in thinking that everything that exists must have an explanation, then his argument that God's existence is explained by his essence is unsound. However, there is an alternative approach available for arguing that God's existence is explained by his essence. In particular, even supposing that one has conceded the possibility of brute facts, it remains true that *one ought to explain as much as one can*. Although this principle of philosophical and scientific method is compatible with the existence of brute facts, it *requires that one not multiply brute facts unnecessarily*. Even if *PSR* is abandoned, the weaker methodological principle that *one should explain as much as one can* is available as an alternative basis for arguing that God's existence is explained by his essence. The difference between Anselm's argument and such an alternative argument is this. Anselm's version of the principle of sufficient reason simply *entails* that *there is an explanation of God's existence*; but our methodological principle only implies that *if* one proposes a viable explanation of God's existence, *then* one has *epistemic justification* for *theorizing* or *hypothesizing* that *there is an explanation of God's existence*. In other words, while this part of Anselm's argument is a straightforward *logical deduction*, the alternative argument is what is known as an **abduction** or *inference to the best explanation*.

Can it be successfully argued that God's existence is explained by his essence *via* an inference to the best explanation? The most promising approach along these lines seems to be this. God's essence is maximal greatness. Thus, we can seek to explain the *necessary* fact *that God exists* in terms of some *necessary* fact about this essence, for instance, the necessary fact that *maximal greatness is necessarily exemplified*. Thus, it might be argued that the fact that *maximal greatness is necessarily exemplified entails*, and thereby *explains*, the fact that *God exists*.

Does such an argument succeed? It is clear enough that a necessary fact of this kind *entails* that God exists. But does such a necessary fact really *explain why* God exists? After all, if God exists, then the necessary fact that *he exists* also *entails* the necessary fact that maximal greatness is necessarily exemplified. Because neither fact seems to be more basic than the other, it appears to be just as plausible that the former fact explains the latter fact, as it is that the latter fact explains the former fact. Still, one might attempt to revive this notion by drawing an analogy between explaining God's existence in terms of his essence and explaining a geometrical theorem in terms of geometrical axioms (as described earlier). In each case, one fact *explains* another even though *both of them* are *necessary*. The trouble with this analogy is that it does not seem that God's essence is *metaphysically more fundamental* than his existence in anything like the way in which straight lines are *geometrically more fundamental* than angles and triangles. One necessary fact explains another only when the first necessary fact is more fundamental than the other. We cannot find an analogy between these theological and geometrical cases that suggests that God's existence is explained by his essence.

Furthermore, it cannot be true *both* that God exists *because* maximal greatness is necessarily exemplified *and* that maximal greatness is necessarily exemplified *because* God exists. Surely, a purported circular system of explanations of this sort is vicious. For these reasons, the notion that God's existence can be explained by his essence does *not* appear to be viable.

Let us take stock. As we have seen, *PSR* is subject to serious doubts. Thus, *PSR* cannot be used to establish that God's existence must have an explanation. It seems that the alternative is to argue that God's existence is explained by his essence by means of an inference to the best explanation. But this alternative approach appears not to succeed. Thus, there seems to be no reason to think that God is self-existent in the sense that his existence is explained by his essence. It seems to be at least equally likely that if God exists, then his existence, although necessary, is a brute fact. However, if the existence of God is a necessary brute fact, then he may be said to be self-existent in the sense that he is a necessary being whose existence is not explained by anything else.[28]

NOTES

1   For example, see Alvin Plantinga, *The Nature of Necessity* (Oxford: Clarendon Press, 1974).

2   For instance, see Roderick Chisholm, *A Realistic Theory of Categories* (Cambridge: Cambridge University Press, 1996).

3   *D2* is schematic, and the letter '*F*' should be replaced by an appropriate predicate expression.

4   *D3* is schematic, and the letter '*F*' should be replaced by an appropriate predicate expression.

5   For a defense of a general account of this kind that employs the concept of haecceity (a kind of individual essence) see Gary S. Rosenkrantz, *Haecceity: An Ontological Essay* (Dordrecht: Kluwer, 1993), pp. 166–7. Such a general account is controversial because the existence of haecceities is controversial.

6   It might appear that this rather extraordinary phenomenon is inconsistent with the Law of Conservation of Energy. However, this phenomenon falls within certain very narrow limits prescribed by Heisenberg's Indeterminacy Principle. Since this principle implies that the amount of energy in the universe is actually indeterminate (given the Copenhagen interpretation of quantum mechanics), it can be argued that the phenomenon in question is consistent with the Law of Conservation of Energy.

7   David Hume, *Dialogues Concerning Natural Religion* (New York: Hafner Publishing Company, 1975), pp. 58–9.

8   Hume's notion of what is *distinctly conceivable* resembles Descartes's notion of *a clear and distinct idea*. According to Descartes, a clear and distinct idea must be true. For example, he claimed that we have a clear and distinct perception of a physical object's extension, but not of its color, taste, or odor. Ironically, though, Descartes never *clearly* explains the difference between the two kinds of ideas in a way that enables us to apply the distinction with any confidence. And Descartes himself regards as clear and distinct ideas that later philosophers have found to be false, for example, that existence comes in three degrees, and that everything must have a sufficient reason or cause.

9   For instance, see Nicholas Rescher, *A Theory of Possibility* (Pittsburgh, Penn.: University of Pittsburgh Press, 1975).

10 The conceptualist model of possibility is subject to this difficulty because it implies that possibility is a *subjective* matter. It should be observed that a similar criticism applies to a subjective theory of truth, for example, the theory that a proposition *p* is true for us if and only if we believe *p*. This theory of truth implies that the proposition *that there are beliefs* is true because we *believe* that there are beliefs. Since nothing can be explanatorily prior to itself, such an explanation of the truth of this proposition is absurd.

11 For example, see Hugh Creswell, "The World is Everything that is the Case," *Australasian Journal of Philosophy* 50 (1972), pp. 1–13.

12 See Plantinga, *The Nature of Necessity.*

13 There are variations upon AWM, depending upon the precise ontology of abstract entities employed, for example, *conjunctions of properties* may be substituted for *conjunctions of propositions*, or *sets* of properties or propositions may be substituted for *conjunctions* of them. Since for our purposes these variations are not particularly important, we ignore them in the text and take Plantinga's version of AWM as representative.

14 David Lewis, "Counter-part Theory and Quantified Modal Logic," *Journal of Philosophy* 65 (1968), pp. 113–26.

15 For an account of the concrete/abstract distinction see section 2.1.

16 Our account of the notion of an abstract entity in section 2.1 is consistent with the intuition that a set is an abstract entity. We would argue that while sets can have members, they cannot have parts. (Parthood is a transitive relation, but membership is not.) Since a set cannot have spatial or temporal parts, a set qualifies as an abstract entity on our account.

17 An *irreducible category* is an ontological category that cannot be reduced to another ontological category; and a *reducible category* is an ontological category that can be reduced to another ontological category. Positing entities of *reducible* categories multiplies entities unnecessarily only if positing entities of the irreducible categories to which they can ultimately be reduced multiplies entities unnecessarily. Thus, what fundamentally needs to be considered in this case is the number of *irreducible categories* of abstract entities.

18 Although Plantinga's possible worlds take propositions as irreducible, alternative schemes define abstract possible worlds in terms of properties, taken as irreducible. So, given our argument in the text, arguably, there are abstract properties, but there are not abstract entities of another irreducible category.

19 For an argument that implies that a formal criterion of transworld identity for concrete entities can be formulated in terms of their haecceities, see *Haecceity: An Ontological Essay.*

20 Note that the kinds of spatiotemporal discontinuities whose intelligibility we countenanced in section 3.2 are different in kind from the ones whose intelligibility we do not countenance. The former only involved discontinuities in the spatial or temporal paths that an object follows within space or time. The latter involves discontinuities between one space-time continuum and another, and the causal inaccessibility of one continuum from another. We are also skeptical of the intelligibility of speculative theories in contemporary physics that posit radically isolated, spatiotemporally discontinuous physical systems, e.g., the many-worlds interpretation of quantum mechanics.

21 For additional considerations that favor AWM, see *Haecceity: An Ontological Essay*, chap. 3.

22 See section 1.2.

23 Lewis, "Counter-part Theory and Quantified Modal Logic," p. 126.
24 Note that saying this does not necessarily commit one to the traditional ideas that the axioms are *more certain* than the theorems, or that the axioms are *self-evident* and the theorems are not.
25 See Anselm's *Monologium* ("Monologue"), chap. VI, in *Saint Anselm, Basic Writings*, trans. Sidney N. Deane (La Salle, Ill.: Open Court Publishing Co., 1962).
26 The divine attribute of self-existence is known as *aseity*, and so traditionally, God is said to exist *a se*.
27 For an account of divine simplicity that does not imply that God = God's essence, see section 3.4.
28 Thus, there is a fourth sense of *self-existence* in addition to the three senses discussed earlier in this section. According to this fourth sense, an entity, x, is self-existent if and only if x is a necessary being whose existence is not explained by anything else.

BIBLIOGRAPHY

Adams, R. M., "Divine Necessity," *Journal of Philosophy* 80 (1983), pp. 741–52.
Anselm, *Monologium*, in *Saint Anselm, Basic Writings*, trans. Sidney N. Deane (La Salle, Ill.: Open Court Publishing Co., 1962).
Chisholm, R. M. (1916–99), *A Realistic Theory of Categories* (Cambridge: Cambridge University Press, 1996).
Creswell, H., "The World is Everything that is the Case," *Australasian Journal of Philosophy* 50 (1972), pp. 1–13.
Hume, D., *Dialogues Concerning Natural Religion* (New York: Hafner Publishing Company, 1975).
Lewis, D., "Counter-part Theory and Quantified Modal Logic," *The Journal of Philosophy* 65 (1968), pp. 113–26.
Loux, M. J. (ed.), *The Possible and the Actual: Readings in the Metaphysics of Modality* (Ithaca, NY: Cornell University Press, 1979).
Plantinga, A., *The Nature of Necessity* (Oxford: Clarendon Press, 1974).
——, *Does God Have a Nature?* (Milwaukee, Wis.: Marquette University Press, 1980).
Rescher, N., *A Theory of Possibility* (Pittsburgh, Penn.: University of Pittsburgh Press, 1975).
Rosenkrantz, G. S., *Haecceity: An Ontological Essay* (Dordrecht: Kluwer, 1993).

5

Eternality

The orthodox view is that God exists outside of time. We will dispute this view, arguing instead that God is temporal and mutable (but nonetheless incorruptible).

5.1 Temporal versus Atemporal Eternality

Philosophers and theologians understand divine eternity in two different ways. In much of traditional theology it is maintained that God is *atemporally eternal*. Influential early figures in this tradition are Augustine and Boethius (475–524). Later important figures in this tradition are Anselm and Aquinas. But others such as the theologian Samuel Clarke (1675–1729) hold that God is *temporally eternal*. A being that has atemporal eternity exists *outside* of time, whereas a being that has temporal eternity exists *in* time. The two relevant senses of eternity can be understood as follows.

First, a substantial being, x, has temporal eternity if and only if (i) x exists at every time, (ii) x has infinite temporal duration, and (iii) x has neither beginning nor end. The point of (iii) is to ensure that x has infinite temporal duration in both of the two temporal directions; since it is not obvious that time has neither a beginning nor an end, it is not obvious that (i) and (ii) entail (iii).

Second, a substantial being, x, has atemporal eternity if and only if (i) x does not exist in time, and (ii) x is a necessary being. It is clear that maximal greatness requires either temporal eternity or atemporal eternity.[1] Thus, if God exists, then he does *not* have *finite* or *limited* duration.

The notion of temporal eternity seems to be coherent: it seems that there could be an everlasting substance of infinite temporal duration.

While the notion of atemporal eternity is the stranger of the two senses
of eternity, there is no obvious *logical* incoherence in that notion. For
example, there is no obvious logical incoherence in the idea of a necessary substance that exists in a static, atemporal universe. Nevertheless, since
temporal and atemporal eternity are incompatible, it is not possible that
God is both temporally and atemporally eternal. So, is God temporally
eternal or atemporally eternal?

If God is in time, then this entails that he has *states* that are ordered
by the *temporal relations* of *earlier than*, *later than*, and *simultaneous with*.
Moreover, according to traditional theologians, if God is in time, then
he has states with the *temporal properties* of *present*, *past*, and *future*. Temporal properties of this kind are *transient*. For example, in 1998 the arrival
of the year 2001 is future (but not present or past), at the arrival of
the year 2001 the arrival of the year 2001 is present (but not past or
future), and in 2004 the arrival of the year 2001 is past (but not present
or future). By contrast, if one state is earlier than, later than, or simultaneous with another, then the relationship in question can never
alter. (For example, insofar as the start of World War I is earlier than the
start of World War II, this relationship can never change.) In this sense,
the temporal relations of earlier than, later than, and simultaneous with
are *fixed*.

However, if God is outside of time, then this entails that he does not
have states that stand in temporal relations. In particular, if God is not in
time, then he does not have states ordered by the relations of earlier than
or later than. This has the further consequence that an atemporal God
does not have states with the transient properties of past, present, or future.
Nevertheless, according to theologians such as Anselm, since an atemporally eternal God does not have states that are ordered by temporal
relations, there is a sense in which all of his states are *present to* him and
simultaneous for him. But notice that if God is an *atemporal* substance, then
logical consistency requires that expressions such as 'present to God' and
'simultaneous for God' do not have a literal *temporal* meaning. Anselm
seems to acknowledge this point.[2] Accordingly, considerations of logical
coherence require that in this context expressions of this kind be given
an alternative interpretation. Similar remarks apply both to the Anselmian
notion that while God does *not* exist *in* time, there is a sense in which
God is entirely *present at* every time, and to the Boethian notion that
although God is *atemporal*, God exists in an *enduring present*. That is, these
ideas are unintelligible unless 'present at', 'enduring', and 'present' have a
meaning other than a literal temporal one.

A number of such meanings might be proposed for such apparently temporally laden terms. First, to say that an atemporal substance, A, "endures" might mean that A is a necessary being. Second, to say that all of the states of an atemporal substance, A, are "present" and "simultaneous" might mean that none of A's states are ordered by the earlier than or later than relations. Third, to say that an atemporal substance, A, is entirely "present at" every time might mean that A has knowledge of, and/or power over, what happens at every time.[3] All three of these interpretations seem to be coherent.

Another possible interpretation is that an atemporal substance, A, is entirely "present at" every time in the sense that for any time t, t is necessarily such that A has atemporal eternity. (Such a time, t, is metaphysically dependent upon A's having atemporal eternity.) The claim that there is an atemporal substance which is entirely "present at" every time in this sense also appears to be coherent.

A further suggestion is although an *atemporal substance*, A, is not in time, A is entirely "present at" every time in virtue of *time's* occurring in A. Unfortunately for this suggestion, however, it appears that time's occurring in A is incompatible with A's being atemporal. To see this, notice that if A is atemporal, then A does *not* undergo intrinsic change. Yet, presumably, change occurs in time. Moreover, it appears that, necessarily, if change occurs *in* time, and time occurs *in* A, then change occurs *in* A. After all, *occurring in* appears to be a transitive relation, that is, necessarily, for any x, y, and z, if x occurs in y, and y occurs in z, then x occurs in z. Hence, it seems that if time occurs in A, then A undergoes intrinsic change. So, this suggestion appears to be incoherent: it appears to imply both that A undergoes intrinsic change, and that A does not undergo intrinsic change.

Stump and Kretzmann argue that there is nothing to prevent an atemporal God from being simultaneous with all events in as well-defined a sense as the sense in which human experience is simultaneous with some events.[4] In particular, Stump and Kretzmann appeal to the notion in theoretical physics that simultaneity is relative to a frame of reference, and argue that if there is an atemporal God, then in addition to temporal frames of reference, there exists an atemporal frame of reference. However, 'simultaneous' literally means to exist or occur *at the same time*. This is a definitional truth that is not open to dispute. Moreover, necessarily, for any x and y, if x and y exist or occur *at the same time*, then x and y are *temporal* beings. Thus, when Stump and Kretzmann say that nothing prevents an *atemporal* God from being simultaneous with all events, they use 'simultaneous' with a coherent meaning only if they do not use 'simultaneous' with a literal temporal meaning.

5.2 A Defense of Temporal Eternality

There are two arguments in favor of divine atemporality that should be considered. The first is *the argument from divine simplicity*:

Argument A

(*Premise A1*) Necessarily, if God is temporal, then he has temporal parts.
(*Premise A2*) Necessarily, if God exists, then he does not have parts.

Therefore, necessarily, if God exists, then he is atemporal.

As we have seen, *Premise A2* is true.[5] Nevertheless, *Argument A* does not succeed. For, as we argued earlier, if God is temporal, then he is an enduring soul that undergoes change, and such a soul does not have temporal parts.[6] It follows that *Premise A1* is false. Hence, *Argument A* is unsound.

The second argument in favor of divine atemporality is *the argument from divine immutability*:

Argument B

(*Premise B1*) Necessarily, if God exists, then he is maximally great.
(*Premise B2*) Necessarily, if God is temporal, then he is mutable.
(*Premise B3*) Maximal greatness entails immutability.
(*Premise B4*) Possibly, God is atemporal.

Therefore, necessarily, if God exists, then he is atemporal.

We have already defended *Premise B1* and *Premise B2*.[7] However, we shall raise doubts about *Premise B3* and *Premise B4*. In other words, we shall question both the notion that maximal greatness entails immutability, and the intelligibility of the notion that God is atemporal.

To begin, it seems that mutability is compatible with maximal greatness. For example, with respect to divine power, maximal greatness includes versatility and creativity, yet both versatility and creative power appear to entail mutability. Moreover, if a thing undergoes change, then its greatness can increase, decrease, or remain constant. For example, possibly, a weightlifter's strength increases, remains constant for a period of time, and then decreases. Although God's necessary maximal greatness precludes a *decrease* or *increase* in his greatness, it does not preclude God's greatness *remaining constant*. A maximally great God can undergo change so long as his degree of greatness remains constant. It may be assumed that a spiritual, temporal, omniscient God who intentionally brings about various states of affairs must undergo changes in his psychological or intentional states, for instance, changes in what he believes or wills. Nevertheless, such changes in God do not appear to require either an increase or a decrease in his greatness.

Why, then, has it so often been thought that mutability is incompatible with maximal greatness? In other words, why has it been traditionally claimed that God's greatness entails immutability? Historically, this claim seems to derive from the metaphysics of Plato (427–347 BC), and in particular, from Plato's Theory of Forms, with Neoplatonism as an intermediary.

According to Plato's Theory of Forms, for things of any possible *kind*, say, things which are *triangular*, or things which are *beautiful*, or things which are *tables*, there is a corresponding original Form which is the exemplar for any things of that kind. Such an exemplar is a maximally great being of the kind in question. Thus, there is a perfect triangle, the exemplar for any possible triangular thing; there is a maximally beautiful being, the exemplar for any possible beautiful thing; there is an ideal table, the exemplar for any earthly table, and so forth. These heavenly, perfect Forms are immutable and necessary. Thus, anything that is imperfect, mutable, and contingent, for example, a sensible thing or a soul, is not a Form, but is rather a *copy* of a Form. Assuming that divine things are possible, Plato's Theory of Forms implies that there is an immutable, necessary, maximally great divinity, the exemplar for any divine things.

But Plato's Theory of Forms appears to be unintelligible. For one thing, this theory seems to be inconsistent. In particular, Plato's Theory of Forms appears to imply that all non-Forms are copies of some original Form of non-Formedness. But this Form of non-Formedness must be both a Form and a non-Form, thereby violating the Law of Non-Contradiction. Another inconsistency follows from the fact that the Form of any kind of living organism, for instance, the Form of living tigers, must be both *incapable of undergoing change* and *alive*. For, necessarily, any *living organism* is *capable of undergoing change*. Similarly, Plato's metaphysical scheme implies that mutable or contingent things are copies of the Forms of mutability or contingency, respectively. Yet, this metaphysical scheme paradoxically entails that the Form of mutability is both immutable and mutable, and that the Form of contingency is both necessary and contingent. Furthermore, the Form of triangularity is itself a triangle, but it is not a triangle of any particular *kind*, for instance, it is neither a right triangle, nor an obtuse triangle, nor a scalene triangle, nor an isosceles triangle, nor an equilateral triangle. But such a triangle is impossible! Thus, there are several good reasons for thinking that Plato's Theory of Forms is incoherent. We conclude that this theory is untenable. Therefore, the contention that maximal greatness requires immutability does not receive any support from Plato's Theory of Forms.

What has gone awry in Plato's Theory of Forms? Our diagnosis is that the source of the theory's incoherence is Plato's conception of a Form as an ideal object. Because it is *ideal*, a Form must be an *abstract entity*. Yet, a Form of a concrete object must also be a *concrete entity*. But it is inconsistent to suppose that an entity is both abstract and concrete. Many contemporary Platonists avoid this inconsistency by rejecting Plato's theory of ideal objects in favor of a theory of abstract attributes, for example, the abstract properties of being a triangle, being a tiger, being a table, and so on.

Still, according to contemporary Platonic theories, abstract entities, like Platonic Forms, are incorporeal, necessary, and incapable of undergoing intrinsic change. Accordingly, one might seek to defend the doctrine of divine immutability as follows.

Argument C

(*Premise C1*) If God exists, then he is necessary and incorporeal.
(*Premise C2*) Whatever is necessary and incorporeal is abstract.
(*Premise C3*) Every abstract entity is immutable.

Therefore, if God exists, then he is immutable.

Premise C1 and *Premise C3* are plausible. Moreover, *Premise C2* is not implausible. After all, contemporary Platonic theories imply that necessary, incorporeal beings such as the empty set, the property of being a triangle, and the property of being a unicorn are abstract entities, and it is not clear that there *is* an incorporeal, necessary, concrete entity. Nevertheless, if God exists, then he is a necessary, incorporeal, *concrete* entity (*not* an abstract entity); and it is evident that concreteness does *not* entail immutability. Hence, *Premise C2* is problematic in a context in which it is supposed that God is a possible being.

Although God might be said to be "abstract" in the sense of *being incorporeal*, or might be said to be "abstract" in the sense of *being theoretical*, neither of these senses of abstractness appears to entail immutability. For instance, mutable, contingent souls seem to be possible,[8] and contemporary physics implies that theoretical entities such as atoms and molecules are mutable. Finally, simplicity seems not to entail immutability: simple, contingent, mutable souls appear to be possible.[9]

Let us take stock. God has traditionally been thought to be atemporal either on the ground that he is simple, or on the ground that he is immutable. But given a proper understanding of divine simplicity, there is no good reason to think that divine simplicity entails divine atemporality. On the other hand, although it appears that if God is immutable, then he is atemporal, there seems to be no good reason to think that if God exists, then he is immutable. Neither Platonic metaphysics nor God's necessity and incorporeality provide such a reason. Nor can we think of any other plausible reason to suppose that God is atemporal. As far as we can see, there is no good reason at all to think that if God exists, then he is atemporal.

We argue next that there are good reasons to think that if God exists, then he is temporal. To begin, if God exists, then he is an active, creative, purposeful being. Furthermore, such a God is a person who intentionally performs actions, and is morally responsible for them. Thus, if God exists, then he is a moral agent. Since atemporality entails *inactivity* or *stasis*, it follows that if God exists, then he is a temporal being.

Let us explore this line of reasoning in greater detail. There are three types of actions which God performs if he exists: (i) *God intentionally creates temporal things*, for example, human beings; (ii) *God intentionally destroys temporal things*, for instance, certain stars; and (iii) *God intentionally brings about events which are not changes in himself*, for example, the coming into existence of matter and the advent of light. The following general principle is applicable to divine actions of these three types:

Necessarily, if an agent, *A*, intentionally creates or destroys a temporal thing, or intentionally brings about an event which is not a change in *A*, then *A* performs such an action either by *deciding* (or *choosing*) to do so or by *endeavoring* (or *willing*) to do so. Thus, if God exists, then he performs actions of the three foregoing types *via* his decisions or endeavorings. Yet, necessarily, for an agent to decide or endeavor to do something is for that agent to engage in a *volitional activity*. And a volitional activity of God would be an *intrinsic change* in him. So, if God exists, then he is mutable. (To say that a substance, x, is mutable is to say that x possibly undergoes intrinsic change.)[10] In addition, necessarily, God's performing an action of any of the three types in question is an *interaction* between him and another temporal entity. Hence, if God exists, then he both undergoes intrinsic changes and interacts with other temporal entities, with the latter implying that he undergoes relational changes. Furthermore, necessarily, any agent who undergoes intrinsic change or interacts with another temporal entity is a temporal entity. Consequently, if God exists, then he is a temporal entity.

Our argument can be summarized in somewhat more general terms as follows:

Argument D

(*Premise D1*) If God exists, then he performs actions.
(*Premise D2*) Necessarily, any action is an event.
(*Premise D3*) Necessarily, any event occurs in time.
(*Premise D4*) Necessarily, if God's actions occur in time, then he is in time.

Therefore, if God exists, then he is in time.

On the other side, there is the traditional notion of God as both active and atemporal. For example, Aquinas claims that God's one atemporal action has consequences at different times. But in the light of *Premise D2* and *Premise D3* above, the notion of an *atemporal action* seems to be incoherent. Thus, the claim that God performs a single atemporal action that has consequences at different times appears to be untenable. A similar critique applies to Augustine's argument that God is atemporal because time does not even exist until God *creates* time. In particular, if the notion of an atemporal action is incoherent, then so is the notion of God's acting to bring it about that time exists. We maintain that our critique of the traditional notion of God as both active and atemporal is general enough to have decisively negative implications for any possible attempt to provide a coherent interpretation of this notion.

It can also be plausibly argued that if God exists, then he undergoes *relational* changes that are distinct from any *intrinsic* changes that he undergoes. Although the distinction between intrinsic change and relational change is difficult to define, it is readily illustrated by means of intuitive examples. For instance, if Socrates is awake at time, t_1, and asleep at time,

t_2, then Socrates thereby undergoes an intrinsic change; but if Socrates is in Athens at t_1, and in Thebes at t_2, then Socrates thereby undergoes relational change. It can be argued that if God exists, then he is temporal because he undergoes relational changes. This *argument from relational change* can be stated as follows.

Argument E

(*Premise E1*) Anything that undergoes relational change is temporal.
(*Premise E2*) If God exists, then he undergoes relational change.

Therefore, if God exists, then he is temporal.

With respect to *Premise E1*, necessarily, if there are things that undergo relational change, then these things are temporal, regardless of whether they undergo intrinsic change or interact with anything temporal. Thus, necessarily, if there are two noninteracting, intrinsically unchanging spheres, and one of them rotates around the other, then both of them are temporal in virtue of their changing relationships. For example, sphere 1 has at one time the relationship of being 3 feet to the left of sphere 2, and at another time the relationship of being 3 feet to the right of sphere 2. Hence, it seems that *Premise E1* is true. In addition, it appears that if God exists, then he undergoes relational changes, regardless of whether God undergoes intrinsic change or interacts with anything temporal. For instance, we may assume that God undergoes relational change when Moses prays to God at time t_1 and Moses *fails* to pray to God at time t_2. At time t_1, God has the relationship of being prayed to by Moses, while at time t_2, God does not have the relationship of being prayed to by Moses. It follows that Moses and God cease to stand in a certain *relation* to one another at some time. Thus, it appears that *Premise E2* is true as well. So, we conclude, once again, that God is temporal.

Let us summarize our argument up to this point. First, there seems to be no good reason to think that if God exists, then he is atemporal. Second, there is every indication that if God exists, then he is temporal. We conclude, therefore, that if God exists, then he is a temporal being, a being who exists in time. Moreover, since a being *has atemporal eternity* only if that being does *not* exist in time, it follows that if God exists, then he does not have atemporal eternity.

It follows that if God exists, then he exists in time. Since God would be a maximally great being, God would exist at every time; he would have infinite temporal duration; and he would not be temporally limited, that is, God would not have either a beginning in time or an end in time.[11] Therefore, if God exists, then he has temporal eternity.[12]

How is the notion of a temporally eternal God to be understood? This depends upon whether time is *relational* or time is *absolute*. Time is relational if and only if (i) the existence of time *entails* the existence of entities that stand in temporal relations to one another, and (ii) time exists *because* there are such entities. In contrast, time is absolute if and only if time exists, but *not* because there are entities which stand in temporal relations to one another.

There are two ways of understanding the notion of a temporally eternal God, G, on the assumption that time is *relational*. According to the first understanding, a time exists only if a *change* occurs *at that time*. Notice that, necessarily, for any entity, e, if e exists in time, and anything other e undergoes change, then e undergoes relational change. Thus, the first understanding of the notion of a temporally eternal God, G, implies that G is *perpetually changing*, either relationally or intrinsically, over an infinite period of time which is without a beginning or an end, for example, by perpetually creating, destroying, or maintaining contingent things. (René Descartes argues that God perpetually acts so as to maintain contingent things.) Another example is that if created beings are perpetually changing, then God's relationships to these beings are perpetually changing.

According to the second understanding, if a change occurs at *some* time, then time is infinitely extended and has neither a beginning nor an end. This second understanding implies that if G acts at even *one* time, then G wholly occupies a time of infinite duration. (*Deism* implies that while God creates material things, he does *not* interact with those things after their creation.)

There is a third way of understanding the notion of a temporally eternal God. This way of understanding the notion in question presupposes that time is *absolute*. If time is *absolute*, then a temporally eternal God wholly occupies a time of infinite duration *independently* of any divine acts. (In the view of Sir Isaac Newton [1642–1727] and Samuel Clarke, God wholly occupies an absolute time of infinite duration.) Each one of the foregoing three understandings of the notion of a temporally eternal God seems to be coherent, and we shall not express a preference among them. Only by justifying a theory of the nature of time could we defend such a preference, but justifying a theory of this kind falls outside the scope of this book.

5.3 Incorruptibility versus Immutability

An *immutable substance* is a substance that cannot undergo intrinsic change. As we have argued in the preceding section, maximal greatness does not entail immutability, and if God exists, then he is mutable. On the other hand, an *incorruptible substance* is one whose degree of greatness could not decrease. Thus, an incorruptible substance cannot undergo diminishment or deterioration. As we have seen, maximal greatness entails incorruptibility. So, necessarily, if God exists, then he is incorruptible.[13]

But how is divine incorruptibility to be understood? Divine incorruptibility requires that God has necessary existence and that his core perfections or great-making qualities are essential to him. Accordingly, divine incorruptibility requires that God is necessarily omnipotent, necessarily omniscient, and necessarily omnibenevolent. It follows from this that the degree of God's power, knowledge, and goodness could not decrease.

Divine incorruptibility has additional implications. For example, even though God has *temporal eternity*, divine incorruptibility entails that he cannot undergo deterioration through *aging*. Divine incorruptibility also entails that God cannot be *sick, injured,* or *harmed*. Thus, God is *invulnerable*. It also appears to follow that God is *impassable* in the sense that *he cannot have a sensation of pain*.

Does divine incorruptibility entail that God is impassable in the sense that *he cannot have any feelings*? It is often thought that *in some sense* God *loves* his creatures. However, is it plausible that God has *feelings of love* for his creatures? God could have these feelings only if his having them is compatible with divine incorruptibility. But it can be argued, not implausibly, that having such *nonrational emotional states* is incompatible with divine incorruptibility. According to this Stoical argument, a morally perfect being lives its life by reason alone; nonrational emotional states such as love impede rational activity by their very nature. Since God is a morally perfect being, he does not love. If this argument is correct, then divine incorruptibility precludes God's having feelings of love for his creatures. Such an argument also implies that if God exists, then he does not have *feelings of surprise, wonderment, joy, anger,* and so on. But even if it *is* possible that God has *positive feelings* such as love on some occasions, it is not possible that he has *negative feelings*, for instance, *feelings of hate, sadness, jealousy, envy, fear,* and so forth. Only a being who is morally imperfect, or who has physical or psychic vulnerabilities, could have negative feelings of this sort; yet God is both morally perfect and invulnerable. Divine incorruptibility, then, precludes God's having such negative feelings.

Still, certain evil deeds or immoral actions are proper objects of *moral disapproval*, for example, the Nazis' extermination of six million Jews; and certain good deeds or righteous actions are proper objects of *moral approval*, for instance, the Allied liberation of the surviving Jews from Nazi concentration camps. Hence, if God *morally disapproves* of an evil deed or immoral action, or if God *morally approves* of a good deed or righteous action, then he does *not* thereby undergo a corruption of some sort, provided that these positive or negative attitudes are *dispassionate*, and therefore *lacking* in any nonrational emotive content. Nonetheless, such dispassionate moral attitudes are motivational in nature and have action-guiding force. Hence, it does seem possible for God to possess dispassionate positive and negative moral attitudes of this kind. Thus, although divine incorruptibility *precludes* divine *hate*, it appears that divine incorruptibility is *compatible* with dispassionate divine *disapproval*; and even if divine incorruptibility *precludes* divine *love*, it seems that divine incorruptibility is *compatible* with dispassionate divine *approval*. And in general, it appears that God's being incorruptible is consistent with his having *anti-attitudes* and *pro-attitudes* of these nonemotive sorts.

NOTES

1   See section 1.2.
2   *Monologium*, chap. XXII, in *Saint Anselm, Basic Writings*, trans. Sidney N. Deane (La Salle, Ill.: Open Court Publishing Co., 1962).
3   For example, see Anselm's *Monologium*, chap. XXII. Also compare the parallel interpretations of God's being entirely present at every place in section 3.1.
4   Eleanor Stump and Norman Kretzmann, "Eternity," *Journal of Philosophy* 78 (1981), pp. 429–58.
5   See section 3.4.
6   See section 3.4.
7   See sections 1.2 and 3.4, respectively.
8   See sections 3.2–3.4.
9   See sections 3.2–3.4.
10 Since whatever is mutable is essentially mutable, it follows that if God exists, then God is essentially mutable.
11 See section 1.2.
12 Since temporal eternity is one of the perfections or great-making qualities of a maximally great being, and since a maximally great being is

incorruptible, it follows that a maximally great being has temporal eternity *essentially*. So, if God exists, then God essentially has temporal eternity. See section 1.2.

13 See section 1.2.

BIBLIOGRAPHY

Alston, W., *Divine Nature and Human Language* (Ithaca, NY: Cornell University Press, 1989).

Anselm, *Monologium*, in *Saint Anselm, Basic Writings*, trans. Sidney N. Deane (La Salle, Ill.: Open Court Publishing Co., 1962).

Boethius, A. M. S., *The Consolation of Philosophy*, trans. H. Stewart, in H. Stewart and E. K. Rand (trans.), *Boethius: The Theological Tractates* (Cambridge, Mass.: Harvard University Press, 1936).

Creel, R. E., *Divine Impassibility* (Cambridge: Cambridge University Press, 1986).

Helm, P., *Eternal God* (New York: Oxford University Press, 1988).

Kretzmann, N. (1928–98), "Omniscience and Immutability," *Journal of Philosophy* 63 (1966), pp. 409–21.

Leftow, B., *Time and Eternity* (Ithaca, NY: Cornell University Press, 1991).

Mann, W., "Divine Simplicity," *Religious Studies* 18 (1982), pp. 451–71.

———, "Simplicity and Immutability in God," *International Philosophical Quarterly* 23 (1983), pp. 267–76.

———, "Immutability and Predication," *International Journal for Philosophy of Religion* 22 (1987), pp. 21–39.

Morris, T. V., "On God and Mann: A View of Divine Simplicity," *Religious Studies* 21 (1985), pp. 299–318.

——— (ed.), *Divine and Human Action* (Ithaca, NY: Cornell University Press, 1988).

Pike, N., *God and Timelessness* (New York: Schocken Books, 1970).

Plato, *Phaedo*, trans. G. Grube (Indianapolis, Ind.: Hackett Publishing Company, 1977).

———, *Republic*, trans. G. Grube and C. Reeve (Indianapolis, Ind.: Hackett Publishing Company, 1992).

Quinn, P. L., "Divine Conservation, Creation, and Human Action," in *The Existence and Nature of God*, ed. A. J. Freddoso (Notre Dame, Ind.: University of Notre Dame Press, 1983), pp. 55–80.

Sorabji, R., *Time, Creation and the Continuum* (Ithaca, NY: Cornell University Press, 1983).

Stump, E. and Kretzmann, N. (1928–98), "Eternity," *Journal of Philosophy* 78 (1981), pp. 429–58.

——— and ———, "Absolute Simplicity," *Faith and Philosophy* 2 (1985), pp. 353–81.

—— and ——, "Eternity, Awareness, and Action," *Faith and Philosophy* 9/4 (1992), pp. 463–82.

Swinburne, R. T., "God and Time," in *Reasoned Faith*, ed. E. Stump (Ithaca, NY: Cornell University Press, 1993), pp. 204–22.

6

Omniscience

We will develop an analysis of omniscience (understood as maximal knowledge) and examine its implications for the nature of God. Our analysis implies that if an omniscient being foreknows the occurrence of a contingent event, then this event is causally determined. As we shall see, our analysis implies that God would not foreknow the occurrence of human actions that are free in the libertarian sense. We will discuss the implications of this analysis for the problem of divine foreknowledge and human freedom.

6.1 Omniscience as Maximal Knowledge

The sort of knowledge that a maximally great being would possess is *omniscience*. There are two related questions about omniscience that need to be explored. First, does an intelligible conception of omniscience place *limitations* upon the knowledge of an omniscient being? Second, how is the concept of omniscience to be analyzed or defined?

To answer these questions, one must have an understanding of the nature of knowledge. First of all, it may be assumed that the objects of knowledge are propositions. So, it may be assumed that the knowledge of an omniscient being is propositional knowledge. Accordingly, whatever is generally required for a person, S, to have knowledge of a proposition, p, is required of an omniscient being to have knowledge of p. Among these general requirements of propositional knowledge are the following three: (i) p is true; (ii) S believes p; and (iii) S has adequate epistemic justification for believing p.[1]

It follows that an omniscient being cannot be said to know *every* proposition. Since only a *true* proposition *could* be known, it is not possible to know a *false* proposition, for example, *that New York City is the capital of the United States*. So, if an omniscient being is understood as a being that knows every proposition whatsoever, then the notion of omniscience is unintelligible.

On the other hand, there is a notion of omniscience, employed by many theists, which is not defective in this way. According to this notion, one is omniscient just when one knows every *true* proposition.[2] But, there are serious doubts about the intelligibility of this notion of omniscience as well. For it can be plausibly argued that, necessarily, for any knower, K, there are true propositions which either K could not *believe* or K could not be *adequately justified* in believing. Two different sorts of examples have been put forward in this regard. The first sort of example involves a true proposition which one can express about *oneself* by using the idiom of the first person, for example, the proposition Mister Jones expresses when he says, "I am thinking." It is argued that an omniscient being other than Jones cannot grasp this proposition, and hence that this proposition, even when true, cannot be believed, and thus cannot be known, by an omniscient being other than Jones. The second sort of example involves a true proposition that predicts the occurrence of a causally undetermined, contingent event, for instance, a true proposition that predicts a free human action, or a true proposition that predicts the occurrence of a random quantum event. It is argued that an omniscient being could not have adequate grounds for making such a claim about the future, a hypothetical example of which might be *that Jones will freely come to the lecture next Friday*, or *that a particular undetermined subatomic motion, m, will occur at a certain time, t.*

These arguments raise serious concerns about the notion of omniscience as knowledge of every true proposition. They suggest that an omniscient being's knowledge must be limited to a *subclass* of true propositions. This situation is analogous to the situation with respect to divine omnipotence. As we shall argue later, it cannot be said that God can bring about *every* state of affairs, or even every *possible* state of affairs. It is relatively uncontroversial that God cannot know a false proposition or bring about an impossible state of affairs, such as *that a spherical cube exists*. It is more controversial and less obvious that God cannot know every true proposition or bring about every possible state of affairs. Nevertheless, we shall argue that the two proposed epistemological limitations upon omniscience are highly plausible, and hence that the notion of omniscience as knowledge of every true proposition is very likely unintelligible.

A preliminary observation is that there is another notion of omniscience available. According to this notion, omniscience is *maximal knowledge*. To say that a being, S, has maximal knowledge is to say that S's overall knowledge could not be exceeded by any being. Possession of maximal knowledge is consistent with ignorance of true propositions of certain kinds, provided that it is impossible for a maximally knowledgeable being to know true propositions of those kinds. Nor does possession of maximal knowledge require knowing whatever anyone else knows. If S_1 knows p, and S_2 does not, it does not follow that S_2 is *not overall* more knowledgeable than S_1, since it could be that S_2 knows more propositions than S_1 does, rather than the other way around. If, as we shall argue, omniscience understood noncomparatively, as knowledge of every true proposition, is of dubious intelligibility, then it is the *comparative* notion of omniscience that has the best chance of being intelligible. Let us proceed to show how the doubts about the intelligibility of the *noncomparative* notion of omniscience can be substantiated.

The first example involves a true proposition that Jones expresses by saying, "I am thinking." It seems that to grasp this proposition about Jones, one must be identical with Jones, and that nobody other than Jones could be identical with him. After all, only someone who possibly has introspective or inner awareness of a mental state of Jones possibly grasps the proposition Jones expresses by saying, "I am thinking," and only Jones possibly has introspective or inner awareness of a mental state of Jones. Introspective or inner awareness is the only possible way in which one can be *directly* aware of a mental state of a person.[3] So, for example, it is impossible for anyone to be directly aware of a mental state of a person by means of any form of sensory or *outer* awareness. Thus, it appears that the proposition Jones expresses by saying, "I am thinking," could only be grasped by Jones.[4] However, one can believe a proposition only if one can grasp that proposition. Hence, it seems to be impossible for a being other than Jones to believe the proposition Jones expresses when he says, "I am thinking." Consequently, it appears to be impossible for an omniscient being other than Jones to believe the proposition in question. Since knowledge requires belief, it seems to be impossible for an omniscient being other than Jones to know the proposition Jones expresses when he says, "I am thinking." On the other hand, it is clear that *Jones* can know this proposition. Of course, an ordinary human being such as Jones is *not* omniscient. Thus, it appears that a non-omniscient being knows certain propositions about himself which no other being, not even an omniscient one, can know.

Thus, we believe that a defensible analysis of omniscience should not imply that an omniscient being knows every true proposition. On the other hand, it would be desirable for such an analysis to be neutral about this highly controversial issue, that is, compatible both with our position *vis-à-vis* the knowability of all true egocentric propositions by an omniscient being *and* with a contrary position. This is, in fact, a feature of the analysis we shall develop later.

The second sort of example involves causally undetermined future contingent events. For us fully to appreciate the significance of such examples, we need better to understand the *character* of the knowledge had by an omniscient being. Such knowledge has *quantitative* and *qualitative* dimensions. The quantitative dimension pertains to *how much* is known by an omniscient being, that is, to the *scope* of this knowledge. The preceding discussion illustrates an issue pertaining to the scope of knowledge that an omniscient being possesses.

The qualitative dimension pertains to the *standards of epistemic justification* for an omniscient being to know a proposition: justification, remember, is the third ingredient of knowledge, along with truth and belief. As we shall see, some kinds of knowledge require a higher standard of epistemic justification than others. However, generally speaking, quality and quantity of knowledge are inversely proportional to one another. That is, the higher the quality of justification required for knowledge, the more difficult it is for knowers to acquire knowledge; and the more knowledge accessible to knowers, the weaker the justification required for knowledge. We expect an omniscient being to have a large amount of high-quality knowledge, but, as we have seen, an omniscient being *cannot* have both maximum quantity and maximum quality of knowledge. How, then, are the quantitative and the qualitative dimensions of omniscience to be balanced? In what follows, we attempt to answer this puzzling question.

We begin by considering the implications of understanding omniscience in terms of kinds of knowledge with differing standards of epistemic justification. According to the first kind of knowledge, S knows p entails that if p is true, then p must be self-evidently obvious to *anyone* who grasps p.[5] To understand omniscience in terms of this extremely strong kind of knowledge would appear to limit an omniscient being's knowledge to relatively simple necessary truths such as logical and mathematical axioms, and its own self-presenting states, for example, "I am thinking" (where 'I' refers to the omniscient being in question). But this would be an undue limitation upon the scope of an omniscient being's knowledge. Few philosophers, including the authors, would understand omniscience in terms of such a strict kind of knowledge.

According to the second kind of knowledge, S knows p only if either p is self-evidently obvious to S, or S deduces p from one or more propositions that are self-evidently obvious to S. Unfortunately, this second kind of knowledge is not much of an improvement over the first. Although understanding omniscience in terms of the second kind of knowledge enlarges the scope of knowledge by allowing knowledge of more complex logical and mathematical theorems, it implies, as in the case of the first kind of knowledge, that an omniscient being does not have knowledge of the past. As we will argue later, God's knowledge of the past requires memory, a source of knowledge other than knowledge of the self-evident and of what is deduced from the self-evident (the faculty which is the source of the latter knowledge has frequently been called *reason*). Moreover, on certain assumptions, understanding omniscience in terms of the second kind of knowledge implies that an omniscient being does not have complete knowledge of physical objects and persons other than itself. The assumptions in question are either that human agents are free in the libertarian sense or that some aspect of the behavior of some physical objects is causally undetermined. If either of these is the case, then an omniscient being could not deduce all of the behavior of human agents or physical objects from a self-evident proposition, say, *that a certain universe is created by that omniscient being and that certain laws of nature govern that universe*. On these assumptions, in order for an omniscient being to have a suitably complete knowledge of the concrete universe (which excludes, for example, egocentric propositions about others), that being would require *perception*, a faculty other than reason (and memory).

To deny an omniscient being knowledge of the past, or the sort of knowledge of the concrete universe discussed, is an undue limitation upon the scope of an omniscient being's knowledge. The second kind of knowledge also is too restrictive.

According to another proposed kind of knowledge, it is possible for S to know p when S is merely justified *beyond a reasonable doubt* in believing p. This standard of epistemic justification can be illustrated by an example from our legal system. When a defendant has been accused of committing a felony, the jury is charged to convict the defendant if and only if there is evidence beyond any reasonable doubt that the defendant committed the crime. But a jury can be justified beyond any reasonable doubt that the defendant is guilty, even though it lacks *conclusive evidence* that the defendant is guilty. And so it could turn out that the defendant is in fact innocent in such a case. Thus, that S is justified in believing p beyond any reasonable doubt does *not* entail that p is true. Therefore, to understand omniscience in terms of this proposed kind of knowledge is to imply that the belief-forming faculties that generate an omniscient being's knowledge include modes of inductive or nondeductive inference. As we have seen, such modes of inference are liable to error or *fallible*.[6] Another instance of a fallible mode of inference of the sort in question is an **enumerative inductive argument**. For example:

(*Premise 1*) The sun rose today.
(*Premise 2*) The sun rose yesterday.
(*Premise 3*) The sun rose the day before yesterday.
.
.
.

Therefore, the sun will rise tomorrow.

Based upon the premises stated, it is probable that the sun will rise tomorrow. Nonetheless, this mode of inference is fallible: it is logically consistent with the premises of the argument that the sun will explode tonight, and therefore fail to rise tomorrow.

Understanding omniscience in terms of the proposed liberal kind of knowledge in question does not unduly limit the scope of omniscience. Nevertheless, we shall argue below that a reasonable constraint on the *quality* of an omniscient being's knowledge is that the belief-forming faculties that generate an omniscient being's knowledge be immune to error or *infallible*.[7] Our argument implies that the standards of justification required by the proposed liberal kind of knowledge are *too lax* for the purposes of understanding omniscience. Parallel remarks apply to any more stringent kind of knowledge that is compatible with knowledge-generation *via* fallible belief-forming faculties.

Is there another kind of knowledge that is neither too strict in its scope implications nor too lax in its qualitative ones *vis-à-vis* omniscience? We shall argue that such a kind of knowledge can be identified in terms of the following list of activities, each of which corresponds to a basic cognitive faculty: (1) *a priori* **intuition**; (2) introspection; (3) perception; (4) memory; and (5) inference. We propose: (i) that an omniscient being possesses each one of these basic cognitive faculties; (ii) that each one of these faculties provides maximum quality *for its particular kind* of output; and (iii) that each one of these faculties affords the maximum scope of knowledge of its kind, consistent with (ii). Proposals (i) and (iii) are needed to ensure that the knowledge of an omniscient being has sufficient scope. Proposal (ii) is needed to ensure that the knowledge of an omniscient being is of sufficient quality. If a being possessed a *scope of knowledge* equal to, or even greater than, that guaranteed by proposals (i) and (iii), but lacked the *quality of knowledge* guaranteed by proposal (ii), then such a being would not possess *maximal knowledge*. There could be a being whose knowledge was more perfect than this. Proposal (ii) requires maximal quality for each kind of output, and for this requirement to be met each of the belief-forming faculties in question must be infallible. Accordingly, in order for an omniscient being to possess the requisite quality of knowledge, its belief-forming faculties must be infallible. In particular, it must have infallible *a priori* intuition, introspection, perception, memory, and inference.

Human faculties of *a priori* intuition and introspection are plausibly thought to be infallible with respect to a *finite* number of *very simple* propositions, such as *that a square is four-sided*, and *that I am thinking*, respectively. Thus, it is conceivable that an omniscient being, with a super-humanly powerful intellect, has infallible intuitive *a priori* access to *infinitely many* necessary truths of *all* degrees of complexity, and infallible introspective access to *all* of its own mental states.[8]

However, human faculties of perception, memory, and inference are not plausibly thought to be infallible.[9] Nevertheless, infallible perception can be coherently conceived as a cognitive faculty that as a matter of a basic, necessary principle, invariably functions so as to produce correct ideas or representations of external things in an omniscient soul. Parallel remarks apply to the possibility of infallible memory. Since nondeductive inference is by its very nature fallible, any inference made by an omniscient being must be deductive. On the other hand, nothing in the nature of deduction precludes an omniscient being from possessing an infallible deductive faculty. After all, a *deductive argument* is *necessarily* such that if its premises are *true*, then its conclusion is *true*.[10] Thus, infallible deduction can consistently be thought of as a cognitive faculty that as a matter of a basic, necessary principle, invariably functions to produce deductive, that is, **valid** reasoning in an omniscient soul. All of these infallible cognitive faculties should be thought of as *instantaneous* in their operations, that is, as not requiring the passage of time in order properly to function.[11] The notion of such a faculty is logically consistent.[12]

Incorporating the quality requirements just described, proposal (iii) implies that the scope of an omniscient being's knowledge at a time, t, is as follows: (1) *a priori* access *via* intuition, infallible memory, and/or infallible deduction to all necessary propositions which it can grasp; (2) infallible introspective access to all of its mental states at t; (3) infallible perceptual access to each of the states, at t, of every concrete thing other than itself;[13] (4) infallible memory of all of its knowledge prior to t; (5) infallible deductive access to the entailments of (1)–(4), though only insofar as these entailments are graspable by it.

To say that one thing can be deduced from another is to say that the latter logically entails the former. If S is omniscient at time t, then at t, S is knowledgeable about the future relative to t only to the extent that the future relative to t is deducible from what S knows at t. The future relative to t can be deduced from the laws of nature, $L_1 \ldots L_n$, together with the initial conditions, $C_1 \ldots C_n$, obtaining at t only if the future relative to t is causally determined by the laws and initial conditions that obtain at t. But a law of nature is *not* a particular matter of fact; such a law is *universal* and has implications concerning merely possible instances. Since only a particular matter of fact can be known by perception or introspection, an omniscient being, S, cannot know the laws of nature by means of perception or introspection. So, it appears that such a being, S, knows that $L_1 \ldots L_n$ are the laws of nature because S *enacts* them in virtue of S's being omnipotent.[14] (Plausibly, if an omniscient being has the power to enact the laws of nature, then this entails that the omniscient being in question is also omnipotent.) In particular, it seems that S knows the laws of nature by deducing them from the following premises: (1) S exists; (2) necessarily, if S exists, then S is omnipotent; (3) necessarily, if an omnipotent agent wills that the laws of nature be $L_1 \ldots L_n$, then that omnipotent agent brings it about that $L_1 \ldots L_n$ are the laws of nature; (4) S wills that the laws of nature be $L_1 \ldots L_n$; (5) if an omnipotent agent brings it about that $L_1 \ldots L_n$ are the laws of nature, then $L_1 \ldots L_n$ are the laws of nature. Since S knows that (1)–(5) are true, and since (1)–(5) logically entail that the laws of nature are $L_1 \ldots L_n$, S knows by deduction that the laws of nature are $L_1 \ldots L_n$.[15] Of course, S also knows what initial conditions obtain at time t, since at t, S has infallible access to each of the states of every concrete thing. We conclude that if S is omniscient at t, then S is knowledgeable about only as much of the future relative to t as is deducible from the laws, $L_1 \ldots L_n$ & the initial conditions, $C_1 \ldots C_n$.[16]

If S is omniscient at time t, then at t, S has infallible memory of the past relative to t. This implies that S exists at every time in the past relative to t. Why must S have such memory? Because, otherwise, S would not know that there was a past at all, or the extent of the past. It might be replied that S could deduce the physical universe's past from its present without using memory. But S could only do this with knowledge of the laws of nature. Yet, as we just argued, S could only know these laws if S *enacted* them. So S must have existed before S enacted the laws of nature. Thus, in order to deduce the past from the present, S must *remember* that S enacted the laws of nature.

While we have discussed several sorts of knowledge, it seems that the sort of knowledge we have ascribed to an omniscient being uniquely balances scope of knowledge with quality of knowledge in a way that befits an omniscient being.

We are now in a position to understand why it is so doubtful that an omniscient being can know a proposition that predicts a causally undetermined contingent event, for instance, a future random quantum event or a future human action that is free in the libertarian sense.

It seems that the only way in which an omniscient agent can have the requisite infallible access to future contingent events is by means of a *deduction* from laws and present conditions. The use of *inductive methods* is ruled out by the requirement that the mode of access be infallible. But the occurrence of an undetermined future contingent event cannot be deduced from laws and present conditions. Thus, it seems that an omniscient being cannot have knowledge of a proposition that predicts an undetermined contingent event.

It might be replied that an omniscient being can obtain such knowledge in some way that we have overlooked. There are two replies that need to be considered. The first reply is that knowledge of a proposition of this kind can be obtained through *foresight*. Foresight is *perception* of a future event. The claim is that an omniscient being has infallible foresight of all future contingent events, including undetermined ones. But the notion of infallible foresight of an undetermined future contingent event is of dubious coherence. Necessarily, if S has infallible foresight of an undetermined future contingent event, e, then S's perception of e must have as its efficient cause an event which is in the *future* relative to S's perception of e, namely, e! But it seems to be a necessary truth that if an event e_1 is an efficient cause of an event e_2, then either e_1 is *before* e_2 or e_1 is *simultaneous* with e_2. Thus, if e_1 causes e_2, then this entails that e_1 is *not* in the future relative to e_2. We conclude that it is impossible for an omniscient being to have infallible foresight of an undetermined future contingent event. Infallible foresight of such an event requires a kind of "backward causation" which appears to be impossible. Yet, it is sometimes claimed that such "backward causation" is possible, for example, that possibly a thing travels backward in time. Nevertheless, if God were to have infallible foresight of every future contingent event, then there would be at least as many events that are backwardly caused, i.e., divine perceptions of future contingent events, as there are events that are forwardly caused, i.e., future contingent events. But, apparently, the temporal order of events as past and future, and earlier and later, requires later events to be caused by earlier events and not *vice versa* (at least for the most part).[17] Thus, it seems absurd to suppose that God has infallible foresight of every future contingent event.

The second reply is inspired by Luis de Molina's sixteenth-century defense of the compatibility of divine providence and human freedom.[18] According to this Molinist position, divine providence is best understood as including both divine foreknowledge of all contingent events, including the free actions of humans, and complete control over the course of contingent events, to the extent that this is compatible with the existence of such free actions. However, the Molinist maintains that *the libertarian account* of human (and divine) freedom is correct. This means that there are free human (and divine) decisions that are *not* causally determined by any antecedent or concurrent events, states, or conditions.[19] Let us assume that a human being, S, freely chooses to ϕ at a time t. The libertarian account of human freedom entails that S has it within her power to refrain, in a very robust sense, from choosing to ϕ at t. This very strong libertarian sense of *having it within one's power to refrain* from choosing to ϕ can be understood in terms of the set of circumstances, C, in which S freely chooses to ϕ at t. This set of circumstances, C, contains all of the causal conditions which obtain in the world up to t. To say that S has it within her power to refrain from choosing to ϕ at t entails that, *possibly*, S is in C and S refrains from choosing to ϕ at t. It follows that according to libertarianism, if a person, S, in circumstances, C, freely chooses to ϕ at t, then this entails that in some possible world, S is in C, and S [freely] refrains from choosing to ϕ at t.[20]

The Molinist account of divine foreknowledge of free human actions depends upon its notion of a **subjunctive conditional** *of human freedom*. For example, let as assume that Jones freely chooses to attend the lecture this Friday. C is the set of circumstances in which Jones makes this libertarian choice; C contains all of the causal conditions which obtain in the world up to this Friday. According to the Molinist, at every time prior to this Friday it is true *that if Jones were in C, then Jones would freely choose to attend the lecture this Friday*. Molinists maintain that this proposition is a true subjunctive conditional of human freedom. Based upon this idea, they propose the following account of divine foreknowledge of free human actions. The proposition *that Jones is in C* in conjunction with the subjunctive conditional of human freedom in question logically entails that Jones freely chooses to attend the lecture this Friday. At every time prior to this Friday God knows that Jones is in *C* and that the aforementioned subjunctive conditional of human freedom is true.[21] Thus, at every time *prior* to this Friday, God knows *that Jones will freely choose to attend the lecture this Friday* by validly deducing this proposition from the conjunction of *Jones is in C* and *if Jones were in C, then Jones would freely choose to attend the lecture this Friday*.

However, the Molinist thesis that God has knowledge of true subjunctive conditionals of human freedom does not seem to be consistent. If the Molinist position were correct, then the proposition expressed by the sentence

(1) 'if Jones were in C, then Jones would freely choose to attend the lecture this Friday',

would entail

(E_1) *possibly*, Jones is in C and Jones freely refrains from choosing to attend the lecture this Friday.

This entailment is a straightforward implication of the Molinist's assumption that Jones's free choice in this case is a libertarian free choice. Libertarian freedom, by definition, requires that in *a given set of circumstances*, in *some* possible worlds the agent does one thing, and in *other* possible worlds, the agent does something else. It also requires that there is no antecedent or concurrent event, state, or condition that causally determines the agent's choice. Thus, given Molinism, (1) entails that it is causally or nomically possible, logically possible, *and* metaphysically possible that Jones is in *C* and Jones freely refrains from choosing to attend the lecture this Friday. Hence, Molinism implies that (1) expresses a *contingent* proposition. Yet, because a subjunctive conditional concerns what *would* be the case if something *were* the case, such a conditional concerns what is the case in *possible worlds* other than the actual world. Thus, a subjunctive conditional *if p were the case, then q would be the case* entails that there is a *necessary* connection of some sort between *p* and *q*, for example, a causally or nomically necessary connection, a logically necessary connection, or a metaphysically necessary connection.[22] Admittedly, in ordinary language the term 'would' sometimes means 'will' or 'probably will'. But the use of 'would' in one of these ways in a sentence does not create a sentence that expresses a subjunctive conditional. Yet, Molinism asserts that (1) *expresses* a subjunctive conditional. Hence, if Molinism is correct, then the proposition expressed by (1) entails

(E₂) *necessarily*, if Jones is in *C*, then Jones freely chooses to attend the lecture this Friday.

It should be emphasized that in (E₂), the prefix '*necessarily*' expresses a necessary connection of *some* kind between *Jones is in C* and *Jones freely chooses to attend the lecture this Friday*. Because what is relevant in this context concerns whether later states of affairs are determined or necessitated by earlier states of affairs, no sort of necessity other than causal or nomic necessity, logical necessity, or metaphysical necessity is relevant here. Thus, (1) entails *both* that, *possibly* (causally or nomically, logically, and metaphysically), Jones is in *C* and Jones freely chooses to refrain from attending the lecture this Friday, and that, *necessarily* (either causally or nomically, logically, or metaphysically), if Jones is in *C*, then Jones freely decides to attend the lecture this Friday. Clearly, these two entailments of (1) are inconsistent. Thus, the notion of a subjunctive conditional, such as (1), that asserts that if one *were* in certain conditions, then one *would freely* choose (in the libertarian sense) to perform a particular action, is inconsistent. Since Molinism implies that the proposition expressed by (1) is true, and since this proposition is incoherent, Molinism is inconsistent.

Since the Molinist notion of a true subjunctive conditional of libertarian human freedom is inconsistent, if (1) does express a subjunctive conditional, then this subjunctive conditional is *necessarily false*.[23] Thus, if the conditional expressed by (1) is *true*, then this conditional is *not* subjunctive. It follows that if the conditional proposition expressed by (1) is true, then this conditional proposition does not involve a necessary connection between *Jones is in C* and *Jones freely chooses to attend the lecture this Friday*. Hence, any true conditional proposition expressed by (1) is contingently true.

But it is difficult to see how an omniscient being can have foreknowledge of such a contingently true proposition. This knowledge cannot derive from pure reason alone, for the proposition in question is neither necessarily true nor introspectively known to an omniscient being, nor deducible from anything which is necessarily true or introspectively known to an omniscient being. Nor can an omniscient being acquire this knowledge by perception or memory. Moreover, the aforementioned proposition cannot be deduced from the laws of nature together with initial conditions known to an omniscient being. Finally, inductive methods cannot be used to provide an omniscient being with knowledge of the proposition under discussion.

Molinists say that knowledge of this kind is "middle knowledge," and falls into a special category of its own. But what sort of *cognitive process* is involved in middle knowledge? On this critical question Molinists are generally silent. Is it the Molinist position, then, that middle knowledge is utterly mysterious to us humans, that it must appear to us to be magical knowledge? Middle knowledge does not seem to involve *a priori* intuition, introspection, perception, memory, deductive inference, or inductive inference. And it is doubtful that there is any other sort of cognitive process that would be relevant in this context. Thus, it is not clear that the Molinist is committed to the authority of reason (broadly understood). Any practitioner of rational theology should be so committed.[24]

Finally, the following argument seems to show that prior to this Friday, an omniscient being could not know a subjunctive conditional of human freedom such as *that if Jones were in C, then Jones would freely choose to attend the lecture this Friday.* Suppose that in the actual world, Jones is in C and Jones freely chooses to attend the lecture this Friday. Yet, there is a possible world, $W^\star$, in which there is a person, Jones*, such that: (i) Jones* in $W^\star$ is *other than* Jones in the actual world; (ii) Jones* in $W^\star$ and Jones in the actual world are qualitatively indistinguishable from one another in their intrinsic properties up to this Friday; and (iii) in $W^\star$, Jones* is in C but Jones* freely chooses to refrain from attending the lecture this Friday. But in the light of condition (ii), prior to this Friday, how can an omniscient being, S, tell whether *in a strict sense* he refers to Jones* or to Jones? How can S tell which is which (in this strict sense)? It appears that prior to this Friday, S can tell in the strict sense whether he refers to Jones* or to Jones only if S can grasp the egocentric propositions that Jones* and Jones would express by saying "I am thinking." A number of Molinists hold that such egocentric propositions involve the differing haecceities or individuating essences of Jones* and Jones, respectively.[25] But as we have argued, it seems that S cannot grasp these egocentric propositions. Hence, it appears that prior to this Friday, S cannot tell in the strict sense in question whether he refers to Jones* or to Jones. Accordingly, it appears that prior to this Friday, S does not know whether *the actual world*, that is to say, *the true maximal proposition*, contains a proposition about Jones* or

Jones.[26] But recall condition (iii): in $W^\star$, Jones* is in C but Jones* freely chooses *to refrain from attending the lecture this Friday*. Thus, if prior to this Friday, S cannot tell in the relevant strict sense whether he refers to Jones* or to Jones, then prior to this Friday, S could not know that if Jones were in C, then Jones would freely choose *to attend the lecture this Friday*. There-fore, it appears that prior to this Friday, an omniscient being could not know a subjunctive conditional of human freedom such as *that if Jones were in C, then Jones would freely choose to attend the lecture this Friday*.

In the light of the foregoing arguments, it seems that there cannot be a cognitive process by means of which an omniscient being has fore-knowledge of a causally undetermined contingent event. Thus, we con-clude that an omniscient being cannot know a proposition which predicts a causally undetermined contingent event, for example, a future random quantum event or a future human action which is free in the libertarian sense.

6.2 The Analysis of Omniscience

We are now in a position to propose an analysis or definition of omni-science in terms of the kind of *knowledge* specified in the preceding section; a sort of knowledge, we argued, which befits an omniscient being. Our proposal can be stated as follows.

> **(D1)** S **is omniscient at time** t **= df. (i) for any proposition**
> p, **if** p **is a necessary truth, or if** p **is a contingent truth that**
> **is not about the future relative to** t, **and either** p **can be**
> **grasped by different individuals, or** p **can be grasped by** S
> **alone,**[27] **then at** t, S **knows** p, **and (ii) for any proposition** p,
> **if** p **is a contingent truth about the future relative to** t **whose**
> **truth is** *causally inevitable* **at** t,[28] **and either** p **can be grasped**
> **by different individuals, or** p **can be grasped by** S **alone, then**
> **at** t, S **knows** p.

Let us explain several of the important features of this analysis of omniscience.

It is obvious that, necessarily, for any proposition p, if p can be grasped, then either *p is graspable by different individuals*, or *p is graspable by one indi-vidual alone*. In particular, the egocentric proposition that Jones expresses when he says "I am thinking" either can be grasped by different individuals or can be grasped by Jones alone. If this egocentric proposition is graspable by Jones alone (as our earlier argument implies), then $D1$ does not require an omniscient being other than Jones to know this egocentric proposition. On the other hand, if the egocentric proposition in question is graspable by different individuals, then $D1$ requires an omniscient being other than Jones to know this egocentric proposition. And the egocentric proposition that an omniscient being, S, would express were S to say, "I am thinking," either can be grasped by different individuals or can be grasped by S alone. Consequently, $D1$ requires an omniscient being, S, to know such an egocentric proposition. Thus, $D1$'s requirement that either p is graspable by different individuals or p is graspable by x alone has two desirable features. First, it allows $D1$ to be neutral on the controversial question of whether an omniscient being knows *another person's* egocentric propositions. Second, it requires an omniscient being to know *its own* egocentric propositions.

Finally, as we argued earlier, it is *impossible* for an omniscient being to know a proposition that predicts a causally undetermined contingent event. $D1$ reflects this necessary limitation on maximal knowledge. That is, clause (ii) of $D1$ implies that a being that is omniscient at t knows a future contingent proposition relative to t *only if* the truth of this proposition is causally determined at t.[29]

$D1$ allows that there might be divine omniscience. This is the omniscience of a maximally great being, i.e., God. However, $D1$ also allows that there might be non-divine omniscience.[30] Of course, since God would be incorruptible, his omniscience would be *essential* omniscience. But a corruptible omniscient being with *accidental* omniscience is conceivable.

Earlier we referred to infallibility with respect to various *modes of cognitive access*, for example, *a priori* intuition, introspection, perception, and memory. However, there is another sense of infallibility that exclusively applies to *persons*. In this sense, a person, S, is infallible if and only if S is incapable of committing an error or making a mistake, that is to say, incapable of having a false belief. There are two questions concerning the relationship between omniscience and infallibility of this sort. First, does divine omniscience entail infallibility of this kind? Second, does non-divine omniscience entail such infallibility?

To begin with, it appears that fallibility is a *defect* or *imperfection* that could be avoided. It also seems that one's possessing maximal knowledge is compatible with one's being infallible. Hence, it appears that *a maximally great* or *perfect being* would be infallible. We conclude that divine omniscience entails divine infallibility. Moreover, since God is essentially omniscient, divine omniscience entails essential infallibility. On the other hand, a non-divine omniscient being would not be a maximally great being. Hence, a non-divine omniscient being would not be free of all defects. For example, an imperfect omniscient being might be cognitively impulsive or foolhardy, and might form a belief about a proposition which that being cannot know – it might form such a belief even though it *knew* that it could not know that belief to be true. Thus, it seems that if there can be a non-divine omniscient being, then there can be a being of this kind who falsely believes a proposition which falls outside of the scope of an omniscient being's knowledge, i.e., a proposition which predicts a causally undetermined future event. Therefore, it appears that non-divine omniscience does not entail non-divine infallibility.[31]

6.3 Divine Foreknowledge and Human Freedom

Our account of omniscience presupposes our argument that it is impossible for an omniscient being to know a proposition that predicts a causally undetermined future contingent event. Our argument implies that divine foreknowledge of a human action that is free in the libertarian sense is impossible. Thus, our account of omniscience entails *incompatibilism*, the thesis that divine foreknowledge of a human action is incompatible with that action's being free in the libertarian sense. The opposing position is known as *compatibilism*, the thesis that divine foreknowledge of a human action is *compatible* with that action's being free in the libertarian sense. Accordingly, the preceding two sections constitute a sustained argument against compatibilism.

However, our argument for incompatibilism differs from the usual incompatibilist arguments, in the central role accorded to *epistemological considerations*. Moreover, our analysis of omniscience allows for a position on divine foreknowledge and human freedom that differs in some important ways from the standard ones. In what follows, we explain these differences as well as the ramifications of our analysis of omniscience for the traditional problem of divine foreknowledge and human freedom. In our discussion, by human *freedom*, we mean libertarian freedom. We begin by setting forth this traditional problem in the form of an argument for incompatibilism, which implies, when generalized, that if there were divine foreknowledge of every human action, then there would be no human freedom.

Argument A

(*Premise A1*) If God has always foreknown that Jones would attend the lecture at noon this Friday, then it is not within Jones's power to refrain from attending the lecture at noon this Friday.
(*Premise A2*) If it is not within Jones's power to refrain from attending the lecture at noon this Friday, then Jones does not *freely* attend the lecture at noon this Friday.

Therefore, if God has always foreknown that Jones would attend the lecture at noon this Friday, then Jones does not freely attend this lecture.

All incompatibilists agree that this argument is cogent, and hence, that if God foreknows that Jones would attend the lecture at noon this Friday, then Jones does not freely attend this lecture. Suppose, for the sake of argument, that Jones will attend the lecture at noon this Friday. In that case, incompatibilism is consistent with either one of the following two positions. First, God foreknows that Jones will attend the lecture at noon this Friday, but Jones does not freely attend this lecture. Second, Jones freely attends the lecture at noon this Friday, so it is not the case that God foreknows that Jones will attend this lecture. Historically, incompatibilists are divided over whether God has foreknowledge of all human actions, and over whether there are any free human actions. Thus, there are historical examples of these two incompatibilist positions.

Calvinism provides an example of the first incompatibilist position. According to Calvinism, since all human actions are causally determined or predestined by God, God foreknows such actions. Therefore, for the Calvinist, there simply are no free human actions.

A more extreme example of the first incompatibilist position is logical fatalism. This very strong form of fatalism claims that every true proposition is *necessarily true*. So, according to logical fatalism, there cannot be a free action because there is no contingency. If the occurrence of actions were necessary or fated in this sense, and if God were to exist, then he would have foreknowledge of human actions by means of *a priori* intuition.[32]

One example of the second kind of incompatibilist position is the view that God knows of the occurrence of free human actions, but that he does not *foreknow* their occurrence, because God is an *atemporal* being. The

Christian philosopher Boethius held this view. But as we have argued, the doctrine that God is an atemporal being is incoherent.[33]

Another example of the second sort of incompatibilist position is the view that there are free human actions, but that God does not foreknow their occurrence because a future contingent proposition is neither true nor false. Aristotle argues for the conclusion that a future contingent proposition is neither true nor false. Based on this conclusion, a traditional theist could develop this second sort of incompatibilist position, on the grounds that no future contingent proposition can be known. Nevertheless, since standard logic presupposes that every proposition is either true or false, the notion that a future contingent proposition is neither true nor false is questionable.[34]

Our version of incompatibilism is different from all four of the foregoing versions. Our version does not imply that all human actions are either predetermined or fated, and is compatible with the thesis that some human actions are free. Thus, it differs from both Calvinism and logical fatalism. Since we do not assert that there are free human actions, our version of incompatibilism is also compatible with the thesis that all human actions are predetermined. In contrast to the Boethian version, our version presupposes a *temporal* God. Unlike a version based on Aristotelianism, it does not imply that future contingent propositions have no truth-value, or imply that all propositions of this kind are unknowable. Thus, our version of incompatibilism has the advantage of being consistent with standard logic.

Calvin (1509–64) held that the reason why human actions are foreknown by God is that they are predetermined, and hence unfree. An Aristotelian incompatibilist holds that human actions cannot be foreknown because propositions predicting them have no truth-value. On the other hand, we hold that divine foreknowledge and human freedom are incompatible because an omniscient being *cannot foreknow* the occurrence of contingent events that are *not causally inevitable*.

Incompatibilists assume, correctly, that *Premise A2* is true in virtue of the definition of libertarian human freedom. However, incompatibilists have advanced two major kinds of arguments for *Premise A1*. According to one kind, if there is divine foreknowledge of free human actions, then humans have *causal power over the past*. Since causal power over the past is impossible, *Premise A1* is inferred: if God has always foreknown that Jones would attend the lecture at noon this Friday, then it is not within Jones's power to refrain from attending the lecture at noon this Friday. According to the second kind of argument, if there is divine foreknowledge of free human actions, then certain past facts **counterfactually** depend upon certain present or future facts. Since the past is fixed in a way that precludes such a relationship of dependence, *Premise A1* is inferred.

To understand the difference between these two kinds of arguments, one can distinguish: (i) having it within one's power to *bring it about* that a possible state of affairs, *p*, obtains; and (ii) having it within one's power *so to act* that *p* obtains.[35] (i) can be understood as an agent's having it within its power to *cause* a state of affairs, *p*, to obtain. But (ii) does *not* imply that an agent has it within its power to cause *p* to obtain. (ii) can be defined in terms of (i) as follows. An agent, *S*, has it within its power so to act that *p* obtains if and only if there is a state of affairs, *q*, such that if *q* were true, then *p* would be true, and *S* has it within its power to bring about *q*. *S*'s having it within its power so to act that *p* obtains is compatible with *S*'s not having it within its power to bring about *p*. For example, consider a necessary proposition, e.g., *that 2 + 2 = 4*. Assume that *S* has it within its power to bring about a contingent proposition, e.g., *that a ball rolls*. Clearly, were a ball to roll, then it would be true that 2 + 2 = 4. But *S* cannot bring it about or cause it to be the case that 2 + 2 = 4. To take another example, consider a past contingent state of affairs such as *that George Washington was the first president of the United States*. It seems that if George W. Bush were to scratch his ear during 2000, then it would be the case that George Washington was the first president of the United States.[36] It also seems that George W. Bush has it within his power to scratch his ear during 2000. So in 2000 George W. Bush has it within his power so to act that George Washington was the first president. But in 2000 George W. Bush cannot bring it about that George Washington was the first president of the United States.

Let us first examine the kind of incompatibilist argument for *Premise A1* that is based on the notion that it is impossible to bring about or cause anything that is in the past.

Argument B

(*Premise B1*) If Jones has it within his power to refrain from attending the lecture at noon this Friday and God has always foreknown that Jones would attend the lecture at noon this Friday, then Jones has it within his power to bring it about that God has always foreknown that Jones would refrain from attending this lecture.

(*Premise B2*) Thus, if Jones has it within his power to refrain from attending the lecture at noon this Friday and God has always foreknown that

Jones would attend the lecture at noon this Friday, then Jones has it within his power to bring it about that a fact about the past, i.e., that God has always foreknown that Jones would attend this lecture, would not have been a fact about the past.

(*Premise B3*) It is impossible to bring about or cause anything that is past.

(*Premise B4*) Hence, Jones does not have it within his power to bring it about that a fact about the past would not have been a fact about the past.

Therefore, if God has always foreknown that Jones would attend the lecture at noon this Friday, then Jones does not have it within his power to refrain from attending this lecture.

Premise B3 and *Premise B4* are unobjectionable. Since *Argument B* is valid, any objection to *Argument B* must be an objection to *Premise B2* (and by implication, to *Premise B1*). How do the proponents of *Argument B* try to justify *Premise B2*? There are two reasons that are put forward, each of which rests on a different, so-called *power entailment principle*.

According to the first power entailment principle,

(PEP1) (*p* entails *q*, and *S* has it within his power at *t* to bring it about that *p* obtains) ⇒ *S* has it within his power at *t* to bring it about that *q* obtains.

On the assumption that there is divine foreknowledge, the state of affairs, *that Jones refrains from attending the lecture at noon this Friday*, entails the state of affairs, *that God has always foreknown that Jones would refrain from attending the lecture at noon this Friday*. This entailment, together with *PEP1*, yields *Premise B1* and, therefore, *Premise B2*.

Since *PEP1* might seem to be plausible, the foregoing argument might lead one to accept *Premise B2*. But because *PEP1* is false, this argument for *Premise B2* is, in fact, unsound. Here is a counter-example to *PEP1*. Suppose that Jones has it within his power to bring it about that the rocket ship in front of him is red. He can do this because he is able to cover the rocket ship with red paint. The state of affairs, *that the rocket ship in front of Jones is red*, entails the state of affairs, *that there is a rocket ship*. But suppose that Jones is not capable of building a rocket ship. In this case, Jones does not have it within his power to bring it about that there is a rocket ship, but this is compatible with his being able to cover the rocket ship with red paint, and hence with his having it within his power to bring it about that the rocket ship in front of Jones is red. This counter-example establishes the falsehood of *PEP1*.[37] Thus, if the justification for *Premise B2* depends on *PEP1*, then there is no reason to accept *Premise B2*.

It might be thought that a strengthened power entailment principle would fare better. According to this second principle,

(PEP2) **(*p* and *q* are necessarily equivalent, and *S* has it within his power at *t* to bring it about that *p* obtains)** ⟹ *S* **has it within his power at *t* to bring it about that *q* obtains.**

On the assumption that there is divine foreknowledge of all human actions, the state of affairs, *that Jones refrains from attending the lecture at noon this Friday*, is necessarily equivalent to the state of affairs, *that God has always foreknown that Jones would refrain from attending the lecture at noon this Friday*. This entailment, together with *PEP2*, yields *Premise B1* and, therefore, *Premise B2*.

Because *PEP2* may appear to be plausible, this line of reasoning may lead one to accept *Premise B2*. But because *PEP2* is false, this line of reasoning in favor of *Premise B2* is also unsound. A counter-example to *PEP2* can be constructed as follows. Suppose that there is a sheet of notebook paper which has three unshaded squares printed on it. We may assume that Jones has it within his power to bring it about that all squares on this sheet of paper are blue. Because he can paint the squares on the piece of paper blue, Jones can do this. However, it is a law of logic that *all A's are B's* is equivalent to *all non-B's are non-A's*. Hence, the state of affairs, *all squares on this sheet of paper are blue*, is necessarily equivalent to the state of affairs, *all non-blue things are not squares on this sheet of paper*. Yet, surely, it is possible that in the situation described Jones does *not* have it within his power to bring it about that *all* non-blue things are not squares on this sheet of paper. Indeed, it is possible that in this situation Jones does not *even* have it within his power to bring it about that *some* non-blue thing is not a square on this sheet of paper. After all, power over the color of the squares in question does not entail power over the shape or location of a non-blue thing. Also observe that Jones cannot *bring it about* or *cause it to be the case* that some non-blue thing is not a square on this sheet of paper when the non-blue thing in question is *already* not such a square! And even if Jones can have the power *so to act* that some non-blue thing is not a square on this sheet of paper when the non-blue thing in question is *already* not such a square, Jones's having this power does not imply that Jones has the power to *bring it about* or *cause it to be the case* that such a non-blue thing is not a square on this sheet of paper. We conclude that this counter-example demonstrates the falsity of *PEP2*.[38]

In the light of the falsity of *PEP2*, it appears that there is no true power entailment principle that an incompatibilist can use to argue for *Premise B2*. Thus, it would seem that there is no reason to accept *Premise B2*. We conclude that *Argument B* in favor of the crucial incompatibilist *Premise A1* does not succeed.

Our critique of *PEP2* and *Argument B* presupposes that a state of affairs, *p*, and a state of affairs, *q*, may be necessarily equivalent without being cognitively equivalent, in which case *p* and *q* are not identical, for example, *2 is the even prime number* and *6 is the smallest perfect number*. (Accordingly, one could believe 2 to be the even prime number without believing 6 to be the smallest perfect number.) If our counter-example to *PEP2* is correct, then *all the squares on this sheet of paper are blue* and *all non-blue things are not squares on this sheet of paper* are not identical despite their necessary equivalence, insofar as Jones has the power to bring about the former state of affairs without having the power to bring about the latter state of affairs. Moreover, on the assumption that there is divine foreknowledge, *Jones refrains from attending the lecture at noon this Friday* and *God has always foreknown that Jones would refrain from attending the lecture at noon this Friday* are necessarily equivalent. Yet, they are not cognitively equivalent, since one could believe that Jones refrains from attending the lecture at noon this Friday without believing that God has always foreknown that Jones would refrain from doing this. Consequently, on the assumption that there is divine foreknowledge, these states of affairs are not identical. This consequence conforms to our critique of the incompatibilist argument based upon *PEP2*.

Let us now turn to the second sort of incompatibilist argument for *Premise A1*. This sort of argument is based upon the notion that the fixity of the past precludes the counterfactual dependence of certain past facts upon certain present or future facts. To say that the past is *fixed* is to say that if there is a fact, *F*, about the past, then it is now not within anybody's power so to act that *F* would not have been a fact about the past. In other words, there is no state of affairs, *p*, such that somebody now has it within his or her power to bring about *p*, and if *p* were to obtain, then *F* would not have been a fact about the past. For example, suppose that at 2 p.m., it is a fact about the past that Jones was thinking at 1 p.m. Surely, at 2 p.m., it is *not* within anybody's power so to act that this fact about the past would not have been a fact about the past. It follows that at 2 p.m., the following fact about the past relative to 2 p.m. is fixed: *that Jones was thinking at 1 p.m.*

We can now state the sort of incompatibilist argument for *Premise A1* that is based upon the idea that the fixity of the past precludes a counterfactual dependence of certain past facts upon certain present or future facts.

Argument C

(*Premise C1*) If Jones has it within his power to refrain from attending the lecture at noon this Friday and God has always foreknown that Jones would attend the lecture at noon this Friday, then Jones has it within his power so to act that God has always foreknown that Jones would refrain from attending this lecture.

(*Premise C2*) Thus, if Jones has it within his power to refrain from attending the lecture at noon this Friday and God has always foreknown that Jones would attend the lecture at noon this Friday, then Jones has it within his power so to act that a fact about the past, i.e., that God has always foreknown that Jones would attend this lecture, would not have been a fact about the past.

(*Premise C3*) It is impossible for anyone so to act that a fact about the past would not have been a fact about the past.

(*Premise C4*) Hence, Jones does not have it within his power so to act that a fact about the past would not have been a fact about the past.

Therefore, if God has always foreknown that Jones would attend the lecture at noon this Friday, then Jones does not have it within his power to refrain from attending this lecture.

Premise C1 and *Premise C2* are unobjectionable. After all, the state of affairs, *that Jones refrains from attending the lecture at noon this Friday*, entails the state of affairs, *that God has always foreknown that Jones would refrain from attending the lecture at noon this Friday*. Hence, the following counterfactual is true: *if Jones were to refrain from attending the lecture at noon this Friday, then God would have always foreknown that Jones would refrain from attending the lecture this Friday*. Moreover, it may be assumed that if an agent refrains from doing something, then he thereby *brings it about* that he refrains from doing that thing. Recall that an agent, S, has it within its power *so to act* that p obtains if and only if there is a state of affairs, q, such that if q were true, then p would be true, and S has it within its power to bring about *q.* It follows that if Jones has it within his power to refrain from attending the lecture at noon this Friday, and God has always foreknown that Jones would attend the lecture at noon this Friday, then Jones has it within his power *so to act* that God has always foreknown that Jones would refrain from attending the lecture at noon this Friday. And this implies that if Jones has it within his power to refrain from attending the lecture at noon this Friday, and God has always foreknown that Jones would attend the lecture at noon this Friday, then Jones has it within his power *so to act* that a fact about the past, i.e., that God has always foreknown that Jones would attend this lecture, would not have been a fact about the past. Since *Argument C* is valid, we conclude that any objection to *Argument C* must be an objection to *Premise C3* (and by implication, to *Premise C4*).

Premise C3 expresses the doctrine of the fixity of the past. However, William of Ockham (ca. 1280–1349) challenged this doctrine. Contemporary Ockhamists argue that the doctrine of the fixity of the past is not generally true, and needs to be qualified. The Ockhamist distinguishes between past facts that are *wholly about the past* and past facts that are *not wholly about the past*.[39] Although Ockhamists concede that a past fact of the *first* sort *must* be fixed, they argue that a past fact of the *second* sort *may not* be fixed.

Relative to 2 p.m., the fact *that Jones was thinking at 1 p.m.* is wholly about the past. As we saw earlier, at 2 p.m., a past fact of this kind is fixed. On the other hand, the following situation provides an example of a past fact which is *not* wholly about the past and which is *not* fixed. Suppose that at 2 p.m., it is a fact about the past *that at 1 p.m., Jones begins to give a lecture that lasts for two hours*, that is, which lasts until 3 p.m. There is a sense in which this fact about the past relative to 2 p.m. is *not* wholly about the past. It *does* seem to be possible that at 2 p.m., it is within Jones's power so to act that this fact about the past would not have been a fact about the past. For it appears to be possible that at 2 p.m., it is within Jones's power to end his lecture earlier than he had planned, for example, at 2:30 p.m. Were Jones to end his lecture at 2:30 p.m., then it would have been a fact about the past relative to 2 p.m. *that at 1 p.m., Jones begins to give a lecture which lasts for an hour and a half.* Thus, possibly, there is a fact about the past which is not wholly about the past and which is *not* fixed. This is consistent with the claim that a fact about the past that is wholly about the past must be fixed.[40]

It follows that *Premise C3* is false. An advocate of *Argument C* would reply that *Argument C* can be revived by consistently replacing 'fact about the past' in the premises of *Argument C* with 'fact wholly about the past'.

But it would appear that God's foreknowing or forebelieving that a particular human action will occur is a fact that is not wholly about the past. For instance, suppose it is a fact *that God has always foreknown or forebelieved that Jones would attend the lecture at noon this Friday*. It would seem that for any time *t*, prior to noon this Friday, this fact is partly about the past relative to *t*, but also *partly* about the future relative to *t*, since it is about noon this Friday. Therefore, a fact of this kind is not wholly about the past. However, if an advocate of *Argument C* rewords its premises in the way suggested, then *Premise C2*, which was true on the earlier reading, becomes false (although *Premise C3* and *Premise C4*, which were false on the earlier reading, become true). Thus, it is problematic whether there is any way to revive *Argument C*.[41]

In conclusion, we have seen that two recent attempts to defend incompatibilism, based either on the impossibility of bringing about the past or on the fixity of the past, are problematic at best. However, rather than relying on *Argument B* or *Argument C* to defend the key incompatibilist assumption, *Premise A1*, we defend *Premise A1* by arguing that it is impossible for an omniscient being, for example, God, to foreknow a true future contingent proposition whose truth is not causally inevitable. Such an argument implies that if God has always foreknown that Jones would attend the lecture at noon this Friday, then it is causally inevitable that Jones would attend the lecture at that time. But if it is causally inevitable that Jones would attend the lecture at that time, then it is not within Jones's power to refrain from attending the lecture at noon this Friday (in the relevant libertarian sense). Hence, *Premise A1* follows from our argument that it is impossible for God to foreknow a true future contingent proposition whose truth is not causally inevitable. Our defense of incompatibilism, unlike the others, rests on *epistemological* theses about the nature of omniscience.

NOTES

1 See the discussion of epistemic justification in the introduction.
2 For instance, see Jonathan Kvanvig, *The Possibility of An All Knowing God* (New York: St. Martin's, 1986), pp. 26–71; and Edward Wierenga, *The Nature of God: An Inquiry into Divine Attributes* (Ithaca, NY: Cornell University Press, 1989), chap. 2.
3 We define the relevant concept of direct awareness in section 3.2.
4 According to Edward Wierenga, the proposition that Jones expresses when he says, "I am thinking," involves the haecceity of Jones. Wierenga argues that

God, like Jones, can grasp Jones's haecceity, the property to which Jones refers when he says, "I have the property of being identical with me." If this were correct, then God would grasp the proposition that Jones expresses when he says, "I am thinking." See Wierenga's *The Nature of God: An Inquiry into Divine Attributes*, chap. 2. Compare Gary S. Rosenkrantz, *Haecceity: An Ontological Essay* (Dordrecht: Kluwer, 1993), pp. 220–4. Rosenkrantz argues that God cannot grasp the haecceity of any physical object or person other than himself.

5   For the purposes of *this* kind of knowledge, we assume that a proposition, p, is self-evident only if p is necessarily such that for *any* person, S, if p is true, and S grasps p, then p is evident to S. Other, person-relative, understandings of 'self-evident' are possible.

6   A belief-forming faculty, F, is fallible if and only if possibly, F forms a false belief.

7   A belief-forming faculty, F, is infallible if and only if necessarily, any belief formed by F is true.

8   It may be assumed that for an omniscient being, S, the deliverances of infallible *a priori* intuition are *basic*, in the sense of being evident to S without support from another belief, and absolutely certain for S. In this sense, these deliverances are self-evident *to* the omniscient being in question. This person-relative sense of self-evidence differs from the non-person-relative sense discussed in note 5 of this chapter. Compare note 2 of the introduction.

9   See section 3.2.

10 Even though God cannot form true beliefs about the future based upon *induction*, he may still be able to form true beliefs about the *probabilities* of future events based upon *deduction*. For example, if the proposition that Jones will *probably* freely decide to come to the lecture tomorrow is *deducible* from what God has observed, then God would know that this *probabilistic* proposition is true. Compare note 29 of this chapter.

11 The claim that these infallible cognitive faculties have this remarkable quality is supported by the following considerations. For any time-gap between something's becoming true and a being's coming to believe that it is true, there could be an even *shorter* time-gap between its becoming true and a being's coming to believe that it is true. But the *less* of a time-gap or delay there is, the *more* knowledgeable a being is. (Note that a *delay* in coming to know something relative to when it became true does *not* entail a *time-gap*, since something could be known *at every time after* it becomes true without its being known *when* it becomes true.) Thus, if the operations of a being's belief-forming faculties involve a time-gap, then that being does not have maximal knowledge. For similar reasons, if there could be infallible belief-forming faculties that form true beliefs about events *simultaneously* with their occurrences, then a being with maximal knowledge must have such belief-forming faculties. In the next note we defend the idea that infallible belief-forming faculties of this kind are possible.

12 See section 3.4, where it is pointed out that even in contemporary physics, lawful *simultaneous* correlations are thought to be possible in the case of "entangled" particles.

13 It follows that an omniscient being would have perceptual access to the mental states of others. This implication is compatible with our claim in section 3.2 that God would *not* be directly aware of the mental states of other souls. After all, we understood *direct* awareness to be awareness that is not causally mediated by a representation. As we have argued, infallible perception can be coherently conceived as a representational cognitive faculty. Thus, an omniscient soul may have infallible perceptual beliefs about things of which it is only *indirectly* aware, i.e., aware of only by means of a representation. Notice that this conclusion is consistent with the thesis that all perception is "direct" in the sense of being non-inferential.

14 This claim presumes that any law of nature would be contingent. It seems *possible* that the behavior of physical objects be governed by fundamental laws that are incompatible with the fundamental laws *actually* governing the behavior of physical objects, for example, instead of the actual fundamental law of gravitational attraction between any two basic particles, there could be a fundamental law of anti-gravitational repulsion between any two basic particles. Apparently, then, any *fundamental* law of nature would be contingent; and this entails that *any* law of nature would be contingent. But some philosophers claim, to the contrary, that the laws of nature are necessary truths. Suppose for the sake of argument that these philosophers are right. In that case, it is impossible for an omniscient being to enact or bring about the laws of nature. For as we shall argue in section 8.1, it is impossible for anyone, even an omnipotent being, to bring about a necessary state of affairs. However, an omniscient being would know any necessarily true laws of nature by means of *a priori* intuition.

15 It follows that an omniscient being must also be *omnipotent*. Moreover, since *S*'s being omnipotent cannot be introspected or perceived by anyone, *S* can know that *S* is omnipotent only if *S* knows *a priori* that, necessarily, if *S* exists, then *S* is omnipotent. This implies that an omniscient being must be *essentially* omnipotent.

16 If an omniscient being, *S*, has already determined its future actions, and if there are no other souls with libertarian freedom or undetermined states, and if there are no undetermined physical events, then *S* will have complete knowledge of the future. On the other hand, the absence of any one of those three conditions limits the extent of *S*'s knowledge of the future. We shall defend this conclusion later in the text.

17 For a defense of this proposition, see E. J. Lowe, *A Survey of Metaphysics* (Oxford: Oxford University Press, forthcoming), chap. 18.

18 Contemporary Molinists include Alvin Plantinga, *The Nature of Necessity* (Oxford: Clarendon Press, 1974), chap. 9; Wierenga, *The Nature of God: An*

Inquiry into Divine Attributes, chap. 5; and Thomas Flint, *Divine Providence: The Molinist Account* (Ithaca, NY: Cornell University Press, 1998). Compare William Hasker, *God, Time, and Knowledge* (Ithaca, NY: Cornell University Press, 1989), chap. 2.

19   There are philosophers who believe that there is another version of libertarianism which holds that when an agent acts freely, it is the agent's beliefs or desires which are not causally determined, while the agent's decisions are causally determined by his or her beliefs and desires. We ignore this version of libertarianism. Any arguments we give concerning libertarianism could be reformulated to take account of this other version.

20   On the other hand, *nonlibertarian* accounts of human freedom are *compatible* with the claim that free human choices are *causally determined*. On accounts of this kind, a human being may perform an action freely by doing what she wants to do, or by doing what she wants to do in the absence of coercion by others, even if her action is causally determined. In such a case, it may not be within the agent's power to refrain, in the libertarian sense, from performing this action. Since a human action which is *free* in a *nonlibertarian* sense at a time t may be *causally determined* by events at an earlier time, $t^\star$, and since a being who is omniscient at $t^\star$ has foreknowledge of *all* future contingent events that are causally determined as of $t^\star$, it is possible for an omniscient being to know a true proposition that predicts a human action which is free in a nonlibertarian sense.

21   In this context, the phrase, 'Jones is in C' is to be understood tenselessly.

22   Unlike a *subjunctive* conditional, a **material conditional**, $p \rightarrow q$, does *not* assert any sort of necessary connection between p and q. The truth-value of a material conditional, $p \rightarrow q$, is wholly a function of the truth-values of p and q. In particular, a material conditional, $p \rightarrow q$, is false just when p is true and q is false; for all of the other combinations of the truth-values of p and q, a material conditional, $p \rightarrow q$, is true.

23   An example of a necessarily false subjunctive conditional is the proposition *that if there were a square, then it would be three-sided.*

24   For an account of rational theology see the introduction.

25   For example, see Wierenga, *The Nature of God: An Inquiry into Divine Attributes*, chap. 2; and Alvin Plantinga, "De Essentia," *Grazer Philosophische Studien* 7/8 (1979), pp. 101–21.

26   The notion of a possible world as a maximal proposition is explained in section 4.3.

27   A proposition, p, can be grasped by different individuals if and only if possibly, $(\exists x)(x$ grasps p & p is possibly such that $(\exists y)(y \neq x$ & y grasps $p))$. A proposition, p, can be grasped by x alone if and only if (i) p is possibly grasped by x, and (ii) $\sim(p$ can be grasped by different individuals).

28   If p is a future contingent proposition relative to a time, t, then p's truth is causally inevitable (in the relevant sense) at t if and only if (i) from t until the

time at which p obtains, there are laws and relevant actual conditions which together entail that p is true, and (ii) an omnipotent agent determines that no supernatural or random causes will contravene the laws in question in the circumstances which obtain from t until the obtaining of p. Clause (i) provides a sense in which a causally inevitable future contingent proposition is causally determined. As for clause (ii), if this clause is satisfied, then an omniscient being, O, would know that it is satisfied in virtue of O's knowledge of the laws and initial conditions. (As we've argued, O must also be omnipotent; and for any contingently true law, L, an omnipotent agent has the power to contravene L, *and* the power to determine that nothing will contravene L.) Of course, in knowing that clause (ii) is satisfied, an omniscient being knows that no contravening cause will occur. Clause (ii) is required for the following reasons. Suppose that only clause (i) is satisfied. Then an omniscient being, O, does not know whether or not p will obtain, since O does not know whether or not the contravening cause in question will occur. And O does not know the latter because an omniscient being does not know any proposition that predicts an undetermined future contingent event.

29 Causal inevitability in the sense required by clause (ii) of $D1$ entails causal determination, but not *vice versa*. See the previous note for more on this distinction.

Also note that if it is causally inevitable that an undetermined future contingent event, e, has a certain probability, P, less than 1, e.g., .93, then $D1$ requires an omniscient being to *know* that the probability that e will occur is P. If the Copenhagen interpretation of quantum mechanics is correct, then there are undetermined future contingent quantum events that have *determinate probabilities* of this kind.

30 We have already argued that if a being is omniscient, then that being was both omniscient and omnipotent when it enacted the laws of nature. We have already argued as well that any omniscient being must exist throughout the past. Later, we will show that there cannot be two coexisting omnipotent beings. Together, these three conclusions entail that there cannot be two omniscient beings in any possible world.

31 Still, it should be noted that, necessarily, a non-divine omniscient being does not falsely believe a proposition, p, which *falls within the scope* of an omniscient being's knowledge. Because knowing p entails that p is true, to suppose otherwise is to imply the possibility of an omniscient being's simultaneously knowing p and believing $\sim p$. But it seems to be impossible for an individual to know a proposition while disbelieving it. Furthermore, even if this were possible, such an irrational and confused state of mind would surely be incompatible with the quality of knowledge required of an omniscient being.

32 Whereas logical fatalism precludes God's having freedom of action, divine predestination of human actions is consistent with God's having freedom of action.

33   See chapter 5.

34   For example, *that the sun will rise tomorrow* is a future contingent proposition; standard logic implies that, necessarily, either it is *true* that the sun will rise tomorrow or it is *false* that the sun will rise tomorrow.

35   We understand possible states of affairs as propositional entities that either obtain or fail to obtain.

36   This subjunctive conditional is true in virtue of the "necessity" or fixity of what is wholly past. In other words, since George Washington's becoming the first president of the United States in 1789 is wholly in the past relative to 2000, there is a sense in which there is nothing which *can* happen in 2000, such that were it to happen George Washington would *not* have become the first president of the United States in 1789. The notion of the fixity of the past will be discussed later in this section.

37   See Joshua Hoffman and Gary Rosenkrantz, "On Divine Foreknowledge and Human Freedom," *Philosophical Studies* 37 (1980), pp. 289–96.

38   According to William Hasker, there is a necessarily true power entailment principle, very much like *PEP2*, which is self-evident. This principle can be paraphrased as follows:

> If it is within *S*'s power to bring it about that *p* is true, and if it is within *S*'s power to bring it about that *p* is false, and if *p* entails *q* and *not-p* entails *not-q*, then it is within *S*'s power to bring it about that *q* is true.

But, far from being self-evident, this principle is subject to the same sort of counter-example we give to *PEP2*. See William Hasker, *God, Time, and Knowledge*, p. 109.

39   Or, in other words, the Ockhamist distinguishes between past facts that are *simply* about the past, and past facts that are *not simply* about the past. See William L. Rowe, *Philosophy of Religion: An Introduction*, 2nd edition (Belmont, Calif.: Wadsworth, 1993), pp. 149–51.

40   Although the distinction between past facts which are wholly about the past and past facts which are not wholly about the past seems to be intuitively clear, analyzing this distinction turns out to be formidably difficult and technical. For an attempt to analyze the distinction, see Joshua Hoffman and Gary Rosenkrantz, "Hard and Soft Facts," *Philosophical Review* 93 (1984), pp. 419–34.

41   John Fischer defends a version of *Argument C*. He reformulates *Argument C* in terms of a further distinction between those facts not wholly about the past which are fixed (which he calls "hard-type soft facts"), and those facts not wholly about the past which are not fixed (which he calls "soft-type soft facts"). He then claims that divine foreknowings are hard-type soft facts. We

agree with Fischer's conclusion that divine foreknowledge is incompatible with human freedom. But we don't think that this conclusion can be plausibly supported on the basis of his distinction, since he provides no criterion of his distinction between the two kinds of facts not wholly about the past. Thus, he cannot show that divine foreknowings are hard-type soft facts rather than soft-type soft facts. See John Fischer, "Hard-Type Soft Facts," *Philosophical Review* 95 (1986), pp. 591–601.

BIBLIOGRAPHY

Boethius, A. M. S., *The Consolation of Philosophy*, trans. H. Stewart, in H. Stewart and E. K. Rand (trans.), *Boethius: The Theological Tractates* (Cambridge, Mass.: Harvard University Press, 1936).

Fischer, J. M., "Freedom and Foreknowledge," *Philosophical Review* 92 (1983), pp. 67–79.

———, "Hard-Type Soft Facts," *Philosophical Review* 95 (1986), pp. 591–601.

——— (ed.), *God, Foreknowledge, and Freedom* (Stanford, Calif.: Stanford University Press, 1989).

Flint, T., *Divine Providence: The Molinist Account* (Ithaca, NY: Cornell University Press, 1998).

Hasker, W., *God, Time, and Knowledge* (Ithaca, NY: Cornell University Press, 1989).

Hoffman, J. and Rosenkrantz, G. S., "On Divine Foreknowledge and Human Freedom," *Philosophical Studies* 37 (1980), pp. 289–96.

——— and ———, "Hard and Soft Facts," *Philosophical Review* 93 (1984), pp. 419–34.

Kvanvig, J., *The Possibility of An All Knowing God* (New York: St. Martin's, 1986).

Lowe, E. J., *A Survey of Metaphysics* (Oxford: Oxford University Press, forthcoming), chap. 18.

Mavrodes, G., "Omniscience," in *A Companion to the Philosophy of Religion*, ed. P. L. Quinn and C. Taliaferro (Oxford: Blackwell, 1997), article 29.

Molina, L. (1535–1600), *On Divine Foreknowledge* (Part IV of the *Concordia*), trans. and introd. A. J. Freddoso (Ithaca, NY: Cornell University Press, 1988).

Ockham, W., *Predestination, God's Foreknowledge and Future Contingents*, trans. M. McC. Adams and N. Kretzmann (Indianapolis, Ind.: Hackett Publishing Company, 1969).

Rosenkrantz, G. S., *Haecceity: An Ontological Essay* (Dordrecht: Kluwer, 1993).

Rowe, W. L., *Philosophy of Religion: An Introduction*, 2nd edition (Belmont, Calif.: Wadsworth, 1993).

Swinburne, R. T., *The Coherence of Theism* (Oxford: Clarendon Press, 1977).

Wierenga, E., *The Nature of God: An Inquiry into Divine Attributes* (Ithaca, NY: Cornell University Press, 1989).

Zagzebski, L. T., *The Dilemma of Freedom and Foreknowledge* (New York: Oxford University Press, 1991).

7

Perfect Goodness, Perfect Virtue, and Moral Admirability

What are the implications of God's moral perfection for the character of what God creates? We will attempt to advance our understanding of these implications by describing the moral principles or rules that guide the actions of a maximally great being. We will also attempt to resolve an alleged paradox that claims that moral perfection is incompatible with moral admirability.

7.1 God and the Nature of Morality

Another one of the core attributes ascribed to God is maximal goodness and/or maximal virtue (or omnibenevolence). In attempting to understand this notion of divine moral perfection, one of the main issues for rational theology is the nature of morality.[1] In this section, we examine a number of different moral theories. In subsequent sections, we explore the implications of some of these theories for the understanding of God's moral perfection.[2]

According to the *divine command theory*, an act is *morally required or obligatory* just when God commands it, an act is *morally wrong* just when God forbids it, and an act is *morally right or permissible* just when God does not forbid it. Moreover, the divine command theory holds that an act is morally required, wrong, or right *because* God has either commanded it, forbidden it, or not forbidden it, respectively.

It is important to emphasize that according to this theory of morality, it is not merely that God's commands *correspond* to what is morally required. Rather, it is that something is morally required *because* God has commanded it. Thus, the divine command theory implies that morality *derives from* God's commands. Divine commands are not a reflection of any independently existing moral standards; these commands *determine* moral standards.

If this moral theory were correct, then morality would have no basis other than God's commands. Furthermore, since there would be no objective, independent moral standards, God's commands would not be guided by any such standards, and God's commands would in that sense be arbitrary. Hence, the divine command theory of morality is a type of *subjective* theory of morality. A subjective theory of morality states that right and wrong, and/or good and evil, are *determined by* the attitudes, beliefs, or feelings of one or more agents.[3] Some types of subjective theories of morality say that it is the attitudes of a group of agents, or of a society, which determine morality. Other, more extreme versions say that what morality is for a particular agent is determined by the attitudes of *that* agent, so that there can be for each agent, equally justified, yet conflicting, moral standards. Finally, there is the version that holds that morality is determined by the attitudes of one, unique agent – the supreme moral authority. The divine command theory is a special case of this third type of subjective moral theory. As a type of subjective moral theory, the divine command theory is open to serious criticism.

In particular, on the supposition that the divine command theory is true, it is difficult to understand how God can be essentially morally admirable at all times. For in that case, since nothing would be good or bad, right or wrong, prior to the issuance of God's commands, God could not be said to be morally admirable prior to his issuance of those commands. Because it seems possible that there is a time, *t*, such that God's first commands were issued at *t*, it appears that if the divine command theory is true, then God could fail to be morally admirable at some time. Yet, God is supposed to be *essentially* morally perfect, and therefore *essentially* morally admirable, at all times.

Furthermore, if the divine command theory were true, then there would be a sense in which morality would be arbitrary. According to this theory, *anything* that God commanded would be morally required, and *anything* that God forbade would be morally impermissible. So, if God were to command us to torture infants, we would be morally required to do so. And if God were to forbid us to act kindly, then it would be morally wrong to be kind. These implications of the divine command theory are clearly absurd. It might be replied that because God is essentially morally perfect, he *could not* command or forbid such things. However, this reply assumes that God's moral perfection has a basis *other than* his issuance of the commands in question, and this contradicts the divine command theory of morality. Thus, this reply is unavailable to those who subscribe to that theory of morality.

Alternatively, a divine command theorist of morality might reply that it is because God is essentially *loving* that he could not issue morally repugnant commands or prohibitions (such as commanding us to torture infants or forbidding us to act kindly).[4] But, if God is essentially loving, then we surely may ask, *why is he essentially loving?*[5] There are two observations that are relevant to answering this question. First, necessarily, God's nature includes being essentially loving if and only if being essentially loving is morally admirable. Second, it is God's *fundamental* nature to be a maximally great being with respect to his worthiness for worship and *moral admiration*. So, if being essentially worthy of moral admiration entails being essentially loving, then since being essentially loving does *not* entail being essentially morally admirable, God's being essentially morally admirable would explain his being essentially loving. We conclude that the answer to our question is that God is essentially loving *because* he is essentially morally perfect.[6] Thus, it appears that being essentially loving is *not* a *primary perfection* of God, that is, a perfection of God that is not further grounded. Yet, necessarily, if it is because God is essentially loving that he could not issue morally repugnant commands or prohibitions, and if it is because God is essentially morally perfect that he is essentially loving, then it is because God is essentially morally perfect that he could not issue commands or prohibitions of this kind. Thus, the alternative reply in question presupposes that God could not issue such commands or prohibitions because he is essentially morally perfect. Hence, this alternative reply presupposes the first reply (the one we answered in the previous paragraph). Since this first reply is unavailable to a divine command theorist, so is the alternative reply.

Although God may *always* command what is required, and may *always* forbid what is wrong, it is not *because* he commands or forbids something that it is required or wrong. Plato made this point in his dialogue, the *Euthyphro*, when he has Socrates argue that something is loved by the gods because it is good, and not good because it is loved by the gods.[7] We conclude that the divine command theory cannot provide an acceptable basis for understanding the nature of morality or God's moral perfection.

Such an understanding should be sought in the form of a moral theory that is *objective*, that is to say, a moral theory that provides a basis for morality not in the attitudes of agents, but in the objective nature of reality. According to an objective theory of morality, right and wrong, good and

Diagram 1

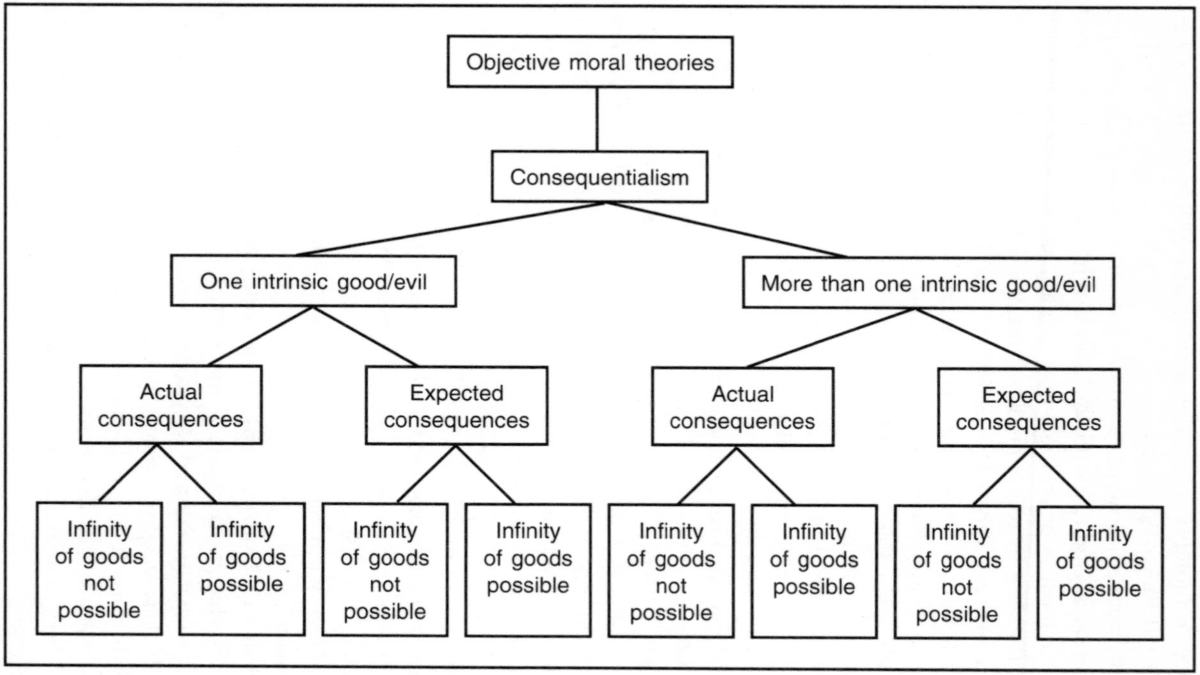
Objective moral theories
Consequentialism
One intrinsic good/evil
More than one intrinsic good/evil
Actual consequences
Expected consequences
Actual consequences
Expected consequences
Infinity of goods not possible
Infinity of goods possible
Infinity of goods not possible
Infinity of goods possible
Infinity of goods not possible
Infinity of goods possible
Infinity of goods not possible
Infinity of goods possible

bad, are in a sense independent of what *anyone* believes, wants, or prefers. This sense of independence will become clearer as we proceed.

Objective moral theories assume various forms. Of these, two types are of special interest: *consequentialist* theories and *deontological* theories. The former hold that right and wrong are determined by the *consequences* of actions, while the latter hold that right and wrong are determined by the *type* of action one performs. Another difference between them is that consequentialist theories define what is *right or wrong* in terms of what is *good or evil*, while deontological theories in general define what is *good or evil* in terms of what is *right or wrong*.

7.2 Perfect Goodness and Consequences

Diagram 1 on page 146 will be useful to the discussion of consequentialist theories that follows.

The first sort of theory to be considered in the attempt to understand God's moral perfection is consequentialism. Simply put, this type of theory claims that an act is obligatory, right, or wrong depending on the consequences of that act. More specifically, an act is obligatory, right, or wrong depending on the amounts of good and evil it produces relative to other acts that one could perform. Consequentialist theories put forward the following sort of *supreme moral principle*: do that act which, among the acts one can perform, produces (or can be expected to produce) the greatest amount of good minus evil, or in other words, has the best consequences. The term 'best' in this formula is defined in terms of an aggregate measure of good and evil, typically, the total amount of intrinsic good minus the total amount of intrinsic evil.

What is meant by 'good' or 'evil' in this context? There are two senses in which something may be good or evil, *intrinsically*, or *as a means*. The intrinsic goods and evils are things which are good or evil in themselves, while things which are good and evil as a means are good or evil insofar as they bring about or lead to intrinsic good or evil.[8] It is intrinsic good and intrinsic evil that figure in the consequentialist's calculations.

Consequentialists differ over which things are intrinsically good or intrinsically evil. *Hedonists* claim that the only intrinsic good is *pleasure*, and that the only intrinsic evil is *pain*.[9] Other consequentialists include one or more of the following as intrinsic goods: *satisfaction, happiness, beauty, knowledge*, and so forth. Of course, the more intrinsic goods one recognizes, the more intrinsic evils one must recognize. But for our purposes, which, and how many, intrinsic goods and evils a consequentialist theory recognizes is not relevant. Therefore, in what follows, we will ignore this difference between consequentialist moral theories.

What sorts of things are the *bearers* of intrinsic good and evil? It would seem that *conscious* beings, whether human or otherwise, are typically capable of pleasure, pain, satisfaction, dissatisfaction, and so forth. Hence, conscious beings, or certain mental states of these beings, are typically bearers of intrinsic good and evil. Thus, such beings or states are typically bearers of intrinsic value. On the other hand, if beauty is an intrinsic good, then whatever is capable of being beautiful would also be a bearer of intrinsic value. Moreover, while it seems that any consequentialist theory must, when assessing consequences, give *some* weight to any state of pleasure and pain, etc., it is not obviously the case that every such state should be given *equal* weight. The states of human beings, presumably, should count more than the states of frogs. Moreover, many consequentialists believe that the states of oneself, one's close relatives, and one's friends, for example, should count more heavily for oneself than those of complete strangers. Finally, some consequentialists accept distributive principles, according to which a world in which every bearer of intrinsic value enjoys no *less* than a certain amount of positive intrinsic value and suffers from no *more* than a certain amount of negative intrinsic value, is morally preferable to one in which not every bearer of intrinsic value does so, even though the latter world contains a greater *aggregate* of intrinsic value than does the former world.

Another important difference between consequentialist theories is between those that are framed in terms of *actual* consequences and those that are framed in terms of *expected* consequences. According to the former, the rightness or wrongness of an act is defined in terms of the total amounts of intrinsic good and evil it would *actually* produce relative to all the other acts one could perform. But according to the latter, the rightness or wrongness of an act is defined in terms of the total amounts of intrinsic good and evil it *could be expected* to produce, relative to all the other acts one could perform. This is an important difference, for an act that could reasonably be expected to produce much good (or evil) might instead actually produce much evil (or good). It is a truism that the best intentions sometimes produce bad, or even terrible, outcomes. It is also obvious that we humans, at least, cannot see very far into the future, and so cannot know, or even have a reasonable expectation of, the remote consequences of our actions. As we have seen, even an omniscient being cannot know the future, free actions of other persons or those future events which are not inevitable. Although we are inclined to think that a consequentialism framed in terms of expected outcomes is more plausible than one framed in terms of actual outcomes, we will not insist on the expected outcomes formulation in the discussion which follows, and, in any event, the distinction is not important for most of that discussion.[10]

A final distinction *is* very significant for our investigation of divine moral perfection. According to one version of consequentialism, an *infinity* of concrete entities is *not* possible.[11] On this assumption, there could not be an infinity of bearers of intrinsic value. Therefore, there could not be a created infinity of pleasure or pain, or of any other kind of created intrinsic value. On the other version, infinities of concrete entities *are* possible, and there *could* exist an infinity of bearers of intrinsic value. Consequently, on this second assumption, there *could* exist an infinite amount of created pleasure or pain, or of other sorts of created intrinsic value.

Given all of these distinctions, we are now in a position to ask what God would be morally obligated to do were a form of consequentialism to be the correct moral theory, and were it *impossible* for there to be an actual infinity of concrete entities. We will then ask what God would be obligated to do were it *possible* for there to be an infinity of concrete entities.

Assume that it is *impossible* that there be an infinity of concrete entities. In that case, God could not bring about a state of affairs that involves an infinity of concrete entities. Thus, God could not create a universe in which the amount of created pleasure, satisfaction, happiness, etc., reached infinity. Suppose, further, that consequentialism is true, so that a perfectly good God would strive to bring about a universe which contained a greater amount of overall or aggregated intrinsic good, that is, intrinsic goodness less intrinsic evil, than any other universe which he could bring about.[12] This combination of factors leads to paradox.

Suppose that God were to create a universe in which the aggregated amount of created good is n, where n is a positive finite number. Let us call this universe U_1. Since a universe in which the aggregated amount of created good is greater than n, yet is still finite, is possible, and since God is omnipotent and omniscient, God could create a universe, U_2, in which the aggregated amount of created good is greater than n, say $n + m$. But since $n + m$ is a finite number, and since a universe in which the aggregated amount of created good is greater than $n + m$, yet still finite, is possible, God could create a universe that contained a finite amount of aggregated, created good greater than $n + m$. No matter how much aggregated, created good a universe contained, so long as the total is finite, God could create a universe with a greater finite aggregated amount of created good.[13]

In this situation, it is not possible for God to create a universe *in which the aggregated amount of created intrinsic goodness exceeded the amount in any other universe that he could create*. That is, God could not conform his actions to the consequentialist supreme moral principle. Since God could not conform his actions to the requirements of morality, he could not exhibit perfect goodness in such a situation. The conclusion that follows is that (1) God's moral perfection, together with (2) consequentialism, and (3) the finitist assumption that an infinity of concrete entities is impossible, are incompatible. Thus, if we are to preserve a coherent idea of God's moral perfection, we must reject any theory of morality which includes (2) and (3).

Suppose, however, that (4) it *is* possible for God to create an infinity of bearers of intrinsic value. This supposition carries us into the realm of the infinite, the subject, in mathematics, which is known as *transfinite arithmetic*. Transfinite arithmetic was fashioned toward the end of the nineteenth century by a group of mathematicians, especially Cantor (1845–1918), and his views have become the standard ones in mathematics. According to Cantor, there are indefinitely many infinite numbers, starting with $\aleph_0$. $\aleph_0$ is the number of elements there are in the set of the natural numbers, that is, the numbers, 1,2,3. . . .[14] Next comes $\aleph_1$, the number of elements in the set of the real numbers (and the number of elements in the set of points between any two given points on a line, and the number of elements in the set of times between any two times). And according to Cantor, there is no limit to the number of infinite numbers, each greater than the preceding one.[15]

Thus, if we accept (4), then it is plausible to suppose that it is not only possible for God to create an infinity of bearers of intrinsic value, but also that for any infinite number, $\aleph_n$, it is possible for God to create that many bearers of intrinsic value. For example, it seems that this is possible for God because, possibly, for any infinite number, $\aleph_n$, God creates $\aleph_n$ souls, each one of which is a concrete entity having states that are of intrinsic value. And it can be argued that for any infinite number, $\aleph_n$, it is possible for God to create $\aleph_n$ bearers of intrinsic value on the ground that, possibly, God creates a space of $\aleph_n$ dimensions, where each one of these dimensions contains concrete entities that are of intrinsic value. A further question arises at this point. Is it possible for God to bring about the state of affairs, *that for any number, n, including any infinite number, there are more concrete entities than n?*[16]

If not, then we should conclude that it is *not* possible for God to create more bearers of intrinsic value than any infinite number. In that case, God could only create any infinite number of such bearers, but not more bearers of intrinsic value than any infinite number, and thus could not bring about an amount of aggregated, created intrinsic goodness that is more than any infinite number. On this assumption, which we call assumption (4a), together with assumptions (1) that God is morally perfect, and (2) that consequentialism is true, we again encounter paradox.

Suppose that God creates an $\aleph_n$ number of bearers of intrinsic value. To simplify things, suppose further that God creates an $\aleph_n$ number of such bearers *at every time*, such that there is an $\aleph_n$ aggregated amount of created intrinsic goodness at every time.[17] But for any created world of this kind, God could create a *better* one, namely one that contained an $\aleph_{n+1}$ amount of aggregate intrinsic goodness at every time. Since (1) and (2) require God to create the *best* world which he can create, and since on assumption (4a), God *cannot* create a possible world which is better than any other world he can create, assumptions (1), (2), and (4a) are inconsistent. Therefore, if we are to accept the possibility of God's moral perfection, we cannot accept any moral theory which includes both (2) and (4a).

On the other hand, is it possible that there be more concrete, created bearers of intrinsic value than any infinite number? It may be possible for God to create more souls than any infinite number. But it might be thought that the nature of space and time limits the amount of physical bearers of intrinsic value that God could create to $\aleph_1$. Yet, some philosophers have thought that a space of any number of dimensions is possible. Thus, perhaps these philosophers would allow for the possibility of there being a space with more dimensions than any infinite number. This hypothesis would certainly allow for the possibility of a space-time that contains more physical bearers of intrinsic value than any infinite number. If it is possible for there to be that many spiritual or physical bearers of intrinsic value, then (4b) God can bring about a possible world which contains (at every time) an amount of aggregated, created intrinsic goodness in spiritual or physical bearers which is *more than* any infinite number. This would be the case if God created more intrinsic good than any infinite number, and no intrinsic evil. Nevertheless, if God created more intrinsic good than any infinite number, and also some amount of intrinsic evil, then a problem arises with respect to evaluating the overall or aggregated intrinsic goodness in such a world. Since the arithmetical operations of addition and subtraction are well-defined only in the case of finite and infinite *numbers*, there is no arithmetically well-defined way to aggregate the intrinsic good and evil contained in such a world. Thus, we cannot say on the basis of arithmetic that any such world is or is not a maximally good world. What are we to say, then, about the aggregated value of possible worlds of this kind? There seem to be two options. First, one could hold that since arithmetical operations are not well-defined in the relevant domain, we are not in a position to assign any definite value to such possible worlds. Second, one could argue that we can determine intuitively, not by an arithmetical operation, that, for example, a world that contained more intrinsic good than any infinite number, and 2 units of evil, still contains more aggregated intrinsic good than any infinite number.

If the foregoing considerations are correct, then God could do what is required by the conjunction of (1) his moral perfection, and (2) consequentialism: God *could* bring about a world which contains more, or *at least no less*, aggregated, created intrinsic goodness than any other world which God can bring about.[18] Thus, unlike the cases of (3) and (4a), (4b) *does seem to be* compatible with (1) God's moral perfection, and (2) consequentialism.

Let us summarize our findings with respect to the attempt to understand God's moral perfection in terms of a consequentialist moral theory. We have argued that if God cannot bring about an infinity of aggregated, created intrinsic goodness, then his moral perfection cannot be understood in terms of consequentialism. We have also argued that if God can bring about any $\aleph_n$ amount of aggregated, created intrinsic goodness, but cannot bring about an amount of aggregated, created intrinsic goodness more than any infinite number, then his moral perfection, once again, cannot be understood in terms of consequentialism. It is only if God can bring about an amount of aggregated, created intrinsic goodness that is more than any infinite number that his moral perfection can be understood in terms of consequentialism. It is only then that God could bring about a world that contained *at least as much* aggregated, created intrinsic goodness as any other world that he could bring about. This result creates considerable doubt about whether or not God's moral perfection *can* be understood in terms of a consequentialist moral theory: as much doubt as one ought to have about the possibility of there being more concrete things than any infinite number. The possibility of there being more concrete entities than any infinite number is truly mind-boggling.

7.3 Perfect Virtue and Moral Rules

As we have said, a deontological, or non-consequentialist, moral theory attempts to define good and evil in terms of right and wrong, and holds that what makes an act right or wrong is the *kind* of act it is, rather than its consequences. The most famous proponent of this sort of moral theory is the German philosopher Immanuel Kant (1724–1804). Kant argued that there is a single, supreme moral principle, which he called *the categorical imperative*. He also claimed that all the other, less general, moral principles that determine the rightness or wrongness of acts can be derived from this ultimate principle. Although he claimed that they are all equivalent, Kant provided at least three different statements of the categorical imperative.[19] Unfortunately, most philosophers do not agree with Kant's judgment that the three versions are equivalent. Moreover, on any of the three versions, the categorical imperative has been found to have undesirable implications, that is, to imply moral conclusions that are unacceptable. Nor has there been any more recent, purely deontological or non-consequentialist moral theory which has earned significant support.[20] Thus, it is not easy to assess the implications of a non-consequentialist moral theory for God's moral perfection in any but the most general terms.

Suppose, however, that (i) there *is* an (as yet, undiscovered) acceptable (true) purely non-consequentialist moral theory. Suppose, further, that (ii) this theory consists of one or more fundamental moral rules, together with a set of derived moral rules. The moral rules implied by our supposed theory would determine which acts were right and which wrong, according to the kinds of acts they are. One such rule might be that it is wrong to murder, another might be that it is wrong to steal (in certain conditions, perhaps), and so forth. Finally, suppose that (iii) all the rules of this supposed moral theory were *negative*, that is, that all of these rules would obligate agents to *refrain* from performing wrong acts. Call the conjunction of (i), (ii), and (iii) condition (5). Assuming (5), it certainly appears that God could perfectly satisfy the requirements of morality by refraining from performing any act prohibited by the theory in question. Thus, (1) God's moral perfection, and (5) are compatible, and if (5) were true, it would provide an understanding of God's moral perfection. However, all of this is purely speculative, since no acceptable moral theory of the sort required by (5) is in the offing.

To continue, let us consider the possibility that (i) and (ii) are the case, but that instead of (iii), our non-consequentialist theory (iv) includes not only negative obligations, but also some *positive* moral obligations, such as

an obligation to show kindness or to be charitable.[21] As long as such obligations are not liable to maximization, that is, as long as one is not required
to maximize kindness by being kind to as many subjects as one can be, or
to maximize charitableness by being as charitable to as many subjects as one
can be, then it would seem that the conjunction of (i), (ii), and (iv), which
we call condition (6), is compatible with (1), God's moral perfection. God
could satisfy all the requirements of the theory in question by refraining
from performing any prohibited acts and by performing as many of the
required positive acts as required. So, if a theory along the lines of (6) were
true, it, too, would provide an understanding of God's moral perfection.
But, once again, no theory of the sort required by (6) is on the horizon.

Some moral philosophers have tried, by combining elements of both
consequentialism and non-consequentialism, to construct a moral theory
containing the best features of each. For example, one might try to frame
a moral theory which held that one ought to do that act which would
have the best consequences, unless that act is one of a number of prohibited kinds of acts. Other, more complicated, versions of this sort of theory
can readily be imagined. Let us call such theories, *mixed moral theories*,[22]
and let us say that condition (7) is *that there is a true mixed moral theory.* It
is not hard to see that the problems we found with consequentialist moral
theories for the understanding of God's moral perfection will also be found
with mixed moral theories. For, while it certainly seems that God could
readily satisfy all of the non-consequentialist moral requirements of any
mixed moral theory, God would also have to satisfy the consequentialist
part of the theory. At this point, if God cannot create an actual infinity of
bearers of intrinsic value, or if he can create such an infinity of bearers,
but cannot create more bearers of intrinsic value than any infinite number,
then it would be impossible for him to satisfy the consequentialist part of
our mixed moral theory. For *humans*, it may be that conflicts between the
consequentialist and non-consequentialist aspects of a mixed moral theory
will often arise, at which point they will have to satisfy one requirement
before the other, depending on what the theory says about such cases of
conflict. But it is difficult to see how such conflicts could arise for an
omnipotent and omniscient God. And if they could arise, it is difficult to
see how these *local* conflicts could relieve God of his consequentialist duty
to an extent which would turn aside the sorts of problems for consequentialism we have discussed. Thus, (1) God's moral perfection, and (7)
the truth of a mixed moral theory, are compatible only if the consequentialist requirements of (7) are themselves compatible with (1).

As we stated at the beginning of this chapter, a full explication of God's
moral perfection requires knowledge of an acceptable moral theory, that

is, a theory that explains the nature of right and wrong, good and evil. To the extent that we lack knowledge of such a theory, the explication of God's moral perfection must remain conditional and sketchy. That actually being the situation, we do not regard our explication of God's moral perfection as being as illuminating as, say, our explications of his omniscience was in chapter 6, or as will be our explication of his omnipotence in chapter 8.

On the other hand, we believe that certain insights into God's moral perfection have been gained. First, we think we have shown that unless one makes the questionable assumption that God can create more bearers of intrinsic value than any infinite number, most forms of moral consequentialism are incompatible with the existence of a morally perfect God. Because many philosophers and theologians have tried to understand God's moral perfection in terms of consequentialism, and because consequentialism remains a very popular theory choice among moral philosophers, this is an important result.

Second, if consequentialism is true, and God *can* create more bearers of intrinsic value than any infinite number, then it appears that the traditional problem of evil is interestingly transformed. Consider the possibility of a universe, U_1, which contains *more* created intrinsic good than any number and which also contains an amount of divinely created intrinsic evil equal to an infinite *number*. Recall that there are two positions one could defend regarding the aggregated value of such a universe. According to the first position, because a universe like U_1 contains an infinity of evil, it is not at all clear that it is a maximally good universe. But, according to the second position, we can determine the aggregated value of a universe of this kind by non-arithmetic intuitive means. On this view it can be argued that, because "subtracting" from it a lesser infinity does not diminish a greater infinity, any such universe, U_1, would be a maximally good universe![23] On the other hand, since we cannot strictly speaking, that is arithmetically, aggregate the intrinsic good and evil contained in a universe such as U_1, it can be argued that we are not in a position to assign any definite value to a universe of this kind. In either case, though, we would not be in a position to claim with respect to any universe such as U_1 that the aggregated amount of created intrinsic good is *not* more than any infinite number. That is, we would not be in a position to assert that the existence of an amount of divinely created intrinsic evil equal to any infinite number is *incompatible* with a universe's being a maximally good universe.

Traditionally, the presence of substantial amounts of intrinsic evil in the world has been thought to create a serious problem for theism, a problem known as *the problem of evil*. But if God's moral perfection is to be understood in terms of consequentialism, and to be compatible with consequentialism, then, it would seem, there would be a problem not so much of (too much observable intrinsic) evil, as a problem of too little (observable, intrinsic) good. The intrinsic good we can observe in the world is certainly not infinite, let alone more than any infinite number; the observable world is not bursting with intrinsic goodness.

Third, in the light of the foregoing results, it seems that God's moral perfection could more readily be understood in terms of a deontological or fully non-consequentialist moral theory than in terms of a consequentialist one. Of course, without a proof of the existence of God, this does not imply that a deontological moral theory is more likely to be *true* than a consequentialist moral theory.

Last, although a mixed moral theory may be more plausible than either a purely consequentialist or a purely deontological moral theory, it does not seem to be more compatible with God's moral perfection than a purely consequentialist moral theory.[24]

7.4 Maximal Greatness and Moral Admirability

It might be argued that because maximal greatness and moral admirability are incompatible, the notion of a maximally great being is incoherent. The first version of this alleged *paradox of maximal greatness and moral admirability* goes as follows.

Argument A

(*Premise A1*) Necessarily, a maximally great being is worthy of moral admiration.
(*Premise A2*) Necessarily, for any person S, if S is worthy of moral admiration, then S is capable of intending to do wrong.
(*Premise A3*) Necessarily, a maximally great being is omnibenevolent and incorruptible.
(*Premise A4*) Necessarily, an omnibenevolent, incorruptible being is incapable of intending to do wrong.
(*Premise A5*) Thus, necessarily, a maximally great being is not worthy of moral admiration.

Therefore, necessarily, a maximally great being is both worthy of moral admiration and not worthy of moral admiration.

If *Argument A* were correct, then it would be impossible that there be a maximally great being.

In response, we maintain that there could be a morally admirable individual who is incapable of intending to do wrong. For example, there could be a human being who becomes a moral sage, but only after overcoming her immoral impulses. It may be assumed that such a sage is incapable of intending to do wrong. After all, it is possible that when this individual becomes a moral sage, her brain chemistry changes in such away that she becomes incapable of forming an intention to do wrong. Surely, though, a sage of this kind is morally admirable. Thus, a being can be morally admirable even if that being is incapable of intending to do wrong. Hence, *Argument A* is unsound because *Premise A2* is false.

A second version of the paradox of maximal greatness and moral admirability can be stated in the following manner.

Argument B

(*Premise B1*) Necessarily, a maximally great being is worthy of moral admiration.

(*Premise B2*) Necessarily, for any person S, if S is worthy of moral admiration, then either S is capable of intending to do wrong, or S has immoral impulses, but has overcome them.

(*Premise B3*) Necessarily, since a maximally great being is omnibenevolent and incorruptible, it could neither be capable of intending to do wrong nor have an immoral impulse.

(*Premise B4*) Thus, necessarily, a maximally great being is not worthy of moral admiration.

Therefore, necessarily, a maximally great being is both worthy of moral admiration and not worthy of moral admiration.

Because of its second premise, *Premise B2*, *Argument B* avoids the criticism we made of *Argument A*. *Premise B2* implies that overcoming one's immoral impulses in the effort to acquire a morally desirable quality is inherently worthy of moral admiration. But if *the effort to acquire some quality* is inherently morally admirable, then it must also be true that *one's possessing that quality* is inherently morally admirable. For example, if *one's striving to be just* is inherently morally admirable, then *one's being just* must also be inherently morally admirable. It follows that an individual can be morally admirable because of its intentions to do right, even if it is incapable of intending to do wrong and it lacks an immoral impulse to overcome, that is, an impulse to do wrong. Consequently, an omnibenevolent, incorruptible God who is incapable of intending to do wrong, and who does not need to overcome an immoral impulse in order to attain moral perfection, *is* morally admirable. It follows that *Argument B* is unsound due to the falsity of *Premise B2*.

We are willing to concede that there is a sense of 'morally admirable' in which one's being morally admirable implies that one has overcome one's immoral impulses. But there being such a sense is consistent with the fact that there is another sense of 'morally admirable' in which one's being morally admirable has no such implication. Rather, in this second sense, the sense in which God is morally admirable, one is morally admirable in virtue of effortlessly and unfailingly intending to do right.

There is a final version of the paradox of maximal greatness and moral admirability that assumes that some form of consequentialism is correct and which takes this form.

Argument C

(*Premise C1*) Necessarily, a maximally great being is worthy of moral admiration.

(*Premise C2*) Necessarily, a maximally great being brings about the best possible world.

(*Premise C3*) Hence, there is only one possible world.

(*Premise C4*) Thus, necessarily, a maximally great being does not have the power to do otherwise.

(*Premise C5*) Necessarily, for any person S, if S is worthy of moral admiration, then S has the power to do otherwise.

(*Premise C6*) So, necessarily, a maximally great being is not worthy of moral admiration.

Therefore, necessarily, a maximally great being is both worthy of moral admiration and not worthy of moral admiration.

However, *Argument C* overlooks the possibility that a maximally great being has the power to bring about *any one* of a number of different possible worlds, each of which would be unsurpassably good were it to obtain. The fact that there are different possible worlds of this kind can be illustrated by means of two sorts of examples.

First, we assume that if there is an unsurpassably good possible world, then there is at least one such world that contains contingently existing substances. But for any possible world, W_1, containing contingently existing substances, there is another possible world, W_2, which is *exactly similar* to W_1, but which contains *different* contingently existing substances. It is evident that the value of W_1 (were it to obtain) and the value of W_2 (were it to obtain) would be equal. Hence, if W_1 is unsurpassably good, then W_2 would be unsurpassably good as well.

Second, different possible goods combined in different possible ways may constitute different, logically independent, possible total goods of the same value. This point can be illustrated by means of the following example. Let us assume that the pleasure which would be produced by Smith's eating a spaghetti dinner tonight and the pleasure which would be produced by Smith's eating a linguini dinner tonight are logically independent possible goods of the same value. All other things being equal, a possible world containing Smith's eating a spaghetti dinner tonight and Smith's not eating a linguini dinner tonight, and a possible world containing Smith's eating a linguini dinner tonight and Smith's not eating a spaghetti dinner tonight, constitute different possible goods of the same value. Generalizing from such examples, it seems that if some possible world, W_1, is unsurpassably good, then there is another possible world, W_2, which is not exactly similar to W_1 and which would also be unsurpassably good.

Based upon our discussion of examples of the two foregoing sorts, we conclude that if some possible world qualifies as unsurpassably good, that is to say, qualifies as *a* best possible world, then there is no world which is [uniquely] *the* best of all possible worlds.[25] Therefore, *Argument C* is unsound because *Premise C2* is false.[26]

As we have seen, all three versions of the alleged paradox of maximal greatness and moral admirability are unsound. Thus, this alleged paradox provides no justification whatsoever for thinking that the concept of a maximally great being is incoherent; there is no apparent reason to think that maximal greatness and moral admirability are incompatible.

NOTES

1   For example, is an action morally obligatory owing to *its effects*, or to *its type*, or to *God's commanding it*?

2   Some in the tradition of Western theism have equated existence with goodness, and degrees of existence with degrees of goodness. Assuming that God

has the highest possible degree of existence, they go on to infer that God has the highest possible degree of goodness. We question both the idea that existence itself is (intrinsically) good, and the idea that existence comes in degrees. In any case, if there were such a sense of goodness, it would not be a *moral* sense, and we judge that the core idea of God as the greatest possible being implies that God is morally perfect.

3   For the sake of brevity, henceforth, when we are discussing moral **subjectivism**, we shall speak only of the attitudes of agents determining morality.

4   For example, see Robert M. Adams, "A Modified Divine Command Theory of Ethical Wrongness," in *Religion and Morality*, ed. G. Outka and J. P. Reeder, Jr. (Garden City, NY: Anchor, 1973), pp. 318–47.

5   It should be noted that it is unclear that divine love is compatible with divine incorruptibility. Hence, if we assume that God exists, then it is not clear that God is essentially loving. See section 5.3.

6   See section 1.2. Also note that God's being essentially loving is insufficient to account for God's being essentially morally perfect; for example, his being essentially loving would not account for his being essentially just.

7   Plato, *Euthyphro*, in *The Trial & Death of Socrates*, trans. G. M. A. Grube (Indianapolis, Ind.: Hackett Publishing Company, 1975).

8   While the immediate result of some dental work might be intrinsically bad, i.e., pain, this dental work might be good as a means, since this dental work can prevent greater pain in the long term. On the other hand, while the immediate result of eating a pizza might be intrinsically good, i.e., pleasure, eating that pizza might be bad as a means, since eating that pizza can cause a painful bout of indigestion at a later time which outweighs that pleasure.

9   Epicurus (341–270 BC) and his followers held that the *absence* of pain was the only intrinsic good. For the sake of simplicity, this version of hedonism will not be distinguished from the more usual version just stated in the text.

10   A further distinction between different forms of consequentialism is that between *act-consequentialism* and *rule-consequentialism*. According to the former, the rightness or wrongness of an act depends on *its* consequences. According to the latter, the rightness or wrongness of an act depends on the overall consequences of conformance to the *rule* of action under which the act falls (e.g., a rule prohibiting lying, or one prohibiting stealing). So a particular act might have bad consequences and still be morally right, if conformance to the rule of action under which it falls were to have better consequences than conformance to alternative rules. It has been shown that some forms of rule-consequentialism do not yield different moral judgments than act-consequentialism. Many other forms of rule-consequentialism only make sense in the context of imperfect beings within a social setting, and thus are inapplicable to God. We know of no form of rule-consequentialism of which we need to take heed in our discussion of consequentialism and God's moral

perfection. For an informative discussion of rule-consequentialism, see Fred Feldman, *Introductory Ethics* (Englewood Cliffs, NJ: Prentice-Hall, 1978), chap. 5.

11   Many scholars attribute this view to Aristotle. Thomas Hobbes (1588–1679) may also be committed to this view. He writes as follows.

> Whatsoever we imagine is *finite*. Therefore there is no idea or conception of anything we call *infinite*. No man can have in his mind an image of infinite magnitude; nor conceive of infinite swiftness, infinite time, or infinite force, or infinite power. (Hobbes, *Leviathan* [Chicago, Ill.: Great Books, Encyclopedia Britannica, 1952], part I, chap. 3, p. 54)

If, as Hobbes argues, there is no idea or conception of anything we call infinite, then 'infinite' is a nonsensical term. But if 'infinite' is a nonsensical term, then no human utterance to the effect that something infinite exists is even possibly true.

12   It may be that to *bring about* a universe of the desired sort, God would have to do more than create a universe. It might also be necessary for God to intervene in the world in order to ensure the desired amount of aggregated goodness. This might be the case if God could not foresee all that would obtain in the future in the universe he creates.

We make no assumptions in the arguments which follow about whether or not consequentialism should include the various complications about which kinds of intrinsic value there are, the relative worth of the states of various subjects, or distributive requirements. These complications do not affect these arguments. Nor do we think the distinction between actual and expected consequences relevant to these arguments.

13   A reply to this assertion might go as follows. Suppose that the existence of free agents is necessary for any created universe to be optimal. Since God cannot foresee the free actions of such agents, he cannot know how much intrinsic good and intrinsic evil they will experience. Thus, it is not the case that God can always create a universe better than any given one. However, this reply is not persuasive. God could always create conscious subjects without free will, causally isolated from any created free agents, so that he could foresee how much intrinsic good and evil such subjects would experience. In order to create a better universe than a given universe, U_1, God could create a universe, U_2, containing as many subjects of this sort as required to increase the aggregated amount of created good beyond that in U_1.

14   $\aleph_0$ is also the number of entities in the set which contains all of the integers. It might seem that the set of all the integers is *greater* than the set of all the natural numbers, but according to Cantor, this is not so. Thus, transfinite arithmetic generates many unintuitive conclusions. Others are that $\aleph_0$

$+ 5 = \aleph_o$, that $5 \times \aleph_o = \aleph_o$, and in general, that $\aleph_o + n = \aleph_o$, for any finite n, and that $\aleph_o \times n = \aleph_o$, for any finite n.

15   Cantor says that there is an "absolute infinity" of infinite numbers. According to Cantor, absolute infinity falls outside of the subject matter of mathematics, and thus there is no infinite *number* corresponding to an absolute infinity.

16   Cantor's account of infinity implies that for any number, n, including any infinite number, there are *more* infinite numbers than n. However, an infinite number is an *abstract* entity. To say that there is such an absolute infinity of *abstract entities* is not to say that there is such an absolute infinity of *concrete entities*. Could there be *that many* concrete entities? See the previous note and the discussion in the text to follow.

17   Some philosophers have argued that if in one possible world, W_1, there is an $\aleph_o$ amount of aggregated intrinsic good, and in another possible world, W_2, also an $\aleph_o$ amount of aggregated intrinsic good, nevertheless, W_1 may be a *better* possible world than W_2. This would be the case if, for example, W_1 has 4 units of aggregated intrinsic good at every time, while W_2 has only 2 units of aggregated intrinsic good at every time. See, for example, Peter Vallentyne and Shelly Kagan, "Infinite Value and Finitely Additive Value Theory," *Journal of Philosophy* 94 (1997), pp. 5–26. However, since the *total* aggregated amount of intrinsic good in each possible world is the same, it would appear that a consequentialist should say that the two worlds have the *same* value. Therefore, in our view, the comparative claim about the two worlds made by Vallentyne and Kagan rests upon principles that are not purely consequentialist. But in any case, we avoid these comparative issues by assuming that when God creates a possible world, W_n, containing an $\aleph_n$ amount of aggregated intrinsic good, he creates an $\aleph_n$ amount of aggregated intrinsic good at *every* time. Given such a world, then even granting the comparative principles of the sort favored by Vallentyne and Kagan, there is no possible world containing an $\aleph_n$ amount of aggregated intrinsic good which is *better* than W_n.

18   Consequentialism does not, strictly speaking, require one to do that act which has literally the *best* consequences. Rather, it only requires one to do an act that has consequences that are *at least as good* as those of any other act one could do. If two acts had consequences equally good but better than any other act one could do, then it would be morally right to do either one of them. If God could bring about a world that had at least as much aggregated, created intrinsic goodness as any other world he could bring about, then it is extremely plausible that God could bring about any number of such worlds. See section 7.4, below, for an argument in support of the claim that if there is a world than which no other world is better, then there are indefinitely many such worlds.

19   Immanuel Kant, *Groundwork of the Metaphysic of Morals*, trans. H. J. Paton (New York: Harper and Row, 1964). Kant's first two formulations of the cat-

egorical imperative can be paraphrased as follows. (i) Follow rules of action that can be consistently willed to be universal laws. (ii) Treat others as ends-in-themselves, and never merely as means-to-an-end. Kant's third formulation is "So act that your will can regard itself at the same time as making universal law through its maxim." According to Kant, the third formulation pertains to the autonomy and freedom of moral agents. It should also be noted that as a deontologist, Kant defines goodness in terms of rightness. More specifically, Kant maintains that what is good without qualification (or intrinsically good) is an act of will to do one's duty for the sake of doing one's duty.

20 One theory that has received a lot of attention is John Rawls's *A Theory of Justice* (Cambridge, Mass.: Harvard University Press, 1971). Rawls, however, offers only a theory of justice, not of morality in general. Furthermore, since Rawls's theory is a kind of *social contract theory*, it is difficult to see how it could apply to God. God has no need to enter into a social contract with any other created beings.

21 Kant's theory, for example, includes an obligation to be charitable.

22 An example of such a theory is that of William David Ross (1877–1971), *The Right and the Good* (Oxford: Oxford University Press, 1930).

23 How should we judge the even more extreme case of a possible universe, U_2, which contains *both* more created intrinsic good than any number and more created intrinsic evil than any number? Since addition and subtraction are well-defined arithmetical operations only in the case of finite and infinite numbers, there is no arithmetical basis for concluding that U_2 is a morally neutral universe. Could U_2 be *both* a maximally good and a maximally evil universe? This appears to be absurd. Nor does there seem to be any intuition that U_2 is a maximally good universe or a maximally evil universe. Finally, it can be argued that we are not in a position to assign any definite value to U_2.

24 It might be thought that *virtue ethics* provides a viable alternative to consequentialism, deontology, and mixed theories. Theories of the latter three sorts advance moral principles or rules that evaluate *actions* as *right* or *wrong*. In contrast, virtue ethics evaluates dispositions of moral agents to act as *virtues* or *vices*. For example, kindness, bravery, justice, and honesty are virtues, and cruelty, cowardice, dishonesty, and injustice are vices. Some forms of virtue ethics presuppose that there is at least one intrinsically good end. For example, Aristotle's virtue ethics assumes that the flourishing of a human being as a rational animal is an intrinsically good end. These forms of virtue theory presuppose the existence of moral principles or rules that evaluate actions as right or wrong. From the perspective of virtue theory, it may be observed that God's perfect virtue includes *certain* virtues, for example, justice, but *not* others, for example, bravery. (Because God is invulnerable, he cannot be brave.) Although such observations may shed some light upon the nature

of divine moral perfection, they are by themselves insufficient for making any progress on the central project of this chapter. This central project is to advance our understanding of the implications of divine moral perfection for the character of divine creation. Identifying God's virtues would not *by itself* advance this understanding. From the perspective of rational theology, to advance that understanding requires the use of moral principles or rules that evaluate actions as right or wrong. However, some forms of virtue ethics deny the existence of such moral principles or rules. But God's being virtuous presupposes that there is an objective moral order involving moral principles or rules of this kind. (For example, see our discussion in section 7.1 concerning the unacceptably subjective nature of divine command theories of morality.) Thus, these forms of virtue ethics are incompatible with the existence of God.

25   Leibniz notoriously held that when God created the actual world he created *the* best of all possible worlds. See Leibniz's *On the Ultimate Origins of Things*, in *Leibniz Selections*, ed. Philip Weiner (New York: Charles Scribner's Sons, 1951), pp. 345–55.

26   See section 8.4 for an argument designed to show that divine omnipotence and divine omnibenevolence together entail divine freedom and the power to do otherwise in the libertarian sense.

BIBLIOGRAPHY

Adams, R. M., "A Modified Divine Command Theory of Ethical Wrongness," in *Religion and Morality*, ed. G. Outka and J. P. Reeder, Jr. (Garden City, NY: Anchor, 1973), pp. 318–47.

Benardete, J. A., *Infinity: An Essay in Metaphysics* (Oxford: Oxford University Press, 1964).

Cantor, G., *Contributions to the Founding of the Theory of Transfinite Numbers*, trans. P. E. B. Jourdain (New York: Dover, 1955).

Feldman, F., *Introductory Ethics* (Englewood Cliffs, NJ: Prentice-Hall, 1978).

Helm, P. (ed.), *Divine Attributes and Morality* (Oxford: Oxford University Press, 1981).

Hilbert, D. (1862–1943), "On the Infinite," trans. S. Bauer-Mengelberg, in J. van Heijenoort (ed.), *From Frege to Gödel: A Source Book in Mathematical Logic, 1879–1931* (Cambridge, Mass.: Harvard University Press, 1967).

Kant, I., *Groundwork of the Metaphysics of Morals*, trans. H. J. Paton (New York: Harper and Row, 1964).

Moore, A. W., *The Infinite* (London: Routledge, 1990).

——(ed.), *Infinity* (Aldershot: Dartmouth, 1993).

Plato, *Euthyphro*, in *The Trial & Death of Socrates*, trans. G. M. A. Grube (Indianapolis, Ind.: Hackett Publishing Company, 1975).

Quinn, P. L., *Divine Commands and Moral Requirements* (Oxford: Clarendon Press, 1978).

8

Omnipotence

The divine attribute of omnipotence seems puzzling, even paradoxical, to many philosophers. They wonder, for example, whether God can create a spherical cube, or make a stone so massive that he cannot move it. We will defend the consistency of omnipotence (understood as maximal power). As a part of this defense, we will analyze omnipotence and examine the implications of this analysis for the nature of God.

8.1 Maximal Power and the Uniqueness of God

The last of the core attributes of a maximally great being that we shall explore is omnipotence. Philosophical reflection upon the notion of omnipotence raises many puzzling questions about whether or not a consistent notion of omnipotence places limitations on the power of an omnipotent agent. Can an omnipotent agent create a stone so massive that that agent cannot move it? Paradoxically, it would seem that however this question is answered, an omnipotent agent turns out not to be all-powerful. Could such an agent have the power to create or overturn necessary truths of logic and mathematics? Can an agent of this kind bring about or alter the past? Is the notion of an omnipotent agent other than God an intelligible one? Could *two* omnipotent agents coexist? If there are states of affairs that an omnipotent agent is powerless to bring about, then how is the notion of omnipotence to be intelligibly defined? Another obstacle to traditional Western theism arises if it is impossible for God to be both omnibenevolent and omnipotent. If an omnipotent God is powerless to do evil, then how can he be omnipotent? As practitioners of rational theology, our aim is to construct an analysis of the concept of omnipotence that resolves all of the puzzles and apparent paradoxes that surround this concept. On the other hand, if the notion of omnipotence were found to be unintelligible, then traditional Western theism would be false.

According to some philosophers, omnipotence should be understood in terms of the power to *perform certain tasks*, for instance, to kill oneself, to make 2 + 2 = 5, or to make oneself non-omniscient. Recent philosophical discussion has revealed this approach to the analysis of omnipotence to be fruitless. More successful is the approach of analyzing omnipotence in terms of the power to *bring about certain possible states of affairs* (understood as propositional entities which either obtain or fail to obtain).[1]

One sense of 'omnipotence' is, literally, that of having the power to bring about *any* state of affairs whatsoever, including necessary and impossible states of affairs. Descartes in the *Meditations* seems to have had such a notion.[2] But, as Aquinas in his *Summa Theologiae* and Maimonides in his *Guide for the Perplexed* recognized, it is *not* possible for an agent to bring about an *impossible* state of affairs (e.g., *that there is a shapeless cube*), since if it were, it would be possible for an impossible state of affairs to obtain, which is a contradiction.[3] Nor is it possible for an agent to bring about a *necessary* state of affairs (e.g., *that all cubes are shaped*). It is possible for an agent, a, to bring about a necessary state of affairs, s, only if possibly, (1) a brings about s, and (2) if a had not acted, then s would have failed to obtain. Because a necessary state of affairs obtains whether or not anyone acts, (2) is false. As a consequence, it is impossible for an agent to bring about either a necessary or an impossible state of affairs. Obviously, an agent's having the *power* to bring about a state of affairs entails that, *possibly*, the agent brings about that state of affairs. Hence, the first sense of 'omnipotence' is incoherent.

A second sense of 'omnipotence' is that of *maximal power*, meaning just that no being could exceed the overall power of an omnipotent being. It does not follow that a maximally powerful being can bring about *any* state of affairs, since, as we have seen, bringing about some such states of affairs is impossible. Nor does it follow that a being with maximal power can bring about whatever any *other* agent can bring about. If a can bring about s, and b cannot, it does not follow that b is *not overall* more powerful than a, since it could be that b can bring about more states of affairs than a can, rather than the other way around. This *comparative* sense of 'omnipotence' as maximal power is the only sense that has a chance of being intelligible. In this respect, omnipotence is analogous to omniscience.[4]

Power should be distinguished from *ability*. Power is ability plus opportunity: a being having maximal ability who is prevented by circumstances from exercising those abilities would not be omnipotent. Nothing could prevent an omnipotent agent from exercising its powers, if it were to endeavor to do so.

In light of the foregoing, is it possible that there be two coexistent omnipotent agents, Dick and Jane? If this were possible, then it could happen that at some time, t, Dick, while retaining his omnipotence, attempts to move a feather, and at t, Jane, while retaining her omnipotence, attempts to keep that feather motionless. Intuitively, in this case, neither Dick nor Jane would affect the feather as to its motion or rest. Thus, in this case, at t, Dick would be powerless to move the feather, and at t, Jane would be powerless to keep the feather motionless! But it is absurd to suppose that an omnipotent agent could lack the power to move a feather or the power to keep it motionless. Therefore, neither Dick nor Jane is omnipotent. As a consequence, it is impossible that there be two coexistent omnipotent agents.

As we have argued, for any x, if x is *maximally great*, then this entails that x is a necessary being who is omnipotent, eternal, and incorruptible. So, for any x, if x is maximally great, then this entails that x has *necessary existence*, x is eternal, and x is *essentially* omnipotent. Since there could not be two coexistent omnipotent agents, it follows that if there is a maximally great being, then it is the *only* omnipotent agent that exists in *any* possible world. So a maximally great being would have a very strong sort of *uniqueness*. This explains why the monotheistic doctrine that there cannot be more than one God is correct. It also explains why the greatness of a maximally great being could neither be surpassed nor *matched*.

Could an agent be *contingently* omnipotent? At first glance, this appears possible, but there is the following argument for the opposite view.

On the assumption that God exists, he has necessary existence and is essentially omnipotent. But there could not be more than one omnipotent being. Thus, on the assumption that God exists, a contingently omnipotent being is impossible.

This argument against the possibility of contingent omnipotence presupposes traditional Western theism. However, if one is engaged in a *purely conceptual* exploration of the notion of maximal greatness, then one should not presuppose either theism or atheism. Since, in this context, we are engaged in an exploration of the notion of maximal greatness *per se*, and not just of divine omnipotence, we should remain neutral about whether theism is true or false. Accordingly, omnipotence will not be assumed to be attributable *only* to the God of traditional Western theism or *only* to an essentially omnipotent being.

8.2 What an Omnipotent Agent Can Do

The intelligibility of the notion of omnipotence has been challenged by the so-called paradox or riddle of the stone. Can an omnipotent agent, Jane, bring it about that there is a stone of some mass, m, which Jane cannot move? If the answer is 'yes', then there is a state of affairs that Jane cannot bring about, namely, (S1) *that a stone of mass m moves*. On the other hand, if the answer is 'no', then there is another state of affairs that Jane cannot bring about, namely, (S2) *that there is a stone of mass m which Jane cannot move*. Thus, it seems that whether or not Jane can make the stone in question, there is some possible state of affairs that an omnipotent agent cannot bring about. And this appears to be paradoxical.

A first resolution of the paradox comes into play when Jane is an *essentially* omnipotent agent. In that case, the state of affairs of Jane's being non-omnipotent is impossible. Therefore, Jane cannot bring it about that she is not omnipotent. Since, necessarily, an omnipotent agent can move any stone, no matter how massive, (S2) is impossible. But, as we have seen, an omnipotent agent is not required to be able to bring about an impossible state of affairs.

If, on the other hand, Jane is an *accidentally* omnipotent agent, both (S1) and (S2) *are* possible, and it *is* possible for some omnipotent agent to bring it about that (S1) obtains at one time, *and* that (S2) obtains at a different time. Thus, there is a second solution to the paradox. In this case, Jane's being non-omnipotent is a possible state of affairs; thus, we may assume that it *is* possible for Jane to bring it about that she is non-omnipotent. So, Jane can create and move a stone, s, of mass, m, while omnipotent, and *subsequently* bring it about that she is not omnipotent and powerless to move s. As a consequence, Jane can bring about both (S1) and (S2), but only if they obtain at different times.[5]

It might now be conjectured that omnipotence can be analyzed simply as the power to bring it about that any *contingent* state of affairs obtains. However, the following list of contingent states of affairs shows that there can be contingent states of affairs that an omnipotent agent is powerless to bring about, and hence that this simple analysis is inadequate:

(a) *that a raindrop fell*;
(b) *that a raindrop falls at t* (where t is a past time);
(c) *that Parmenides lectures for the first time*;
(d) *that the Amazon River floods an odd number of times less than four*;

(e) *that a snowflake falls and no omnipotent agent ever exists*; and
(f) *that Plato freely decides to write a dialogue.*

Note that (a) is a past state of affairs. As we saw earlier, it is impossible for an efficient cause to occur *later* than its effect.[6] However, an agent's bringing about a state of affairs is a kind of efficient causation. Therefore, it is not possible for an agent to bring about anything that is in the *past*. In other words, it is impossible for *any* agent to have power over what is past. Hence, no agent, not even an omnipotent one, can bring it about that (a) obtains. Likewise, despite the fact that (b) can be brought about *prior to* t, the impossibility of an agent's having power over what is past implies that *after* t even an omnipotent agent cannot bring it about that (b) obtains. In the case of (c), prior to Parmenides's first lecture, an omnipotent agent can bring about (c). But once Parmenides has lectured, even an omnipotent agent cannot bring it about that (c) obtains. As for (d), prior to the Amazon's third flooding, an omnipotent agent can bring it about that (d) obtains, while after the Amazon's third flooding, even an omnipotent agent cannot bring it about that (d) obtains. (e) introduces a special difficulty. Although it is obvious that (e) could *not* be brought about by an omnipotent agent, it can be argued plausibly that it *is* possible for a non-omnipotent agent to bring about (e) by causing a snowflake to fall, *provided that* no omnipotent agent ever exists.[7] But, as we argued earlier, a maximally powerful being need not have the power to bring about every state of affairs that any other being could. Lastly, while if the libertarian theory of free will is correct, an omnipotent agent (who is, of course, *other than Plato*) cannot bring about (f), apparently a non-omnipotent agent, namely, Plato, can bring it about that (f) obtains.

Consequently, a satisfactory analysis of omnipotence ought not to require that an omnipotent agent have the power to bring about (a), (b), (c), (d), (e), or (f), if it is assumed, *arguendo*, in the case of (f), that libertarianism is true.

Because of the wide disparity among contingent states of affairs, (a)–(f), one might despair of finding an analysis of omnipotence that both deals satisfactorily with all of these states of affairs and implies that an omnipotent being has, intuitively speaking, sufficient power. Yet, the following reflections show that such pessimism is unwarranted.

By identifying certain features of (a)–(f), we will be able to find a feature that none of them possesses, and in terms of which an analysis of omnipotence can be stated. To begin, unless it is possible for *some* agent to bring about a given state of affairs an omnipotent agent ought not to be required to be able to bring about that state of affairs. But (a) is not possibly brought about by any agent.

Next, while (b) and (c) are possibly brought about by some agent, they are not *repeatable*: it is not possible for either one of them to obtain, subsequently fail to obtain, and then obtain again. Note that if, because (a) is not possibly brought about by someone, an omnipotent agent is not required to be able to bring about (a), then for the same reason, that agent is also not required to be able to bring about impossible or necessary states of affairs. Moreover, if, because (b) and (c) are not repeatable, an omnipotent agent is not required to bring about (b) or (c), then for the same reason, that agent is also not required to be able to bring about impossible or necessary states of affairs.

Third, while (d) *is* repeatable, it is *not unrestrictedly* repeatable, that is, it cannot obtain, then fail to obtain, then obtain again, and so on, eternally.

Fourth, while (e) *is* unrestrictedly repeatable, it is a *complex* state of affairs, namely, a *conjunctive* state of affairs whose second conjunct is *not* repeatable. These examples suggest a hypothesis about repeatability and its relation to power, namely, that an omnipotent agent should *not* be required to have the power to bring about *either* a state of affairs that is not unrestrictedly repeatable, *or* a conjunctive state of affairs one of whose conjuncts is not unrestrictedly repeatable.

Lastly, although (f) *is* unrestrictedly repeatable, (f) is another type of complex state of affairs. In particular, it is identifiable with or analyzable as a conjunctive state of affairs. This state of affairs has three conjuncts, the second of which is not possibly brought about by anyone. The conjunctive state of affairs in question can be informally expressed as follows: Plato decides to write a dialogue; and there is no *antecedent* sufficient causal condition of Plato's deciding to write a dialogue; and there is no concurrent sufficient causal condition of Plato's deciding to write a dialogue. Because it is impossible for an agent to have power over what is *past*, the second conjunct of this state of affairs is not possibly brought about by anyone. Thus, an omnipotent agent ought not to be required to have the power to bring about a state of affairs that is identifiable with or analyzable as a conjunctive state of affairs one of whose conjuncts is not possibly brought about by anyone.

8.3 The Analysis of Omnipotence

In light of the foregoing discussion, omnipotence can now be analyzed in terms of the following three definitions.

(D1) The period of time t is a sufficient interval for s = df. s is a state of affairs such that: it is possible that s obtains at a time-period which has the duration of t.

For example, any period of time with a duration of 7 seconds is a sufficient interval for the state of affairs *that a ball rolls for 7 seconds*.

(D2) A state of affairs, s, is unrestrictedly repeatable = df. s is possibly such that: $(n)(\exists t_1)(\exists t_2)(\exists t_3) \ldots (\exists t_n)(t_1 < t_2 < t_3 < \ldots t_n$ are periods of time which are sufficient intervals for s & s obtains at t_1, s doesn't obtain at t_2, s obtains at t_3, $\ldots s$ obtains at $t_n \equiv n$ is odd).[8]

For instance, the state of affairs *that a ball rolls for 7 seconds* is unrestrictedly repeatable.

(D3) x is omnipotent at t = df. (s)(it is possible for some agent to bring about $s \rightarrow$ at t, x has it within his power to bring about s).

In *D3*, x ranges over agents, and s over states of affairs that satisfy the following condition:

(C) (i) s is unrestrictedly repeatable, and of the form 'in n minutes, p', & p is a complex state of affairs $\rightarrow$ (each of the parts of p is unrestrictedly repeatable & possibly brought about by someone), or (ii) p is of the form 'q forever after', where q is a state of affairs which satisfies (i).[9]

In applying *D3* to states of affairs like (e) and (f) it should be observed that a *conjunct* of a conjunctive state of affairs is a *part* of such a complex state of affairs.[10]

As intended, *D3* does not require an omnipotent agent to have the power to bring about either impossible or necessary states of affairs, or states of affairs such as (a)–(f). Furthermore, *D3* does not unduly limit the power of an omnipotent agent, since an agent's bringing about a state of affairs can always be "cashed out" in terms of that agent's bringing about an unrestrictedly repeatable state of affairs that it is possible for some agent to bring about. That is, necessarily, for any state of affairs, s, if an agent, a, brings about s, then either s is an unrestrictedly repeatable state of affairs which it is possible for some agent to bring about, or else *a* brings about *s by* bringing about *q*, where *q* is an unrestrictedly repeatable state of affairs which it is possible for some agent to bring about. For instance, an omnipotent agent can bring about the state of affairs, *that in one hour, Parmenides lectures for the first time*, by bringing about the state of affairs, *that in one hour, Parmenides lectures*, when this lecture is Parmenides's first. And although the former state of affairs is a nonrepeatable one that *D3* does *not* require an omnipotent agent to be able to bring about, the latter state of affairs *is* an unrestrictedly repeatable state of affairs that *D3 does* require an omnipotent agent to be able to bring about.

8.4 Divine Omnibenevolence, Omnipotence, and Freedom

It has been argued that the traditional God has incompatible attributes, namely, necessary existence, essential omnipotence, essential omniscience, and essential omnibenevolence.[11] The contention has been that it is impossible for God to have the power to bring about evil, while non-omnipotent (and non-omnibenevolent) beings may have this power. The precise form of such an argument varies depending on what precisely the relation between God and evil is assumed to be. However, generally speaking, it is argued that divine omnibenevolence and omnipotence are incompatible because divine omnipotence entails that God has the power to bring about evil, whereas divine omnibenevolence entails that God is powerless to bring about evil.

We reply to arguments of this kind as follows. Assume that if God exists, then this is a best possible world.[12] In that case, if God exists, there could not be an evil unless it were necessary for some greater good, in which case any state of affairs containing evil incompatible with there being a maximally good world is *impossible*. As we have argued, it is not possible that *any* agent bring about an impossible state of affairs. Thus, if God exists, any moral evil, that is, any evil brought about by anyone, and any natural evil, or any evil which has an impersonal, natural cause, must be necessary for some greater good.

Suppose that God exists and that some other person, for example, Cain, brings it about that an evil, *E*, exists. There are two possibilities that need to be considered here. The first is that Cain's decisions and actions are causally determined, as are all occurrences in the created universe. Then, given our assumptions, since Cain's bringing it about that *E* exists is necessary for some good which more than compensates for *E*'s existence, it is consistent with God's omnibenevolence that God [remotely] brings it about that Cain brings it about that E exists.

The second possibility is that Cain's decision to do evil is uncaused by anything other than Cain and free in the libertarian sense. In that case, God did *not* [remotely cause Cain freely to] bring it about that E exists, while [let us assume] Cain *did* freely bring it about that E exists. If so, then it must be the case that God's creating Cain and permitting Cain freely to do what he chooses to do [in the context of the entire creation] brings about more good than his *not* creating Cain and thus *not* permitting him freely to do what he chooses to do. It might be objected that if Cain can bring about a state of affairs that God cannot, namely, *that E exists*, then God is not omnipotent. But, as we have seen, an agent's being omnipotent does not require of that agent that it be able to bring about *every* state of affairs which *any* other agent can bring about. It *does*, of course, require that an omnipotent agent have more power than any other agent. And God, of course, *would* have more power than Cain, even though Cain could bring about something that God could not. For there are many more states of affairs which God could bring about and which Cain could not, than *vice versa*. At this point, it might further be objected that an omnipotent agent, one that was not omnibenevolent, who *could* bring it about that E exists, as well as all the other states of affairs that God could bring about, would be more powerful than God. But recall that if God exists, then he exists eternally in every possible world. Recall, too, that there cannot be more than one omnipotent agent. Thus, if God exists, then an omnipotent agent who is not omnibenevolent is *impossible*. Thus, this second objection is based on an assumption that is impossible, namely, that if God exists there could exist another omnipotent agent who is not omnibenevolent and who is therefore more powerful than God.

Of course, if God exists, then any evil state of affairs, s, which *is* incompatible with a maximally good world is *impossible*. And if s is impossible, then neither God nor any other agent has the power to bring it about that s obtains. God would lack the power to bring it about that s obtains because of his moral perfection, and any created agent would lack the power to bring it about that s obtains either because (i) God would not create an agent who had the power to bring it about that s obtains, or (ii) God would not permit any created agent to bring it about that s obtains. Thus, to the extent indicated, if God's attributes impose moral restrictions on the nature of the universe and on what he can bring about, then they impose parallel restrictions on what any other agents can bring about.

We conclude that God's omnibenevolence and omnipotence are not incompatible.[13]

This position about God and the possibility of evil has been disputed by theists such as Alvin Plantinga, who do not hold that God's existence implies the existence of a maximally good world, but do hold that God seeks to create as good a world as he can.[14] Theists such as Plantinga allow for there to be evil that is *unnecessary* for any greater good that outweighs it. An evil of this kind involves free decisions of non-divine agents, which God does not prevent, but which these other agents can prevent. Plantinga contends that God is not wrong to permit an evil of this kind, since God cannot bring about a vital good, the existence of free human agents, without there being such an evil. Alternatively, it might be argued that God does no wrong in this sort of case, because he does not know how to do better (knowledge of the future free actions of created agents being impossible). However, as an omnipotent God is *not* required to have power over the free decisions of non-divine agents, it follows that on these views, his omnipotence and omnibenevolence are compatible, roughly to the extent indicated earlier in our discussion of the view that God's existence implies a maximally good world. Of course, nothing that has been said here answers the question of how much, if any, evil is compatible with the existence of the traditional God. This question is central to the problem of evil for theism.

Finally, the following considerations support the idea that divine omnibenevolence and omnipotence together entail *divine freedom*. As we have seen, if there is a maximally good world, then there are indefinitely many maximally good possible worlds.[15] Let us assume that God exists, and that there are maximally good possible worlds. In that case, since God is omnipotent, there are indefinitely many possible worlds such that he has it within his power to create each one of these worlds. For any two of these possible worlds W_1 and W_2, God's creating W_1 and God's creating W_2 are *equally rational* for God. However, each one of these worlds is incompatible with the others. Hence, it is impossible that *two* of these possible worlds *both* obtain. Because it is impossible for even an omnipotent being to bring about what is impossible, God is powerless to create more than one of these possible worlds. Since there can be no *reason* for God to prefer creating any *one* of these worlds, and since it seems possible for him to create any one of them without his being compelled or determined to do so, it appears that God would be *defective* if he were compelled or determined to create a particular one of them. Of course, as a maximally great being, God could not be defective in this way. Hence, it seems that in creating one of the possible worlds in question, God acts without being compelled or determined to do so. We conclude that in creating one of these worlds, God has it within his power (in the libertarian sense) to create any of the *alternative* possible worlds. In other words, God has it within his power to do *otherwise* in the requisite sense. Thus, it appears that God's creation of the world is a *free action* in the libertarian sense. If this is correct, then God enjoys *freedom of action* in a robust sense.[16]

NOTES

1 This approach is taken by Gary Rosenkrantz and Joshua Hoffman, "What An Omnipotent Agent Can Do," *International Journal for Philosophy of Religion* 11 (1980), pp. 1–19; Thomas Flint and Alfred Freddoso, "Maximal Power," in *The Existence and Nature of God*, ed. Alfred Freddoso (Notre Dame, Ind.: University of Notre Dame Press, 1983), pp. 81–113; and Edward Wierenga, *The Nature of God: An Inquiry into Divine Attributes* (Ithaca, NY: Cornell University Press, 1989), pp. 12–35.

2 René Descartes, *Meditations on First Philosophy*, trans. John Cottingham, Robert Stoothoff, and Dugald Murdoch, in *The Philosophical Writings of Descartes, Volume 2* (Cambridge: Cambridge University Press, 1984), meditation 1.

3 St. Thomas Aquinas, *Summa Theologiae* (New York: Benziger Brothers, 1948), Ia, 25, 3; and Maimonides, *Guide for the Perplexed*, trans. M. Friedlander (London: George Routledge and Sons, 1904), part I, chap. 15.

4 See the discussion of omniscience as maximal knowledge in section 6.1.

5 For a discussion of the paradox of the stone and a useful bibliography concerning this paradox, see Gary Rosenkrantz and Joshua Hoffman, "The Omnipotence Paradox, Modality, and Time," *Southern Journal of Philosophy* 18 (1980), pp. 473–9.

6 See the argument in section 6.1.

7 Such an argument is based on two premises. The first premise is a plausible version of the principle of *the diffusiveness of power* which implies that for any agent, A, and for any states of affairs p & q, if A brings about p, q obtains, and $\sim q$ is not within the power of any agent other than A, then A brings about $(p$ & $q)$. The second premise is that possibly [(a non-omnipotent agent brings it about that a snowflake falls) & (no omnipotent agent ever exists) & (it is not within the power of any agent to bring it about that an omnipotent agent exists at some time)]. It is plausible that this conjunction is possible provided that a contingently omnipotent agent is possible. See Joshua Hoffman and Gary Rosenkrantz, "Omnipotence Redux," *Philosophy and Phenomenological Research* 49 (1988), pp. 283–301.

8   In *D2*, '*n*' ranges over all natural numbers, and $t_1 \ldots t_n$ are nonoverlapping. In addition, it is assumed for the purposes of *D2* that either it is possible for time to have no beginning, or it is possible for time to have no end (or both).

9   It should be noted that in (C), '*n*' ranges over real numbers, and *p* is not itself equivalent to a state of affairs of the form 'in *n* minutes, *r*', where *n* is not equal to zero.

10 A complex state of affairs is one which is either constructible out of other states of affairs by use of the logical apparatus of first-order logic enriched with whatever modalities one chooses to employ, or else analyzable (in the sense of a philosophical analysis) into a state of affairs which is so constructible. Therefore, a *part* of a complex state of affairs, *s*, is one of those states of affairs out of which *s*, or an analysis of *s*, is constructed. We discuss the relevant notion of a *logical part* in section 2.1.

11 See Nelson Pike, "Omnipotence and God's Ability to Sin," *American Philosophical Quarterly* 6 (1969), pp. 208–16. Pike argues that divine omnipotence and omnibenevolence are incompatible. For a discussion of the compatibility of divine omnipotence and omnibenevolence, see Joshua Hoffman, "Can God Do Evil?," *Southern Journal of Philosophy* 17 (1979), pp. 213–20.

12 As we have seen, whether divine omnibenevolence or moral perfection should be understood as perfect goodness, perfect virtue, or an optimal combination of goodness and virtue, depends upon whether the correct theory of morality is consequentialist, deontological, or *mixed* (that is, a mixture of core elements of consequentialist and deontological moral theories). To preserve our neutrality on this controversial question in this context, in our argument in the text we use expressions such as 'best possible world' and 'maximally good possible world' to refer to *either* a possible world of unsurpassable goodness, a possible world governed by a being of unsurpassable virtue, or a possible world with an optimal balance of goodness and virtuous governance. See chapter 7 for a discussion of these alternative conceptions of divine moral perfection.

13 Although from what we have said about the restrictions that any coherent account of God's knowledge and power must place on this knowledge and power, a better term for God's knowledge than 'omniscience' would be 'maxiscience', and a better term than 'omnipotence' would be 'maxipotence'.

14 Alvin Plantinga, *God, Freedom, and Evil* (New York: Harper and Row, 1974). This work is an influential free will defense of theism against the problem of evil. We have argued against some of the presuppositions of Plantinga's view, and in particular, against the acceptance of so-called "counterfactuals of freedom." See our discussion of such subjunctive conditionals of freedom in section 6.1.

15 See section 7.4.

16 This chapter is largely based upon our article "Omnipotence" in *A Companion to the Philosophy of Religion*, ed. Philip L. Quinn and Charles Taliaferro (Oxford: Blackwell, 1997), article 28.

BIBLIOGRAPHY

Aquinas, T., *Summa Theologiae* (New York: Benziger Brothers, 1948).

Curley, E. M., "Descartes On the Creation of the Eternal Truths," *Philosophical Review* 93 (1984), pp. 569–97.

Descartes, R., *Meditations on First Philosophy*, trans. John Cottingham, Robert Stoothoff, and Dugald Murdoch, in *The Philosophical Writings of Descartes, Volume 2* (Cambridge: Cambridge University Press, 1984).

Flint, T. and Freddoso, A., "Maximal Power," in *The Existence and Nature of God*, ed. A. Freddoso (Notre Dame, Ind.: University of Notre Dame Press, 1983), pp. 81–113.

Frankfurt, H., "Descartes on the Creation of the Eternal Truths," *Philosophical Review* 86 (1977), pp. 36–57.

Hoffman, J., "Can God Do Evil?," *Southern Journal of Philosophy* 17 (1979), pp. 213–20.

—— and Rosenkrantz, G. S., "Omnipotence Redux," *Philosophy and Phenomenological Research* 49 (1988), pp. 283–301.

—— and ——, "Omnipotence," in *A Companion to the Philosophy of Religion*, ed. P. L. Quinn and C. Taliaferro (Oxford: Blackwell, 1997), article 28.

Maimonides, *Guide for the Perplexed*, trans. M. Friedlander (London: George Routledge and Sons, 1904).

Pike, N., "Omnipotence and God's Ability to Sin," *American Philosophical Quarterly* 6 (1969), pp. 208–16.

Plantinga, A., *God, Freedom, and Evil* (New York: Harper and Row, 1974).

Rosenkrantz, G. S. and Hoffman, J., "The Omnipotence Paradox, Modality, and Time," *Southern Journal of Philosophy* 18 (1980), pp. 473–9.

—— and ——, "What An Omnipotent Agent Can Do," *International Journal for Philosophy of Religion* 11 (1980), pp. 1–19.

Wierenga, E., *The Nature of God: An Inquiry into Divine Attributes* (Ithaca, NY: Cornell University Press, 1989).

Concluding Remarks and Prolegomena to Future Rational Theology

Rational theology begins with the question, *is the concept of God coherent?* Having completed our exploration of the divine attributes, we can now give our answer to this question. We have not detected any inconsistency or incoherence in the divine attributes, either individually or in combination. Although God could not possess some of the attributes traditionally ascribed to him, for example, omnipresence, atemporal eternity, self-existence, and immutability, the possession of maximal greatness does not entail having any of these problematical attributes. In addition, there are other analogous attributes that can be coherently ascribed to God, for instance, knowledge of, or power over, what occurs at every place, temporal eternity, necessarily existing and not being explained by anything else, and incorruptibility, respectively. Thus, as far as we can tell, the concept of God is coherent, and the nonexistence of God cannot be established by means of *a priori* argumentation alone.

Assuming that the concept of God is coherent, rational theology next asks the question, *is this concept instantiated?*, or, in other words, *does God exist?* While this question is a very important and difficult one, the attempt to answer it falls outside the scope of the present study. Nevertheless, we would like to indicate something of the philosophical context within which rational theology deals with the question of the existence of God.

Broadly speaking, when rational theology asks, *does God exist?*, there are three possible answers. The first possibility is that the evidence from reason and experience favors *belief in the existence of God*. Henceforth, we shall call this position *theism*. In that case, one ought rationally to believe in the existence of God. The second possibility is that the evidence from reason and experience favors *belief in the non-existence of God*. Henceforth, we shall call this position *atheism*. In this case, one ought rationally to disbelieve in the existence of God. The third possibility is that the totality of evidence from reason and experience favors neither theism nor atheism. This outcome implies that any evidence that appears to favor theism is counterbalanced by evidence that appears to favor atheism, and *vice versa*. In that case, reason requires that one *withhold judgment concerning both theism and atheism*, that is, one should neither accept nor reject either of them. This is the position known as *agnosticism* with respect to the proposition that God exists.

One attempt to justify the belief that God exists by means of purely *a priori* argumentation is known as *the ontological argument*. A representative version of this argument goes as follows. A maximally great being, i.e., God, is by definition a necessary being. Hence, (1) God's existing in *some* possible world implies that he exists in *every* possible world. Yet, since the concept of God is coherent, it might appear that the existence of God *is* possible, that is to say, it might seem that (2) God exists in some possible world. Of course, (3) if God exists in every possible world, then he actually exists. Thus, this version of the ontological argument might seem to show that if the concept of God is coherent, then God actually exists. This version of the ontological argument can be formally stated as follows:

Argument A

(*Premise A1*) If God exists in some possible world, then he exists in every possible world.
(*Premise A2*) God is possible, i.e., he exists in some possible world.
(*Premise A3*) If God exists in every possible world, then he actually exists.

Therefore, God actually exists.

The difficulty with this ontological argument is that there seems to be a counter-argument which is at least as plausible and which implies that God does *not* actually exist. The first premise of this counter-argument is the same as the first premise of the ontological argument, namely, that if God exists in some possible world, then he exists in every possible world. The second premise of the counter-argument is that the *nonexistence* of God is possible, that is, God fails to exist in some possible world. Surely, the proposition *that God fails to exist in some possible world* is no less plausible than the proposition *that God exists in some possible world*. Yet, the two premises of the counter-argument together imply that God fails to exist in every possible world. Of course, if God fails to exist in every possible world, then God does not actually exist. This counter-argument may be formally expressed as follows:

Argument B

(*Premise B1*) If God exists in some possible world, then he exists in every possible world.
(*Premise B2*) It is possible that God does not exist, that is, God fails to exist in some possible world.
(*Premise B3*) If God does not exist in some possible world, then God fails to exist in every possible world.
(*Premise B4*) If God fails to exist in every possible world, then God does not exist in the actual world.

Therefore, God does not exist.

As we have shown, *Premise A2* of *Argument A*, the ontological argument, is not justified. In other words, the claim that the existence of God is possible is not justified. So, it seems that the proposition *that the concept of God is coherent implies that the existence of God is possible* cannot be established by means of *a priori* argumentation alone. To justify the former, *epistemic* claim, that the concept of God is *coherent*, is *not* to justify the latter, *metaphysical* claim, that the existence of God is *possible*.

Another way of attempting to justify the belief that God exists is by arguing that divine creation is the *best explanation* of the existence of contingent entities of certain sorts.[1] In particular, it might be argued that divine creation is the best explanation of the existence of the following three interrelated domains: (i) the domain of concrete, contingent entities in general; (ii) the domain of contingently true laws of nature; and (iii) the domain of biological life and the consciousness and subjective experiential qualities sometimes associated with biological life. To explain the existence of these domains would be to explain why it is that there are any concrete, contingent entities, why the contingent laws of nature are what they are, and why consciousness exists, respectively. How promising is an argument for theism based on the claim that theism is the best explanation of the existence of these three domains?

Apparently, it would be desirable to have a *unified* explanation of the existence of the three domains in question. Since an abstract entity does not have causal power, we can infer that the three domains were not caused or created by one or more abstract entities. And since nothing can be causally prior to itself, the existence of the domain of contingent concrete entities cannot be explained by the hypothesis that one or more concrete, *contingent* entities created this domain. Because every entity is either concrete or abstract, it follows that the existence of the three domains can be explained only if these three domains are created by one or more *necessarily* existing concrete entities. The alternative to there being such an explanation is that the existence of the three domains is an inexplicable, or brute, fact. But from a rational point of view, the more we can explain, the better. So, the hypothesis that the existence of the three domains can be explained by one or more creative, necessarily existing, concrete entities has some evidence in its favor. Furthermore, according to Ockham's Razor, one should not multiply entities needlessly. Since there seems to be no need to posit more than one necessarily existing, creative, concrete entity, it seems more reasonable to suppose that there is a *unique*, necessarily existing, creative, concrete entity than more than one.

By considering the nature of living organisms this line of reasoning can be expanded. The astonishing order and functional organization that naturally obtains among the parts of a living organism resembles that which obtains among the parts of a machine, though far exceeding it in complexity and subtlety.[2] Since machines are the products of intelligent design, the analogy between living organisms and machines suggests that a concrete entity which created the contingently true laws of nature and biological life has an attribute which in some respects resembles human intelligence, but which is much more powerful. Yet, the degree of resemblance or analogy between the attribute in question and human intelligence is obscure.[3]

Is there any way in which it can plausibly be argued that there is a primal, creative, concrete entity that is spiritual, omnipotent, and omniscient? During the eighteenth century, advocates of theism often argued that the order and functional organization which obtains among the parts of living organisms could not be satisfactorily explained without the hypothesis of a supernatural, intelligent designer. This is traditionally known as *the teleological argument* or *the argument from design*. But from a twenty-first-century perspective, it seems that molecular and evolutionary biology together can provide a satisfactory explanation of the biological phenomena in question. Thus, the argument from design does not have much weight today.

On the other hand, consciousness and the subjective experiential qualities associated with it have yet to be adequately explained in wholly naturalistic terms. In particular, it remains something of a mystery how the mental qualities of a human person, such as consciousness, pain, and pleasure, derive from the basic properties of physical objects, for instance, shape, size, mass, motion, order and arrangement of parts, and so on. As Leibniz observed in the seventeenth century:

> *Perception* and that which depends upon it are *inexplicable* by *mechanical causes*, that is, by figures and motions. And supposing that there were a machine so constructed as to think, feel, and have perception, we could conceive of it as enlarged and yet preserving the same proportions, so that we might enter it as into a mill. And this granted, we should only find on visiting it, pieces which push against another, but never anything by which to explain a perception. This must be sought for, therefore, in the simple substance and not in the composite or in the machine.[4]

Moreover, as we have argued, both souls and body–soul interaction are possible.[5] Thus, it *might* be the case that mental qualities of a human person inhere in a soul. If we were to *solve* the mystery of how mental qualities such as consciousness, pain, and pleasure derive from the basic properties of physical objects, then we would have a powerful argument against the existence of human souls.[6] But if we were to learn that this mystery is *insoluble*, then this would lend credence to the idea that human souls exist.[7] And it appears that if there are human souls, then a primal concrete entity that created the three domains might itself be a soul. Finally, it would seem that a soul that created the three domains would be both omnipotent and omniscient.

On the other hand, given the modern scientific picture of the nature of human beings and their place in the natural world, it does not seem to be necessary to suppose that human souls exist. After all, since mysteries often can be solved, the mystery of how mental qualities such as consciousness, pain, and pleasure derive from the basic properties of physical objects may be soluble. Since the modern scientific picture of the nature of human beings and their place in the natural world is extremely plausible, it appears unlikely that human souls exist. In other words, it is plausible that some sort of physicalism or naturalism is the best explanation of our experience. This physicalistic or naturalistic picture of the world implies that human persons are physical things of some kind, for example, carbon-based life-forms. As long as such a picture of human persons and their place in the natural world remains viable, it does not seem plausible to argue that the best explanation of the existence of the three domains is a primal, creative, omnipotent, omniscient soul.

Another kind of argument for theism is based on the evidence of *religious experience*. There are two varieties of religious experience that might be thought to justify belief in the existence of God. The first variety is *apparent perceptions of God*, for example, the experiences Moses is said to have had when he saw the burning bush and conversed with God. An apparent perception of God is an experience involving a perceptual belief that God is present. The second variety of religious experience is *mystical experiences of universal oneness*. Experiences of this kind are sometimes produced by certain ascetic and meditative practices. A mystical experience of universal oneness involves an apparent awareness that the universe is atemporal, unchanging, and undifferentiated.

Most apparent perceptions of God occur within the context of a religious tradition, for instance, some form of Judaism, Christianity, Islam, or Hinduism. Since these religious traditions disagree with one another on various theological points, it sometimes happens that an apparent perception of God in one religious tradition involves elements that are inconsistent with elements of an apparent perception of God in another religious tradition. For example, Christians sometimes have an experience of God as a trinity, whereas Jews would have an experience of God as a unity. But since it would appear that these conflicting experiences are equally credible, it would seem that none of them is likely to be correct.[8]

A related factor affecting the degree of credibility of apparent perceptions of God is the extent to which they are *shared* experiences. It appears that in at least most cases, if an individual has an apparent perception of God, then this apparent perception is not shared with anybody else. However, all other things being equal, the larger the community of observers who share an apparent perception of something, for example, God, the more likely it is that this apparent perception is correct. There could be a case in which there are apparent perceptions of God which are shared by a large community of observers and which are not contradicted by an apparent perception of anyone else. It seems that in such a case the members of that community of observers can be justified in believing that God exists.

On the other hand, mystics from a variety of religious backgrounds have a considerable degree of unanimity about the character of the ultimate reality that they claim to experience. Specifically, based upon similar mystical experiences of universal oneness, these mystics agree that reality is *atemporal, unchanging,* and *undifferentiated.* But the claim that reality is atemporal, unchanging, and undifferentiated is inconsistent with our everyday experiences of concrete entities such as space, time, and physical objects; and it seems that these everyday experiences are *far more widely shared* than mystical experiences. Moreover, in the light of our characterization of the nature of God as a maximally great being, we can see that the mystic's claim is also inconsistent with the existence of God. After all, this characterization implies that if God exists, then he is temporal and intrinsically changing. Furthermore, both our characterization and the core of traditional theology imply that God is diverse from other things. Thus, it appears that mystical experiences of universal oneness neither justify a belief that reality is atemporal, unchanging, and undifferentiated nor justify a belief in God.

Finally, Alvin Plantinga has argued that a belief in a proposition such as *God loves us and cares for us* can be *properly basic* or have intrinsic credibility for an individual. A proposition of this sort obviously entails the existence of God. In Plantinga's view, a belief in such a proposition can be properly basic for an individual even if that individual never has an apparent perception of God. Plantinga supports this claim with the example of a 14-year-old theist raised to believe in God within a community of believers.

> The 14-year-old theist, we may suppose, doesn't believe in God on the basis of evidence. He has never heard of the cosmological, teleological, or ontological arguments; in fact no one has ever presented him with any evidence at all. And although he has often been told about God, he doesn't take that testimony as evidence; he doesn't reason thus: everyone one around here says that God loves us and cares for us; most of what everyone says around here is true; so probably *that's* true. Instead, he simply believes what he's taught.[9]

Plantinga's position is highly controversial, and is not accepted by most epistemologists. In any case, since a properly **basic belief** about God such as Plantinga envisions is not self-evidently true, any credibility it might have can be *defeated* if it does not cohere with other beliefs or experiences, for example, those presupposed by the form of the problem of evil discussed below.

Even if it is assumed that there is a necessarily existing, omnipotent, omniscient soul, it is not easy to see how the claim that this soul is morally perfect and incorruptible can be justified. In other words, it is not easy to see how one can justify the claim that the soul in question is a maximally great being, i.e., God. Indeed, while the fact that there are conscious living organisms coheres with the existence of God, it seems that the fact that there is such a large quantity and variety of evils that befall these conscious living organisms does not. Granted, the existence of God is consistent with the existence of an evil that he has no choice but to allow in order to obtain a greater good. But it appears that there are many cases in which an evil occurs which God would *not need to allow* in order to obtain such a good and which he would be *obligated to prevent*. It also seems that since God is omnipotent, omniscient, and morally perfect, he would prevent the occurrence of any evil of this sort. Thus, what we observe of good and evil in the world provides a powerful challenge to the proposition that God exists.

Of course, this *a posteriori* argument in favor of atheism is a form of the problem of evil. The theist can decisively answer this form of the problem of evil only if she can justify the claim that every evil falls into one or more of the following three categories: (i) an evil that God has no choice but to allow in order to obtain a greater good; (ii) an evil which God is not obligated to prevent given the nature of moral perfection; and (iii) an evil which God fails to prevent due to God's ignorance (since there are limitations upon omniscience). The complex question of whether theism can provide a satisfactory answer to this form of the problem of evil is a fitting subject for further philosophical exploration.[10]

NOTES

1 This line of reasoning resembles what is traditionally known as *the cosmological argument*, with the important difference that it relies on an inference to the best explanation, rather than on a deductive argument, one of whose premises is the principle of sufficient reason. According to one version of the principle of sufficient reason, necessarily, for any F, if F is a positive fact, then there is a logically sufficient reason for the existence of F.

2 For a naturalistic account of the principle of order and functional organization of the parts of a carbon-based living organism, see Joshua Hoffman and Gary S. Rosenkrantz, *Substance: Its Nature and Existence* (London: Routledge, 1997), chap. 4.

3 The character, Philo, makes this point in David Hume's *Dialogues Concerning Natural Religion* (New York: Hafner Publishing Company, 1975), part XII.

4 *The Monadology*, in *Leibniz Selections*, ed. Philip Weiner (New York: Charles Scribner's Sons, 1951), 17.

5 See sections 3.2 and 3.3.

6 Another powerful argument against the claim that human beings with mental qualities have souls would be provided by the empirical discovery that physical conditions and the laws of nature explain all of the workings of the human brain. Were this discovery to be made, then the nonexistence of human brain–human soul interaction would be empirically well-confirmed.

7 Apparently, a more powerful argument in favor of the claim that human beings with mental qualities have souls would be provided by the empirical discovery that physical conditions and the laws of nature cannot explain the workings of the human brain. Were this discovery to be made, then the existence of human brain–human soul interaction would be empirically well-confirmed. Compare the previous note.

8 This line of reasoning parallels the argument of Xenophanes discussed in section 1.1.

9 Alvin Plantinga, "Reason and Belief in God," in *Faith and Rationality*, ed. Alvin Plantinga and Nicholas Wolterstorff (Notre Dame, Ind.: University of Notre Dame Press, 1983), p. 33.

10 For a recent philosophical defense of the existence of God, including a response to the problem of evil, see Richard Swinburne, *Is There a God?* (Oxford: Oxford University Press, 1996). Contrast Bertrand Russell, *Religion and Science* (New York: Oxford University Press, 1997), and William L. Rowe, *Philosophy of Religion: An Introduction*, 2nd edition (Belmont, Calif.: Wadsworth, 1993).

BIBLIOGRAPHY

Alston, W. P., *Perceiving God: The Epistemology of Religious Experience* (Ithaca, NY: Cornell University Press, 1991).

Anselm, *Proslogium II and Response to Gaunilo*, in *Saint Anselm, Basic Writings*, trans. Sidney N. Deane (La Salle, Ill.: Open Court Publishing Co., 1962).

Audi, R., "Theism and the Scientific Understanding of the Mind," in *A Companion to the Philosophy of Religion*, ed. P. L. Quinn and C. Taliaferro (Oxford: Blackwell, 1997), article 55.

Beardsworth, T., *A Sense of Presence* (Oxford: Religious Experience Research Unit, 1977).

Bowker, J., *The Sense of God* (Oxford: Clarendon Press, 1973).

Clarke, S., *A Discourse Concerning the Being and Attributes of God*, 9th edition (London, 1738).

—— and Leibniz, G. W., *The Leibniz–Clarke Correspondence*, ed. H. G. Alexander (Manchester: Manchester University Press, 1956).

Craig, W., *The Cosmological Argument from Plato to Leibniz* (London: Macmillan, 1980).

Flew, A., *God and Philosophy* (New York: Delta Books, 1966).

Gale, R. M., *On the Nature and Existence of God* (New York: Cambridge University Press, 1991).

Hoitenga, D., *From Plato to Plantinga: An Introduction to Reformed Epistemology* (Albany, NY: State University of New York Press, 1991).

Hume, D., *Dialogues Concerning Natural Religion* (New York: Hafner Publishing Company, 1975).

James, W. (1842–1910), *The Varieties of Religious Experience* (London: Collier Macmillan Publishers, 1961).

Leibniz, G. W., *Monadology*, in *Leibniz Selections*, ed. P. Wiener (New York: Charles Scribner's Sons, 1951).

Paley, W. (1743–1805), *Natural Theology* (Houston, Tex.: St. Thomas Press, 1972).

Peterson, M. L. (ed.), *The Problem of Evil: Selected Readings* (Notre Dame, Ind.: University of Notre Dame Press, 1992).

——, *God and Evil: An Introduction to the Issues* (Boulder, Colo.: Westview Press, 1998).

Pike, N., *Mystic Union: An Essay in the Phenomenology of Mysticism* (Ithaca, NY: Cornell University Press, 1992).

Plantinga, A. (ed.), *The Ontological Argument from St. Anselm to Contemporary Philosophers* (New York: Doubleday, 1965).

——, *God and Other Minds: A Study of the Rational Justification of Belief in God* (Ithaca, NY: Cornell University Press, 1967).

——, *The Nature of Necessity* (Oxford: Clarendon Press, 1974).

—— and Wolterstorff, N. (eds.), *Faith and Rationality* (Notre Dame, Ind.: University of Notre Dame Press, 1983).

Ross, J., *Philosophical Theology* (Indianapolis, Ind.: Bobbs-Merrill, 1969).

Rowe, W. L., "The Problem of Evil and Some Varieties of Atheism," *American Philosophical Quarterly* 16 (1979), pp. 335–41.

——, *The Cosmological Argument* (Princeton, NJ: Princeton University Press, 1975).

——, *Philosophy of Religion: An Introduction*, 2nd edition (Belmont, Calif.: Wadsworth, 1993).

Russell, B., *Religion and Science* (New York: Oxford University Press, 1997).

Swinburne, R. T., *The Coherence of Theism* (Oxford: Oxford University Press, 1977).

——, *The Existence of God* (Oxford: Oxford University Press, 1979).

——, *Is There a God?* (Oxford: Oxford University Press, 1996).

Wainwright, W. J., *Mysticism: A Study of its Nature, Cognitive Value, and Moral Implications* (Madison, Wis.: University of Wisconsin Press, 1981).

Yandell, K. E., *The Epistemology of Religious Experience* (Cambridge: Cambridge University Press, 1993).

Glossary

Glossary entries appear in **bold face** when they first occur in the main text or in the notes.

a posteriori **knowledge/***a priori* **knowledge** According to the traditional conception of *a priori* knowledge, a person, *S*, has *a priori* knowledge of a proposition, *p*, if and only if (i) *p* is necessarily true, and (ii) *S* knows *p* independently of any evidence for *p* acquired *via* sense-perception. Note that while (ii) is an epistemological requirement, (i) is a metaphysical one. For example, in this sense of *a priori* knowledge, most people have *a priori* knowledge of necessarily true propositions such as *if something is red, then it is colored*, *if something is square, then it is four-sided*, and *7 + 5 = 12*. But there is an alternative conception of *a priori* knowledge. According to this broader conception of the *a priori*, *S* knows *p a priori* if and only if *S* knows *p* independently of any evidence for *p* acquired *via* sense-perception. This purely epistemic conception of the *a priori* is consistent with one's having *a priori* knowledge of contingent propositions such as *oneself exists* and *oneself thinks*. Since on either conception of the *a priori* we can have *a priori* knowledge of comprehensive systems of logical and mathematical truths, logic and mathematics are classified as *a priori* sciences. A notion of the *a posteriori* or the empirical is relative to *one* of the two foregoing senses of *a priori* knowledge: *S* knows *p a posteriori* if and only if (i) *S* knows *p*, and (ii) *S* does not know *p a priori* in the sense in question. For example, in either sense of the *a posteriori*, most people have *a posteriori* knowledge of the propositions *that there are elephants*, *that the Sun is bigger than the Earth*, and *that some water is frozen*. Since on either conception of the *a priori*, none of us can have *a priori* knowledge of a comprehensive system of physical, chemical, or biological truths, physics, chemistry, and biology are classified as *a posteriori* or empirical sciences.

abduction An inductive argument or inference of the form: *p* is actual; *q* is the best available explanation of *p*; therefore *q* is actual. For example, contingent things actually exist; the best available explanation of the existence of contingent things is that they were created by a necessarily existing concrete thing; therefore contingent things were actually created by a necessarily existing concrete thing. See **argument**.

accidental property (accident) A property, *P*, is accidental to an entity, *e*, if and only if (i) *e* has *P*, and (ii) *e* possibly exists while lacking *P*. For example, the property of being hungry is an accidental property of a hungry mouse. An accidental property of a thing is also called a contingent property of a thing.

analysans The analytical or defining conditions offered by a proposed philosophical analysis. The *analysandum* is that for which these analytical or defining conditions are offered. See **analysis**.

analysis An analysis (or analytical definition) of a concept, *c*, provides an explanatory logically necessary and sufficient condition for the satisfaction of *c*. To be sufficiently explanatory such a necessary and sufficient condition must be noncircular, that is, it must not have *c* as a part. For example, the concept of a square can be analyzed or defined as a four-sided closed plane figure that is equilateral and equiangular. See *analysans*.

argument An inference from one or more premises to a conclusion. Every deductive or formally valid argument is such that, *necessarily*, if its premise or premises are true, then its conclusion is true, e.g., *All men are mortal and Socrates is a man, therefore Socrates is mortal*. An inductive or invalid argument is an argument in which *possibly*, its premise or premises are true and its conclusion is false. An argument is sound if and only if it is valid and all of its premises are true; and an argument is unsound if and only if it is either invalid or has at least one false premise. An invalid or inductive argument is nevertheless good if its premise or premises make its conclusion probable. Otherwise an inductive argument is bad, e.g., *The sky is blue, therefore George W. Bush is the president of the USA*. An enumerative inductive argument extrapolates or generalizes from observations, inferring that in some particular respect what we have not observed resembles what we have observed, e.g., *We have repeatedly observed, without exception, that water freezes when it is sufficiently cold, therefore All water freezes when it is sufficiently cold*.

axiomatic Having the status of an axiom, i.e., a self-evident truth. Compare **theorem**.

basic belief A belief which one is epistemically justified in holding independently of any evidence in favor of that belief provided by another belief, e.g., a belief in a self-evident truth such as the proposition *that a square is a square*. See **justification, epistemic**.

brute fact A fact which lacks a cause or any other explanation.

coextensive Applicable to the same class of entities.

complex entity An entity which has parts. Contrast **simple entity**.

conceptualism A form of nominalism advocated by, e.g., William of Ockham, which eliminates properties in favor of mental constructions or concepts. See **eliminative**.

condition, [logically] necessary or sufficient To say that a condition, C_1, is a [logically] necessary condition for a condition, C_2, is to say that, *necessarily*, C_2 is satisfied *only if* C_1 is satisfied. For example, a thing's being four-sided is a necessary condition for a thing's being square. To say that a condition, C_1, is a [logically] sufficient condition for a condition, C_2, is to say that, *necessarily*, *if* C_1 is satisfied, *then* C_2 is satisfied. For example, a thing's being a cat is a sufficient condition for a thing's being an animal. To say that a condition, C_1, is a [logically] sufficient and necessary condition for a condition, C_2, is to say that, *necessarily*, C_1 is satisfied, *if and only if* C_2 is satisfied. For example, a thing's being a four-sided closed plane figure which is equilateral and equiangular is a necessary and sufficient condition for a thing's being square. See *analysans* and **analysis**.

conditional A hypothetical proposition, that is, one of the form *if p, then q*, e.g., *if Bush is the president of the USA, then a Republican is the president of the USA*. A material or weak conditional is false when *p* is true and *q* is false, otherwise it is true. A subjunctive or strong conditional is expressed in the subjunctive mood and indicates a necessary or causal connection of some sort between *p* and *q*. Thus, in contrast with a material conditional, the mere falsehood of *p*, or the mere truth of both *p* and *q*, is not sufficient to account for the truth of a subjunctive conditional. A counterfactual or contrary-to-fact conditional is a subjunctive conditional in which *p* is false, e.g., *if all snow were brown, then polar bears would be brown*.

conjunction A conjunction of properties consists of two or more properties joined by the logical connective *and*, e.g., being red and square. A conjunction of propositions consists of two or more propositions joined by the logical connective *and*, e.g., *that the sky is blue and Bush is the president of the USA.*

consequentialist moral theory A theory which holds that what is morally required, prohibited, and permitted is determined by the consequences of one's actions and which defines what is morally required, prohibited, or permitted in terms of what is good or evil.

contingency See **proposition**.

contingent being An entity whose nonexistence is possible. Such an entity is said to have **contingent existence**.

contingent property See **accidental property (accident)**.

counterfactual See **conditional**.

deduction See **argument**.

deontological moral theory A theory which holds that moral requirements and prohibitions are determined by the type of action one performs and which defines what is good or evil in terms of what is morally permitted, required, or prohibited.

diverse See **identical**.

divine command theory A theory of morality which holds that an act is morally required just when God commands it, an act is morally prohibited just when God forbids it, and an act is morally permissible just when God does not forbid it.

dualism In reference to substance, the doctrine that there exist both material substances (bodies) and spiritual substances (souls or spirits). The classical dualistic theory of Descartes maintains that bodies and souls interact.

empirical See *a posteriori* **knowledge**.

eliminative An eliminative theory denies the reality of entities belonging to a certain category. It maintains that any term that appears to refer to an entity belonging to that category is actually nonreferential. Compare and contrast **reductionist**.

entails To say that a proposition, p, entails a proposition, q, is to say that, *necessarily*, if p is true, then q is true. Symbolically expressed, $p \Rightarrow q$. For example, *Horses exist* $\Rightarrow$ *organisms exist*. To say that one thing *logically entails* another is to say that it is a necessary truth of deductive logic that if the first is true, then the second is true. For example, *all diamonds are hard and some diamonds are gems* logically entails *some gems are hard.*

enumerative inductive argument See **argument**.

epistemic Pertaining to knowledge. See **justification, epistemic**.

epistemology The theory of knowledge: the philosophical inquiry into the nature and extent of human knowledge.

essential property (essence) A property, *P*, is essential to an entity, *e*, if and only if (i) *e* has *P*, and (ii) *e* cannot exist without having *P*. For example, the property of being alive is an essential property of a living organism. An essential property of a thing is also called a necessary property of a thing.

equivalence To say that a proposition, *p*, and a proposition, *q*, are equivalent is to say that, *necessarily*, *p* is true if and only if *q* is true. Symbolically expressed, $p \Leftrightarrow q$. For example, *All crows are black* $\Leftrightarrow$ *all non-black things are non-crows.*

exemplification An entity is said to exemplify or instantiate a property or relation if and only if that entity *has* that property or *bears* that relation to something. In an extended sense, a concept or the like may be said to be instantiated or exemplified by any item to which it applies.

ethics The study of the nature of morality and of what actions are morally required, prohibited, and permitted.

freedom According to the libertarian account of freedom, an action, *A*, performed by an agent, *S*, is free only if *S*'s decision to perform *A* is *not* causally determined by any prior or concurrent event, state, or condition. Thus, nothing other than the agent is causally responsible for the agent's decision to perform *A*. On the other hand, a nonlibertarian account of freedom is *compatible* with the claim that a free decision to perform an action is *causally determined* by some prior event, state, or condition. According to such an account, a person may perform an action freely by doing what he wants to do, or by doing what he wants to do in the absence of coercion by others, even if his action is causally determined by some prior event, state, or condition.

haecceity Thisness. The haecceity of an entity is the property of being identical with that entity. For example, George Washington's haecceity is the property of being identical with George Washington. The concept of haecceity can be formally defined by using the logical device of existential quantification as follows. *H* is a haecceity if and only if *H* is possibly such that: $(\exists x)$ (*H* is the property of being identical with *x*). The haecceity of an entity, *e*, is an individual essence of *e*, that is, an essential property of *e* which is necessarily repugnant to anything other than *e*.

idealism In reference to substance, the doctrine that only spiritual substances exist.

identical To say that a is identical with b, or symbolically expressed, that $a = b$, is to say that a is numerically one and the same thing as b. For example, George Washington = the first president of the USA. The relation of identity is contradictory to the relation of diversity, a relation that implies duality. For example, Bill Clinton is diverse from Al Gore, or symbolically expressed, Bill Clinton $\neq$ Al Gore.

impossibility See **proposition**.

individual essence See **haecceity**.

induction See **argument**.

instantiation See **exemplification**.

interaction, body–soul There are two sorts of body–soul interaction. The first sort consists in a physical event, state, or condition, e.g., a bodily injury, producing a spiritual event, state, or condition, e.g., a pain. The second sort of body–soul interaction consists in a spiritual event, state, or condition, e.g., worry, producing a physical, event, state, or condition, e.g., frowning.

intrinsic change A concrete entity's undergoing an intrinsic change may be thought of as its exchanging, over time, one of its *intrinsic qualities* for another, incompatible intrinsic quality, e.g., a particle's changing from *being spheroid* at a time, t_1, to *being ovoid* at a time, t_2. As a general rule, an intrinsic qualitative change in a concrete entity, e_1, is *not* a change in how e_1 is related to some *other* entity, e_2 (with possible exceptions for other entities like e_1's parts, boundaries, tropes, properties, etc.). Another sort of intrinsic change is the creation or destruction of a thing, x, at a time, t. Aristotle calls such an intrinsic change in x a *substantial change*. A substantial change involves an intrinsic quality of x that is essential to x. If x comes into being at t, then at t it becomes *true* that x has all of its essential intrinsic qualities; and if x ceases to be at t, then at t it becomes *false* that x has any essential intrinsic qualities. For example, when a living thing comes into being it becomes true that it is essentially a living thing, and when a living thing ceases to be it becomes false that it is essentially a living thing. Compare **qualitative change** and **relational change**.

intrinsic credibility To say that a proposition is intrinsically credible for someone is to say that someone is epistemically justified in believing that proposition independently of any evidence in favor of believing that proposition. See **justification, epistemic**.

intuition, *a priori* The epistemic faculty whereby one apprehends the truth of a self-evident or intrinsically credible proposition of which one has *a priori* knowledge. See *a priori* **knowledge** and **intrinsic credibility**.

invalid See **argument**.

irreflexive relation A relation which nothing can bear to itself, e.g., the relation of being a sibling.

justification, epistemic The sort of justification needed if a belief is to be acceptable from the perspective of a truth-seeking and error-avoiding rational being. This is the sort of justification that a belief must have in order for that belief to count as knowledge.

Law of Non-Contradiction See **Non-Contradiction, Law of**.

libertarianism See **freedom**.

material conditional See **conditional**.

materialism In reference to substance, the doctrine that only material substances exist. Compare **physicalism**.

mereological sum A concrete collection of two or more concrete entities which has these concrete entities as parts.

metaphysics The primary or first philosophical science. It is largely concerned with **ontology**, the study of the fundamental categories of existence.

modal logic The study of logical **modalities** such as possibility, necessity, impossibility, and contingency. These modalities may be either *de dicto* or *de re*. Modalities *de dicto* apply to propositions, e.g., it is necessarily true *that 2 + 2 = 4*. Modalities *de re* apply to things and their attributes, e.g., a living organism is necessarily a living organism.

natural thing or event A concrete substance or event which exists inside of the natural or physical world, that is, inside of space, and which thereby is subject to the laws of nature.

necessity See **proposition**.

necessary being An entity whose nonexistence is impossible. Such an *ens necessarium* is said to have **necessary existence**.

necessary property See **essential property (essence)**.

nominalism The doctrine that only concrete entities exist. Thus, nominalism denies the existence of abstract entities such as properties, relations, propositions, sets, and numbers.

Non-Contradiction, Law of This logical law asserts that in general it is not possible for something to both be and not be. Thus, it is not possible for a thing to both exist at a time and not exist at that time. Nor is it possible for an item to both have a property at a time and not have that property at that time. Thus, it is not possible for a proposition to both be true at a time and not be true at that time.

(It should be noted that although it is *nowadays* usually called the *Law of Non-Contradiction*, the logical law in question was *traditionally* known as the *Law of Contradiction*.)

objective Mind–independent. Contrast **subjective**.

Ockham's Razor William of Ockham's methodological principle that in formulating a theory one should not multiply entities unnecessarily.

ontology The science of being. See **metaphysics**.

paradox A paradox arises when one or more apparently true assumptions entail a contradiction.

physicalism The doctrine that there are only physical entities, that is, entities which stand in spatial relations.

point-particle A substantial, spatially located entity which lacks length, width, and depth, but which has causal powers.

point-position (or point) A place which lacks length, width, and depth. Such a concrete entity is physical, but insubstantial.

possibility See **proposition**.

proposition An abstract entity which is either true or false. A proposition is impossible if and only if it implies a contradiction, e.g., *that there exists a spherical cube*. A proposition is possible if and only if it is not impossible, e.g., *that it is raining somewhere*. A proposition is necessary if and only if it is impossible for it to be false, e.g., *that if something is square, then it is four-sided*. Finally, a proposition is contingent if and only if it is possibly true and it is possibly false, e.g., *that elephants exist*.

qualitative change A change in something's intrinsic qualities or features. Qualitative change is to be distinguished from substantial change, i.e., something's creation or destruction. See **intrinsic change**.

qualitative indistinguishability Two concrete entities e_1 and e_2 are qualitatively indistinguishable if and only if e_1 and e_2 are exactly similar and are related to other entities in an exactly similar fashion.

qualitative universal In reference to abstract entities, a property or relation which can be expressed without naming a specific concrete entity, e.g., an abstract entity such as sphericity or betweenness. (See **universal**.) Thus, a *nonqualitative* property, e.g., being identical with George Washington, or being beside *that* sphere, cannot be expressed without naming a specific concrete entity, e.g., George Washington, or *that* sphere. Compare **haecceity** and **relational quality**.

quantification There are two basic kinds of quantification in logic: existential quantification, and universal quantification. For example, the existentially quantified proposition that $(\exists x)(x$ is red) says that there exists an x such that x is red, in other words, that there exists at least one red thing; and the universally quantified proposition that $(\forall x)(x$ is square $\rightarrow x$ is equilateral) says that for any x, if x is square, then x is equilateral, in other words, that all squares are equilateral.

random event An event which lacks a sufficient causal condition, that is, an event which is not causally determined by any prior or concurrent event, state, or condition.

realism In reference to properties, the doctrine that abstract properties exist. Realism takes two forms. Extreme realism holds that some properties are unexemplified, e.g., perfect squareness. Moderate realism maintains that a property exists just when it is exemplified. Thus, whereas extreme and moderate realism both imply that being a tiger exists, moderate realism implies that being a sabertooth tiger no longer exists.

reductionist A reductionist theory accepts the reality of entities which belong to a certain category, but claims that their existence can be reduced to, that is, analyzed in terms of, the existence of entities which do not belong to that category. Compare and contrast **eliminative**.

relation A multi-term abstract entity whose exemplification would relate something to one or more items. For example, identity, diversity, betweenness, etc. Contrast **relational quality**.

relational change An entity's undergoing a relational change may be thought of as its ceasing to stand in some *relation* to some entity at some time, e.g., a cat's changing from *being on* that mat at a time, t_1, to *being off* that mat at a time, t_2. A relational change of an entity, e_1, is a change in how e_1 is related to some *other* entity, e_2. See **relation**. Compare and contrast **intrinsic change**.

relational quality A quality consisting of being related in some way, e.g., *identical with, on, beside,* or *between,* to one or more entities, either specifically or generally. For example, being identical with George Washington, being on *that* mat, being beside a sphere, being between a block and a slab, etc. See **haecceity**.

schema (plural schemata) A logical formula containing variables which may or may not represent individuals, properties, or relations. When the variables do *not* represent, the schema is said to be *uninterpreted*. When the variables *do* represent, the schema is said to be *interpreted*.

sense-datum (plural sense-data) A sense-datum is a concrete entity which can be identified with a sensation, e.g., an after-image.

set A set is an abstract collection. The null or empty set has no elements. Any other set has one or more concrete or abstract elements.

simple entity An entity which lacks parts. Contrast **complex entity**.

sound See **argument**.

space-time continuum A four-dimensional physical system consisting of three mathematically continuous spatial dimensions and one mathematically continuous temporal dimension.

state A concrete state is a concrete entity's having some feature, and an abstract state is an abstract entity's having some feature.

state of affairs An abstract propositional entity which either obtains or fails to obtain. See **proposition**.

subjective Dependent for its reality upon one or more minds. Contrast **objective**.

subjectivism With respect to some quality, the doctrine that this quality is mind-dependent. For example, subjectivism about truth states that truth and falsehood are mind-dependent; subjectivism about possibility asserts that possibility and impossibility are mind-dependent; and subjectivism in ethics says that moral rightness and wrongness are mind-dependent.

subjunctive conditional See **conditional**.

supernatural thing or event A concrete substance or event which exists outside of the natural or physical world, that is, outside of space, and which thereby is not subject to the laws of nature.

supervenience A relation of dependence of one class of properties or relations upon another, more basic class of properties or relations whereby the instantiation of the first class of properties or relations is determined by the instantiation of the second class of properties or relations.

synthetic 'Synthetic' and 'analytic' are antonyms. An analytic connection is one that holds solely in virtue of the laws of formal deductive logic and/or the definitions of terms, e.g., the connection expressed by the *analytic sentence* 'All squares are four-sided'. A synthetic connection is a connection that is *not* analytic, e.g., the connection expressed by the *synthetic sentence* 'All crows are black'. It is evident that all analytic connections are necessary, and that all contingent connections are synthetic. But the claim that there are synthetic necessary connections is highly controversial within philosophy.

theorem A proposition which is proved or provable by deduction from axioms. See **axiomatic**.

thisness See **haecceity**.

trope A concrete entity which resembles an abstract property in some respects but which is incapable of multiple exemplification, e.g., the particular roundness of *that* ball, the particular wisdom of Socrates, etc.

truth-value Truth or falsehood. According to classical logic, every proposition must have one or the other of these two truth-values.

universal According to a usage established during the Middle Ages, a 'universal' is what is predicated of many. In this very broad sense, entities of such very different sorts as the predicate 'sphere', the concept of sphericity, the Platonic Form of sphericity, and the abstract property of sphericity all count as universals. But in contemporary usage, a 'universal' is an abstract property or relation that is capable of multiple exemplification, e.g., sphericity or betweenness.

unsound See **argument**.

valid See **argument**.

will to believe According to the pragmatist William James, one can have practical reasons for believing in God even if the proposition that God exists is intellectually undecidable. In James's view, under such conditions it is intellectually permissible for one to choose or "will to believe" that God exists.

Index